Computer Graphics

Using

Object-Oriented

Programming

Computer Graphics

Using

Object-Oriented

Programming

Edited by:

Steve Cunningham
California State University Stanislaus

Nancy Knolle Craighill
Sony Corporation of America

Martin W. Fong
SRI International

Judith R. Brown
The University of Iowa

JOHN WILEY & SONS, INC.
New York • Chichester • Brisbane • Toronto • Singapore

In recognition of the importance of preserving what has been written, it is a policy of John Wiley & Sons, Inc., to have books of enduring value published in the United States printed on acid-free paper, and we exert our best efforts to that end.

Library of Congress Cataloging in Publication Data

Computer graphics using object-oriented programming / editors, Steve Cunningham ... [et al.].
    p.   cm.
  Includes bibliographical references and index.
  ISBN 0-471-54199-0 (pbk.)
  1. Computer graphics. 2. Object-oriented programming. I. Cunningham, Steve.
  T385.C5925 1992
  006.6—dc20   91-35774

Printed in the United States of America

10 9 8 7 6 5 4 3 2 1

Trademarks

About the Editors

Judith R. Brown is a visualization consultant for Advanced Research Computing Services, Weeg Computing Center, The University of Iowa. She holds a B.A. in mathematics and education and an M.S. in mathematics, both from The University of Iowa. She is co-author (with Steve Cunningham) of *Programming the User Interface: Principles and Examples*, John Wiley & Sons, 1989; co-author of a chapter in *Visualization in Scientific Computing*, IEEE Computer Society Press, 1990; author of a chapter in *Interactive Learning Through Visualization: The Impact of Computer Graphics in Education*, Springer-Verlag, 1992; and of other articles on computer graphics, visualization, and education. She has given many invited presentations on visualization and education, nationally and internationally, and taught computer graphics in Instructional Design and Technology for six years. She served as Vice Chair of the ACM SIGGRAPH Education Committee for four years, chaired the first two SIGGRAPH Educators' Workshops, and currently serves as SIGGRAPH Vice Chair. She is a member of ACM, SIGGRAPH, SIGCAPH, SIGCHI, IEEE Computer Society, and Eurographics.

Nancy Knolle Craighill is a Senior Development Engineer at Sony Corporation of America in the Advanced Video Technology Center. She holds a B.S. in Computer Science and Mathematics from the University of California at Davis. She has over seven years' experience in software engineering developing military command and control systems, commercial graphics packages, video editing systems, and managing large software projects. Her primary expertise is in object-oriented programming, user interface design, and computer graphics. She was the Objective-C columnist for the *Journal of Object-Oriented Programming*. She co-developed (with Martin Fong) and then productized the GraphPak object-oriented graphics class library appearing in this book. She is co-author (with Martin Fong) of a chapter in *Applications in Object-Oriented Programming*, Addison-Wesley, 1990. She was the panel chair for "Object-Oriented Graphics," SIGGRAPH '91, and is both an ACM and SIGGRAPH member.

Steve Cunningham is Professor of Computer Science at California State University Stanislaus. He holds a Ph.D. in mathematics from the University of Oregon and a M.S. in computer science from Oregon State University. His primary interests are computer graphics algorithms, computer graphics education, and the use of computer graphics in science and mathematics education. He is the co-author (with Judith R. Brown) of *Programming the User Interface: Principles and Examples*, John Wiley & Sons, 1989, and co-editor (with Walter Zimmermann) of *Visualization in Teaching and Learning Mathematics*, Mathematical Association of America, 1991, and (with Roger Hubbold) of *Interactive Learning Through Visualization: The Impact of Computer Graphics in Education*, Springer-Verlag, 1992. He chaired the ACM SIGGRAPH Education Committee from 1984 to 1990, the SIGGRAPH '91 educators' program, and was co-chair of the Computer Graphics & Education '91 conference. He is currently SIGGRAPH's Director for Publications. He is a member of Eurographics, IFIP Working Group 5.10 (computer graphics), ACM SIGCHI, the IEEE Computer Society, and is on the Board of Governors of the Mathematical Association of America and the Board of Directors of ACM SIGCSE.

Martin W. Fong is a Senior Software Engineer at SRI International. He holds a B.A. in Astronomy from the University of California at Berkeley. He has 19 years' experience in software engineering, ranging from designing and implementing data analysis codes to leading large software efforts. He has worked on several object-oriented graphics applications, is the primary developer of the GraphPak commercial 2D object-oriented class library, and is involved in the development of new commercial Macintosh applications. He is co-author (with Nancy Knolle) of a chapter in *Applications in Object-Oriented Programming*, Addison-Wesley, 1990. His interests include object-oriented programming, computer graphics, and special effects cinematography. He was a panelist for "Object-Oriented Graphics," SIGGRAPH '91, and is both an ACM and SIGGRAPH member.

Contributors

Peter C. Bahrs, IBM, Boca System Design, MS 1422, 1000 NW 51st Street, Boca Raton, FL 33431. peterb@bcrvmpc1.vnet.ibm.com

M. Pauline Baker, National Center for Supercomputing Applications, University of Illinois at Urbana-Champaign, 5600 Beckman Institute, Drawer 25, 405 North Mathews Avenue, Urbana, IL 61801. baker@ncsa.uiuc.edu

Nancy Knolle Craighill, Advanced Video Technology Center, MD 35, Sony Corporation of America, 677 River Oaks Parkway, San Jose, CA 95134. craighil@renoir.sfc.sony.com

Wayne C. Dominick, Center for Advanced Computer Studies, University of Southwest Louisiana, Lafayette, LA 70504. wdd@gumbo.cacs.usl.edu

Parris K. Egbert, Department of Computer Science, University of Illinois at Urbana-Champaign, 1304 W. Springfield Ave, Urbana, IL 61801. egbert@cs.uiuc.edu

Martin W. Fong, Senior Software Engineer, SRI International, 333 Ravenswood Avenue, Menlo Park, CA 94025. fong@erg.sri.com

Robert Howard, The Whitewater Group, 1800 Ridge Avenue, Evanston, IL 60201.

William J. Kubitz, Department of Computer Science, University of Illinois at Urbana-Champaign, 1304 W. Springfield Ave, Urbana, IL 61801. kubitz@cs.uiuc.edu

Karl D. Melcher, 4046-G Dunwoody Park, Dunwoody, GA 30338.

Dennis R. Moreau, Center for Advanced Computer Studies, University of Southwest Louisiana, Lafayette, LA 70504. drm@gator.cacs.usl.edu

G. Scott Owen, Mathematics and Computer Science, Georgia State University, Atlanta, GA 30303. matgso@gsusgi1.gsu.edu

Richard L. Peskin, CCAIP, Dept. of Mechanical and Aerospace Engineering, Rutgers University, Piscataway, NJ 08855-1390. peskin@caip.rutgers.edu

Dennis Roseman, Department of Mathematics, University of Iowa, Iowa City, IA 52242. roseman@dimension4.math.uiowa.edu

Spencer Thomas, EECS, University of Michigan, Ann Arbor, MI 48109. spencer@eecs.umich.edu

Sandra S. Walther, CCAIP, Dept. of Mechanical and Aerospace Engineering, Rutgers University, Piscataway, NJ 08855-1390. walther@caip.rutgers.edu

Peter Wisskirchen, GMD, Schloss Birlinghoven, Postfach 1240, D-5205 Sankt Augustin 1, Germany. wisskirchen@f3.gmd.dbp.de

Robert L. Young, Schlumberger Laboratory for Computer Science, 8311 North RR 620, P.O. Box 200015, Austin, TX 78720-0015. byoung@slcs.slb.com

Frank Zinghini, Applied Visions, Inc., 75 Laurel Hill Road, Centerport, NY 11721.

Contents

Computer Graphics

Using

Object-Oriented

Programming

Introduction

Conventional approaches to computer graphics are failing—they are causing a bottleneck in the industry, preventing state-of-the-art computer graphics techniques from reaching the mainstream. With the current awareness of object-oriented programming, many promoters claim their graphic systems to be object-oriented, leaving the false impression that they are implemented in object-oriented languages. More significantly, because neither the implementation nor the Application Programming Interface (API) of these packages are object-oriented, many programmers have been disappointed by so-called "object-oriented" graphics systems. However, as this book shows, and given our collective experiences, the editors feel that object-oriented programming is the solution that will make sophisticated computer graphics technology available to everyone.

Computer graphics is an explosive and complex field, with rapid advances in both theory and practice. There are many important techniques in rendering, including ray tracing, radiosity, volume visualization, and a host of special effects such as fur and anisotropic lighting. There are a number of modeling systems using both polygonal and non-polygonal techniques, constructive solid geometry, NURBS, fractal surfaces, height fields, and four or more dimensions. There are a host of new and growing graphics application areas, including scientific visualization, special effects, virtual reality, hypermedia, and publishing. There is also a continuing stream of new graphics devices and systems, such as silicon viewing pipelines and accelerators, 3D displays, and exotic input devices, and an increasing trend toward more interaction. Many of these are just in the laboratory, but more and more are becoming available to the general graphics programmer.

Taking advantage of these new techniques and capabilities is very difficult for programmers. Each new rendering technique, each new modeling system, and each new device requires a major programming effort to incorporate into a new or existing application. An alternative to implementing these from scratch is to share or purchase source code from friends, contacts, and vendors, but such code is of highly variable quality and almost always needs to be adapted to satisfy the requirements of the target application. Even when graphics packages provide sophisticated capabilities, there is a mismatch between what is offered by a graphics system API and what is required by most application programmers, because graphics systems must be managed at an extremely low level. In short, computer graphics is ripe for a new software technology that addresses these problems and makes it easier to incorporate advanced graphics technology into applications.

Object-oriented programming is a revolutionary and mature approach to designing and implementing software. Object-oriented programming languages impose an engineering discipline that allows software to be built from reusable, interchangeable, and extensible parts. Imagine being able to put together a graphics application much like putting together a stereo sound system, by buying software components off the shelf and plugging them together. Imagine also that you can add the latest in graphics capability by replacing or upgrading selective components that you either construct yourself by extending current ones, have constructed for you by specialty shops, or buy off the shelf as they become available in standard catalogs. The object-oriented approach is revolutionary in providing improved productivity and effective software engineering by dividing software manufacturing into part suppliers and part assemblers.

Although object-oriented programming is evolving, and class libraries marketed as parts are just beginning to appear, very few graphics object libraries (beyond user interface toolkits) are available, and none are produced by vendors other than language providers. As the industry adopts the object-oriented paradigm, the demand for advanced graphics parts will substantially increase.

This book shows how to apply object-oriented techniques to computer graphics, and, through examples, illustrates the benefits gained when comparing object-oriented techniques against conventional computer graphics approaches. The chapters include descriptions of the facilities and APIs provided by two vendor-specific graphics object libraries; descriptions of several graphics kernels developed in research settings to study the nature and capabilities of graphics object libraries for high-level work and for distributed systems; and descriptions of some graphics applications built with object-oriented programming languages.

Thus, this book provides a representative sample of how object-oriented design and programming techniques have been used to solve a variety of practical computer graphics problems. We hope that this will shed some light on the current state of technology and why some people, including the editors and authors, find object-oriented programming applied to computer graphics both exciting and very productive.

Overview of Object-Oriented Programming Terminology

Although there are many different object-oriented programming languages, the underlying principles of object-oriented programming including encapsulation, class inheritance, polymorphism, and dynamic binding remain the same. These principles, combined with good design, produce reusable, extensible, and maintainable code.

Objects encapsulate their data structures and algorithms by defining a public interface that specifies *what* an object does, not *how* it does it. Objects then communicate via *messages* without incurring interdependencies between object implementations. Thus, an object-oriented program is essentially a network of objects with a message flow between them. Once an object interface is specified, the object is essentially a reusable, pluggable module that can be improved or replaced without affecting the rest of the program.

Class inheritance facilitates reuse in a slightly different way by means of a class or abstract data type. A *class* defines a template for creating object instances. For example, a **Lamp** class defines data fields such as wattage, color and style, and implements methods such as "on" and "off." These data are called *instance variables*, and the algorithms or routines that operate on the data are called *methods*. The application uses these templates to create actual instances of a lamp, such as a green floor lamp or a brass desk lamp.

Common data structures and algorithms can be abstracted into a super-class where *subclasses* inherit these characteristics. For example, the **Lamp** class may have **FloorLamp** and **DeskLamp** subclasses, each inheriting the wattage data and the **on** and **off** methods. Thus, software is reused because common code is not replicated in each subclass. Programmer productivity is improved because only additional and/or different data and methods need to be defined in each subclass, such as having **DeskLamps** jump on red rubber balls. Some languages support both single and multiple inheritance. *Multiple inheritance* allows classes to inherit data and methods from more than one class.

Polymorphism is the ability to send the same messages to disparate object types. For example, "on" could be sent to an instance of **Lamp** and to an instance of **Stove**. Each class may define an "on" method even though

Lamp and **Stove** have no common ancestors in the class hierarchy. (Note that conventional languages cannot have multiple functions with the same name.)

Dynamic binding allows programmers to create generic data structures and algorithms which can be more reusable than type-specific data structures and algorithms. For example, sorting algorithms can be type independent. *Dynamic binding* or *weak typing* is the ability to bind a message to an implementation (method) at runtime. For example, the Smalltalk-80™ class **OrderedCollection** is a collection of arbitrary objects; it can contain instances of entirely different classes. The kind of objects contained in the ordered collection is not defined until runtime; therefore, messages sent to these objects are bound dynamically at runtime. For example, to make all elements in the collection (for example, cats, kangaroos, and desk lamps) jump, we simply send **jump** to each element and let the system decide at runtime which **jump** method implementation to execute:

```
for x in aCollection do [x jump]
```

Class inheritance is also very powerful in building *frameworks*, reusable designs that define a common protocol and message flow among a group of objects. For example, the dependency mechanism in Smalltalk-80 is a reusable design. The dependency mechanism allows each object to register itself as a dependent of another object and be notified if that object changes state. Each object maintains a list of dependents, and when it changes state, it broadcasts update messages to its dependents. Thus, new objects that respond to this protocol become part of a much larger object-oriented design.

There are two distinct styles of object-oriented programming languages: those that are class-based and those that are type-based. *Class-based languages* include the family of Smalltalk-like and LISP-derived languages (such as Objective-C® and Actor™), which fully support dynamic binding and the notion of a factory object. In class-based languages, a class is a special object called a *factory object* that may define its own methods and instance variables. On the other hand, *type-based languages* derived from Simula (such as C++ and Object Pascal) support abstract data types, but rely primarily upon compile-time type checking. Type-based languages tend to be less flexible in implementing dynamic runtime behavior and have difficulty producing generic classes. Thus, as you may notice when reading these chapters, the language of choice does influence the design and implementation of both object-oriented graphics libraries and applications. Because of this, some programmers have even designed and implemented new languages.

Chapter 1

GraphPak: A 2D Graphics Class Library

Nancy Knolle Craighill
Martin W. Fong

GraphPak is a sophisticated graphics tool that combines structured graphics with object-oriented programming. (GraphPak is now a commercial product marketed by the Stepstone Corp.) GraphPak's structured graphics allows programmers to conveniently construct interactive displays, and its object-oriented Application Programming Interface (API) allows these structures to be easily reused and extended, thus allowing more flexibility to model application-specific graphics. In other words, you don't need to be a computer graphics expert to use it. This chapter presents GraphPak programming examples, describes powerful object-oriented design principles (frameworks) related to graphics programming, and details GraphPak's kernel implementation.

Background

GraphPak was designed to support a situation map application in a military command and control system. The situation map graphically displays tactical data, allows users to draw interactively on top of color map backgrounds, and subsequently distributes these graphics electronically. The user-drawn graphics (namely, overlays or "grease-pencil graphics") represent weather reports, engineering plans, or a battle area and are constructed from well-established military symbology. Consequently, one application requirement was to provide a graphics editor that allows users to install application-specific palettes. Because the user-drawn graphics are meaningful application objects, these objects also contain semantic information that may not have a graphical representation; additionally, they may also exhibit their own behavior when manipulated by users.

Thus, because the user interface required direct manipulation of graphical objects that had real-world counterparts, we decided to use object-oriented programming technology. We also selected object-oriented programming because it more easily adapts to changing application requirements. However, none of the object-oriented toolkits we evaluated in early 1988 supported all of our graphics needs. Specifically, we needed a toolkit that would support the building of application-specific graphics structures and storage/retrieval of these structures; we also needed support for interactive drawing and editing. (Our first choice would have been Smalltalk if it could have produced applications for our specific hardware and window system.) Therefore, we selected the environment that came closest to meeting our requirements (Stepstone's Objective-C, ICpak™ 101, and ICpak 201) and implemented the structured graphics extensions ourselves.

Paradoxically, because GraphPak was implemented as an extension to a preexisting graphical user interface toolkit (ICpak 201), GraphPak's design and implementation was made both easier and more difficult. For example, although ICpak 201 supports the building of structures from components and provides a sophisticated way of handling user events, it supports only rectangular opaque objects. Thus, as part of GraphPak's implementation, ICpak 201's clipping and display logic had to be modified to support such graphical objects as circles and polygons. Nevertheless, our efforts produced a unique, straightforward, and powerful API for interactive computer graphics.

Application Programming Interface

This section highlights GraphPak's API, which supports structured graphics, custom primitives, the definition of application semantics and behavior, and drawing and editing. We will use object-oriented design and programming examples centered around the adventures of a fugitive robot named George to describe GraphPak's API. For those unfamiliar with Objective-C, we use class specifications to describe object-oriented design in combination with Objective-C programming examples.

Objective-C

Objective-C is a C-hybrid object-oriented programming language that supports class definitions and messaging by adding Smalltalk-like syntax extensions to the proposed American National Standards Institute (ANSI) C language definition. Objective-C is class-oriented, not type-oriented; it fully supports classes as factory objects.

Factory objects may have both factory methods and instance variables. Therefore, within example code, factory methods are prefixed by "+," whereas instance methods are prefixed by "–." This chapter also uses these prefixes to distinguish between instance and factory methods. In this chapter, all method names appear in bold face.

The Objective-C message syntax is:

```
[object message];
```

where *object* will be sent the message *message*. Message arguments appear after the ":" as in:

```
[anObject moveTo:newLocation];
```

where ":" is part of the message name, **–moveTo:**.

Primitive Objects

In GraphPak, primitives are autonomous objects that can be rendered (see Figure 1.1). For example, a circle primitive is created by specifying a radius

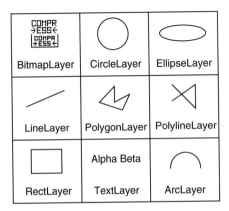

Figure 1.1: GraphPak primitives

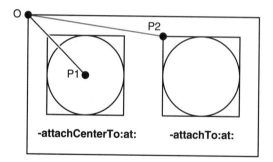

Figure 1.2: Methods for attaching circles

to the **CircleLayer** class:

```
aCircle = [CircleLayer radius:20];
```

However, until the circle is attached to a drawing surface, its center is *not* defined. Similarly, lines, polygons, and polylines are independently created by defining a sequence of points relative to their own origins.

After a primitive is defined, it can be attached to another graphical object using several methods. For example, a circle can be attached by specifying either its origin (upper left corner) or its center relative to the origin of the parent object (see Figure 1.2). Note that GraphPak has no formal concept of a world coordinate system.

Unlike other graphics systems, GraphPak allows any graphical shape to be attached to another, including such user interface objects as menus and buttons. Thus, the graphics package and the user interface toolkit are implicitly integrated.

Graphics Structures

The **Layer** class is the backbone of the GraphPak and ICpak 201 user interface toolkits. Layers are displayable objects that are analogous to sheets of acetate; as such, they can be successively stacked upon one another. The collective set of layers forms a directed tree data structure called a *layer hierarchy*. The entire user interface is modeled with a single layer hierarchy that defines the appearance of the application. The system window, an instance of **BaseLayer**, is the root of this layer hierarchy. Each layer has a list of **frontLayers** that are its children and a **backLayer** that points to the parent in the layer hierarchy (similar to Smalltalk-80 subviews and super-

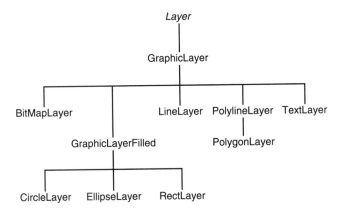

Figure 1.3: GraphicLayer class hierarchy

views).

Layers are the foundation for GraphPak's structured graphics, where objects are constructed using building blocks; each block is an instance of **GraphicLayer** or of one of GraphicLayer's subclasses (see class hierarchy, Figure 1.3). Primitives are then logically grouped to form composites. In turn, composites are represented by layer hierarchies whose leaf nodes are primitives and whose parent nodes are transparent layers (that is, instances of **GraphicLayer** that render their frontLayers, not themselves), as shown in Figure 1.4. Thus, **GraphicLayer** is an abstract superclass for all primitives *and* a factory object for composite instances.

Figure 1.5 shows a composite of George's head made up of three rec-

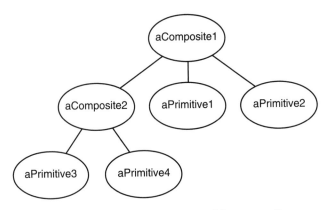

Figure 1.4: Composite graphic example

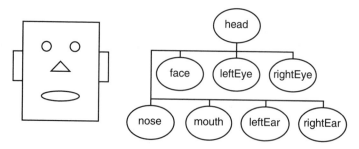

Figure 1.5: Robot head composite and part-whole graph

tangles, two circles, a polygon, and an ellipse using the classes **BRectLayer**, **BCircleLayer**, **BPolygonLayer**, and **BEllipseLayer**, respectively. The geometry of George's head, shown in Figure 1.6, is implemented in Listing 1.1.

Each layer has an origin and extent instance variable. Therefore, after the primitives are attached to the head (an instance of **GraphicLayer**), its bounding box must be adjusted to include the union of its frontLayers' extents. This is done by sending **–adjustBoundingBox** to **head**, which in turn adjusts its origin and extent. This guarantees that it will not be inadvertently clipped when displayed. As a more dramatic example, Figure 1.7 illustrates the effect of invoking **–adjustBoundingBox** after placing a hat on George's head.

Graphics Attributes

Paint attributes (pattern, color, line thickness, and font) alter the appearance

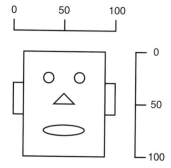

Figure 1.6: Robot head geometry

of layers. Although only primitives retain paint attribute values because they are the only renderable layers, setting the paint attribute of a composite changes the paint attribute of all its frontLayers. For example, we can show

```
/* Create the face rectangular region */
face = [[[[BRectLayer rect:pt(80,100)] filled:YES]
    pattern:GA_GRAY_25] fgColor:GA_WHITE];
[face attachTo:self];
[self adjustBoundingBox];

/* Create the eyes -- left eye first */
leftEye = [[Eye new] attachCenterTo:self
    at:pt([face width]/3, [face height]/4)];
[leftEye addDependent:self];
/* then the right eye */
rightEye = [[Eye new] attachCenterTo:self
    at:pt(2*[face width]/3,[face height]/4)];
[rightEye addDependent:self];

/* Create the nose */
nose = [[[BTriangle width:25 height:10] filled:YES]
    fgColor:GA_WHITE];
[nose attachCenterTo:self];

/* Create the mouth */
mouth = [[[BEllipseLayer xAxis:20 yAxis:5] filled:YES]
    fgColor:GA_WHITE];
[mouth attachCenterTo:self at:pt([face width]/2,
    1*[face height]/4)];

/* Create the ears -- left ear first */
leftEar = [[[[BRectLayer rect:pt(10,25)] filled:YES]
    fgColor:GA_WHITE] pattern:GA_GRAY_25];
[leftEar attachCenterTo:self at:pt(-5,[face height]/2)];
/* then the right ear */
rightEar = [[[[BRectLayer rect:pt(10,25)] filled:YES]
    fgColor:GA_WHITE] pattern:GA_GRAY_25];
[rightEar attachCenterTo:self at:pt([face width]+5,
    [face height]/2)];

/* adjust the bounding box to include all the
    frontLayers */
[self adjustBoundingBox];
```

Listing 1.1: Creating George's head

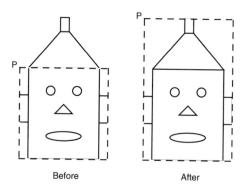

Figure 1.7: Bounding box adjustment

anger by coloring George's head red:

```
[head fgColor:GA_RED];
```

Then we can give George a black eye by increasing the thickness of the left eye, as shown in Figure 1.8:

```
[leftEye insideThickness:2];
```

If a primitive is filled, the pattern attribute applies to the filled region; otherwise, it applies to the border. The *foreground color* applies to the nonzero bits in a pattern, whereas the *background color* applies to the zero bits in a pattern.

Clear is a special color that is used to create translucent objects. If either the foreground or the background color is set to clear, patterned objects will appear translucent (objects behind are partially visible). If a fine mesh is used as the pattern, then objects have the appearance of colored acetate. For example, suppose George has the ability to vanish when he gets in trouble. By setting the pattern to a gray mesh and the background to clear, George will appear translucent (see Figure 1.9):

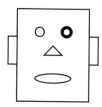

Figure 1.8: George with a black eye

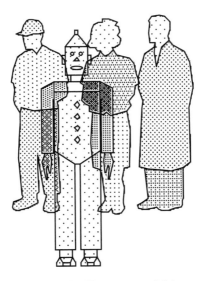

Figure 1.9: George vanishing

```
[george pattern:GA_GRAY_50];
[george bgColor:GA_CLEAR];
```

If the foreground color is also set to clear, George will "vanish." However, he will *still* receive events if pursued by an inquisitive user because he is still a displayable entity in the layer hierarchy. Because layers also have a visibility attribute, George will not be displayed and will not receive events if his visibility is set to NO.

Rendering

After a layer is attached to the root layer hierarchy, it can be displayed by sending it the **–show** message. **–show** sets a layer's visibility to YES and displays the layer. **–erase** sets the visibility to NO and removes the layer. For example, George enters the local saloon:

```
[george attachTo:localSaloon at:pt(20,0)];
[george show];
```

The second statement, which sends **–show** to George, causes him to be rendered in the **localSaloon**. (Of course, this is how our wayward and naive robot first gets into trouble.)

   –repaint is used to update a displayed graphic that has been changed.

–repaint uses a clipping list to display only the damaged regions. For example, because George fell hopelessly in love with the saloon's jukebox and became involved in an altercation with the proprietor, who had more practical uses for it, he was punched in the eye:

```
[leftEye thickness:2];      // create the black eye
[leftEye repaint];          // update the display
```

George quickly escaped by turning invisible and leaving, but not before blundering into tables, barstools, and patrons:

```
// George turns translucent
[george pattern:GA_GRAY_50];
[george bgColor:GA_CLEAR];
[localSaloon repaint];

// George turns invisible
[george fgColor:GA_CLEAR];
[localSaloon repaint];

// George leaves the premises
[george erase];
[george removeFromBackLayer];
```

Creating New Shapes

New shapes can be created by simply subclassing GraphPak primitives. For example, George's diamond-shaped buttons (see Figure 1.10) can be easily created using a **Diamond** class, a subclass of **PolygonLayer**. **Diamond** simply adds new methods for conveniently defining a diamond shape, as shown in Listing 1.2.

Now George's buttons can be created as follows:

Figure 1.10: Robot torso

```
for ( i=1; i<= 4; i++ )
  [[Diamond width:10 height:20] attachCenterTo:torso
      at:pt([torso width]/2, i*[torso height]/5)];
```

As shown above, the return value from most methods is the pseudovariable self; therefore method invocations may be nested.

Creating Application Objects

In traditional graphics packages, such as GKS or PHIGS, the interface

---

```
// Diamond Implementation File

#import "graphpak.h"
#import "Diamond.h"
#import "Points.h"

@implementation Diamond : PolygonLayer

/* Creates and returns a w by h diamond shape. */
+width:(int)w height:(int)h
{
    self = [super new];
    [self width:w height:h];

    return self;
}

/* Sets the receiver's dimensions to w and h.
   Returns self. */
-width:(int)w height:(int)h
{
    id points;

    points = [Points new];
    [points appendPoint:pt(0,h/2)];
    [points appendPoint:pt(w/2,0)];
    [points appendPoint:pt(w,h/2)];
    [points appendPoint:pt(w/2,h)];
    [self setPoints:points];
}

@end
```

Listing 1.2: Diamond implementation

between the package and application is clumsy because the internal display list is not accessible to programmers. For example, because GKS returns a picked graphic's segment identifier, application programmers must resolve what "logical" application object corresponds to it. This requires programmers to replicate data structures that are deliberately inaccessible and internal to the graphics package. Thus, it is extremely difficult to add application semantics to graphics with traditional graphics implementations. However, the power of object-oriented design and programming allows programmers to solve this problem in a straightforward way.

Application objects are created by subclassing **GraphicLayer**. For example, all the code fragments shown above could be encapsulated in the class called **Robot** as specified in Listing 1.3. Using this class, we can create instances of George, Bob, and Jill.

The default geometry and paint attributes are set in **–initialize**, which is automatically called whenever a new instance is created. **–createHead** will contain some of the same code shown above, but it is implemented as a separate method so that subclasses of **Robot** can override the default implementation and create robots with different heads. For example, a robot might have a "smiley face."

Application semantics (such as the robot's name, height, and weight) can be directly added to the graphics object by defining additional instance variables and methods in the **Robot** class. *There are no restrictions on the kinds of data or the methods that may be added to graphics objects!*

Similarly, the implementation of heads and eyes could be encapsulated in classes, as specified in Listing 1.4 and Listing 1.5.

Adding Application Behavior

Suppose that when the robot is hit in an eye by clicking the left mouse button on the eye, the eye turns black. This is implemented by overriding **Eye**'s **–leftButtonUp** method, which is called when the eye is selected with the left mouse button:

```
- (BOOL) leftButtonUp
{
    /* create a black eye */
    [border insideThickness:2];
    [self adjustBoundingBox];
    [self repaint];

    return YES;
}
```

Robot

Superclass: GraphicLayer

Classes used: Diamond, GraphicLayer, Head, RectLayer

Instance variables:

head
   The head graphic for this instance (an instance of
   Head).

height
   The height of this instance.

name
   The name of this instance.

weight
   The weight of this instance.

Methods:

-createHead
   Creates and returns the receiver's face. Should be
   overridden by subclasses wishing to change the
   default face.

-initialize
   Initializes receiver's instance variables
   (constructs its graphics). Returns self.

-(int)height
   Returns the receiver's height.

-name
   Returns the receiver's name.

-(int)weight
   Returns the receiver's weight.

-height:(int)h
   Sets the receiver's height to h. Returns self.

-name:(STR)aName
   Sets the receiver's name to aName. Returns self.

-weight:(int)w
   Sets the receiver's weight to w. Returns self.

Listing 1.3: Robot class specification

Head

Superclass: GraphicLayer

Classes used:
BEllipseLayer, Eye, BRectLayer, BTriangle

Instance variables:

face
the rectangle region that defines the face.

leftEye
a bordered circle that defines the left eye.

rightEye
a bordered circle that defines the right eye.

leftEar
a bordered rectangle that defines the left ear.

rightEar
a bordered rectangle that defines the right ear.

nose
a bordered triangle that defines the nose.

mouth
a bordered ellipse that defines the mouth.

Methods:

-initialize
Initializes the receiver's instance variables. Creates the composite graphic (frontLayers) for this instance. Returns self.

-getMad
Sets the paint attributes to show anger. Returns self.

-(BOOL)leftButtonUp
Overridden to color the face red to show anger. Returns YES.

-update:sendingObject because:(SEL)aMessage
Overridden to update the face condition if an eye is hit (i.e., if the receiver gets a black eye then the face will turn red).

Listing 1.4: Head class specification

Eye

Superclass: GraphicLayer

Classes used: CircleLayer

Instance variables:

border
   The border circle for this instance.

Methods:

-initialize
   Initializes the receiver's instance variables; sets
   the eye-specific paint attributes. Returns self.

-(BOOL)leftButtonUp
   Overridden to give the receiver a black eye, if hit.
   Returns YES.

Listing 1.5: Eye class specification

On the other hand, if we click anywhere else on his face, he becomes angry, and his face turns red (Color Plate 1 shows George with a red face and black eye). This behavior is implemented by overriding the **Head** class's **–leftButtonUp** method:

```
-(BOOL)leftButtonUp
{
    [self getMad];
    return YES;
}

-getMad
{
    /* color the face red */
    [face fgColor:GA_RED];
    [leftEar fgColor:GA_RED];
    [rightEar fgColor:GA_RED];
    [self repaint];
}
```

When a user event occurs, GraphPak transparently handles all event processing and notifies the application by sending an event message (that is, **–leftButtonUp**) to the picked object. Any object in the layer hierarchy can receive event messages by simply overriding the corresponding method and performing object-specific actions. *That's all there is to adding application-specific behavior to graphics.*

Drawing and Editing

One of GraphPak's unique features is that it supports interactive drawing and editing, direct benefits from our object-oriented design and implementation. Each primitive contains methods that define how to draw or edit itself interactively. These methods effectively encapsulate the user interaction semantics and specify what mouse and keyboard actions define and redefine primitives, correct errors, and cancel user interactions.

As an example of the API's simplicity, once the message **–userCreate:whenComplete:do:** is sent to a primitive (for example, a **PolylineLayer** instance), the user can interactively define the primitive (that is, polyline points are selected in sequence by moving the mouse and clicking). All the programmer needs to do is specify the drawing surface and an object/message pair as the callback. The primitive will then interact with the user until the interaction is either successfully completed or canceled by the user. (Although this feature was originally designed for graphics editing, because it is part of GraphPak's kernel, it can be used by *any* application.)

For example, as illustrated in Figure 1.11, an FBI agent can plot our fugitive robot's movement on a map by interactively defining a **Polyline-Layer** instance, with each vertex corresponding to a sighting in a particular location. However, note that the user-drawn polyline can be more than a simple geometric shape—it can be an *application object* that represents George's path and that contains application-specific data and behavior (see class specification in Listing 1.6). Thus, after the agent has interactively drawn the path, the path could prompt for more information, such as the agent's starting point, and then solve the "traveling salesman" problem so

Figure 1.11: George's last reported locations

Path

Superclass: `PolylineLayer`

Methods:

```
-travelingSalesman
    Returns a sequence of locations whose total distance
    constitutes the shortest possible travel path.
...
```

Listing 1.6: Path class specification

that the agent could efficiently conduct interviews with local residents and law enforcement representatives without excessive travel.

GraphPak also supports the re-editing of primitives. Therefore, when the FBI agent receives a late-breaking report from a disgruntled saloon proprietor that an abusive and clumsy robot has attacked him without provocation, he can add another point to the fugitive's path.

Application Frameworks

A *framework* is essentially a reusable design that establishes a protocol and message flow within a group of objects. Objects that support the protocol increase their own reusability by being part of a framework. This section presents frameworks within GraphPak that can be used to model application data and behavior.

Part-Whole Relationship

An object-oriented program can be represented by a graph of interconnecting objects with a single thread of runtime messages. Because instance variables constitute the connections between objects, the aggregate object relationship graph is called the "part-whole" relationship. Because of the heterogeneous nature of objects, object-oriented implementations allow an arbitrary object, even a graphical object, to be a part of another object (compare this to strongly typed procedural languages). In fact, objects can even have multiple references. As a consequence, when using GraphPak, nongraphical data structures can contain graphical objects.

In Objective-C, classes are also objects and therefore can contain their own class variables and methods. Thus, because the **Robot** class is a factory object for all robot instances, it can maintain an inventory of all robots it creates. This can be done by adding a reference to the Robot factory's inventory list whenever a new robot is created. This is implemented in Robot's **+new** method, in which **inventory** is an instance of **OrdCltn** (an ICpak 101 foundation class):

```
+ new
{
   self = [super new];
   [inventory add:self];
   return self;
}
```

Note that **inventory** was initialized in **Robot**'s **+initialize** method; this method is called automatically as part of the **Robot** class runtime initialization.

Dependency Mechanism

Whenever two or more objects are interdependent, there is a need to propagate changes when the value of a shared instance variable or attribute is changed. (For example, if you change your residence, you need to notify the U.S. Postal Service, the drivers license bureau, your local newspaper, and a plethora of others.) Within Objective-C, this notification is supported by a dependency mechanism that allows any object to be notified when an object it depends upon changes state. Internally, each object manages a list of dependents, allowing objects to be added or removed. Whenever its internal state is changed, an object simply sends itself the **–changed** or **–changed:** message to notify its dependents. In turn, all of the object's dependents are sent an **–update:because:** message to allow each dependent to respond.

In a previous example, if George's left eye is hit, it turns black; if George is hit anywhere else in the face, he becomes angry, and his face turns red. This implementation does not make his face turn red when his left eye is hit (the left eye receives the event, not the face). Although one approach is to have the eye instance set the face to red, this hack defeats object encapsulation! Therefore, we now describe an implementation that uses the general purpose dependency mechanism.

For example, the face registers itself as a dependent of the left eye, so that it is notified when the eye changes state. When the left eye is hit, it sends itself the **–changed** message. This causes the left eye to implicitly send the message **–update:because:** to its dependents:

```
-(BOOL)leftButtonUp
{
    /* notify dependents */
    [self changed];

    /* create a black eye */
    [border insideThickness:2];
    [self adjustBoundingBox];
    [self repaint];

    return YES;
}
```

To complete the implementation, **Head** overrides **–update:because:** to set the face to red (**–update:because:** passes both the sending object and a method name as arguments to allow dependent objects to determine what data have changed):

```
-update:sendingObject because:(SEL)aMessage
{
    if ([sendingObject isKindOf:Eye])
        [self getMad];
    else
        return [super update:sendingObject
                because:aMessage];
}
```

Figure 1.12 illustrates the resultant flow of messages when the left eye is

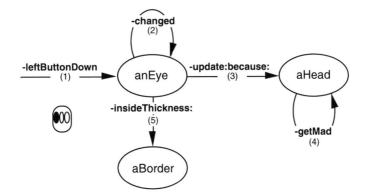

Figure 1.12: -leftButtonDown message flow

hit. By using this mechanism, the previously proposed interdependency between the **Eye** and **Face** classes is *completely eliminated.*

The dependency mechanism has many applications, including the implementation of the model-view-controller framework.

Model-View-Controller

The model-view-controller (MVC) paradigm originated as a Smalltalk-80 user interface design strategy for representing information. (The MVC framework described here is a variation of that used in Smalltalk-80. See [Knolle 89]). Although GraphPak and ICpak 201 support MVC, neither require its use.

The MVC separates user interface applications into three components. *Model* contains application-specific data, *views* display the data on the screen, and *controllers* handle user interactions that affect both models and views. Figure 1.13 shows the relationships between model, view, and controller objects.

The advantages of using MVC include (1) a single model can have multiple views (statistical data can be simultaneously represented by a spreadsheet, a pie chart, and a bar chart); (2) MVC allows and encourages component reuse, because views are built from subviews; and (3) controllers can be easily interchanged during runtime to modify an application's behavior.

MVC Implementation

Models maintain a list of views and, whenever their data change, broadcast

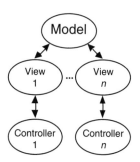

Figure 1.13: Model-view-controller relationship

changes to their views using the general dependency mechanism. The model-view protocol is implemented by having views be dependent upon their models and by overriding their **–update:because:** method to update the display.

In GraphPak, **Layer** and **GraphicLayer** are abstract superclasses for all views, which are responsible for managing the graphical display. **GraphicLayer** has a **model** instance variable that allows views to communicate with their model.

Controllers implement the behavior of views. Each layer has an associated controller that handles all events (such as keyboard and mouse input) from the underlying window system that occur within the layer's bounding box. When a controller receives an event, it can either directly consume it or pass it to its layer's **backLayer**. Controllers consume events by overriding distinct methods for each type of event they wish to consume. Because a controller's methods define the interactive behavior of its layer, this behavior can be arbitrarily changed by replacing a layer's controller.

Typically, controllers are subclasses of **TransCtlr**, **OpaqCtlr**, or any class that responds to the controller protocol. Because **Layer** also responds to the controller protocol, the default controller for a **Layer** instance is itself. Thus, behavior can be encapsulated in a layer without using controllers at all. This feature makes GraphPak's MVC framework both easy and flexible to use.

Controllers also allow generic behavior to be reused by disparate objects. For example, GraphPak provides a class, **LayerCtlr**, that allows users to move a layer to the front when clicked and to drag a layer to a new location. The following example shows how an instance of **LayerCtlr** can be attached to George so that he can be moved by the user:

```
[robot controller:[LayerCtlr new]];
```

MVC Example

Models and Views

Suppose we want multiple views of George, a full length view and a mug shot view (see Figure 1.14). It now makes little sense to couple the robot's model information with the graphical view, particularly because we now have multiple views. Therefore, we separate the robot data in a class, **Robot**, and view-specific data into the classes **RobotView** and **RobotMugShot**. The **Robot** class will contain the name, height, and weight instance variables. **RobotView** and **RobotMugShot** are subclasses of **GraphicLayer** (see the class specifications in Listings 1.7 – 1.9).

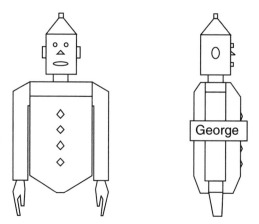

Figure 1.14: Multiple George views

Updating Multiple Views

Suppose George assumes a different name, then changing the name in the model should be reflected in the mug shot view. This is achieved by having mug shot views establish dependency on their models:

```
aView = [[RobotMugShot new] model:george];
[george addDependent:aView];
```

Additionally, **RobotMugShot** must override **–update:because:** to update its display when the model changes:

```
-update:sendingObject because:(SEL)aMessage
{
    if ([sendingObject isEqual:myModel] &&
        @selector(name:) == aMessage){
      [self updateName:sendingObject];
      return self;
    }
    else
        return [super update:sendingObject
            because:aMessage];
}
```

where **–updateName:** changes the name plate. Figure 1.15 shows the flow of messages when the robot's name changes. Although **RobotView** instances also receive these broadcast messages, RobotViews will ignore them because the class did not override **–update:because:** (the default implementation does nothing).

Using Controllers

How controllers communicate with views and models is an application-specific design choice. Suppose we want the robot's black eye to be reflected in all its views. The fact that the robot is in pain and has a black eye should be retained in the model and not in the view. The best implementation is to have the **Robot** class define submodels that are analogous to how robot views are constructed from subviews. In fact, the model part-whole diagram is an exact parallel of the view part-whole diagram.

Robot

Superclass: Object

Instance variables:

height
　　The height of this instance.

name
　　The name of this instance.

weight
　　The weight of this instance.

Methods:

-initialize
　　Initializes the receiver's instance variables (sets
　　the default weight and height). Returns self.

-(int)height
　　Returns the receiver's height.

-name
　　Returns the receiver's name.

-(int)weight
　　Returns the receiver's weight.

-height:(int)h
　　Sets the receiver's height to h. Returns self.

-name:(STR)aName
　　Sets the receiver's name to aName. Returns self.

-weight:(int)w
　　Sets the receiver's weight to w. Returns self.

Listing 1.7: Robot class specification

RobotView

Superclass: GraphicLayer

Classes used: Diamond, GraphicLayer, Head, RectLayer

Instance variables:

head
  The head graphic for this instance (an instance of Head).

Methods:

-createHead
  Creates and returns the receiver's head. Should be overridden by subclasses wishing to change the default face.

-initialize
  Initializes the receiver's instance variables (constructs its graphics). Returns self.

Listing 1.8: RobotView class specification

RobotMugShot

Superclass: GraphicLayer

Classes used: Eye, Face

Instance variables:

head
  The head graphic for this instance.

Methods:

-createHead
  Creates and returns the receiver's head. Should be overridden by subclasses wishing to change the default face.

-initialize
  Initializes the receiver's instance variables (constructs its graphics). Returns self.

-update:anObject because:(SEL)aSelector
  Updates the display if the model changes (i.e., updates the name plate if the model's name changes).

- updateName:anObject;
  Updates the receiver's name plate. Returns self.

Listing 1.9: RobotMugShot class specification

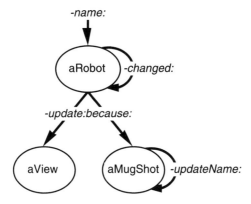

Figure 1.15: Update message flow

Each view and subview is registered as a dependent of its respective model and submodel. Therefore, EyeView's **–leftButtonUp** directly updates its model:

```
-leftButtonUp
{
    [model blackEye];
    return YES;
}
```

In turn, this changes the model's state, causing the model to broadcast **–update:because:** to all its views, assuming each view implements **–update:because:** to update the display:

```
-blackEye
{
    blackEye = TRUE;    /* set internal model state */
    [self changed];     /* broadcast change to views */
    return self;
}
```

Changing Controllers
In addition, suppose we want the robot to cry if he is hit a second time after receiving a black eye. Remember that each view overrides event methods (such as **–leftButtonUp**) to implement its default behavior. By replacing a view's controller with a specialized controller, we can arbitrarily override this default behavior at runtime! This is the power that controllers provide within the MVC framework.

Thus, because ICpak 201 layers are also controllers, we begin by defining an **EyeView** subclass, **CryCtlr**, which overrides **–leftButtonUp** to add a tear to the display when its view is hit. After the eye has turned black, the **Eye** instance replaces the controller for its views with **CryCtlr** instances

```
[views elementsPerform:@selector(controller:)
    with:[CryCtlr new]];
```

Note that **views** is an instance of **OrdCltn**, while **–elementsPerform:** will send the message **–controller:** to each element in **views**, passing a new instance of **CryCtlr** .

The original behavior is not lost. If the eye later heals, the model can restore the views' default behavior by broadcasting the **–defaultController** message to its views (the default implementation returns itself).

Fundamental Frameworks

Whereas the frameworks in the previous section concern modeling application objects and their behavior, this section discusses fundamental frameworks that support software engineering. Specifically, GraphPak supports frameworks for initializing, copying, storing, retrieving, and freeing instances.

These frameworks make extensive use of the Objective-C pseudovariable *super*, which refers to the superclass of the receiver. For example,

```
[super aMessage]
```

will execute the superclass's implementation of **-aMessage**.

Instance Initialization

When a new instance is created, its memory is allocated from the heap via standard C library functions. However, the allocated memory needs to be prepared for its first use through object initialization. The initialization framework ensures that all inherited instance variables are initialized before subclass instance variables. This ordering is very important, because subclasses typically have dependencies on their superclasses, even when they initialize their instances.

Typically, a high level class (such as **Object**) overrides **+new** to send

Figure 1.16: An "OOPS" TopHat

the new instance **–initialize** and provides a default implementation for **–initialize**. Each class then overrides **–initialize** to call **[super initialize]** and initializes its subclass-specific instance variables.

For example, suppose for all types of hats, we have an abstract superclass, **Hat**, that has a subclass **TopHat**. **Hat** overrides **–initialize** to set its default hat size. **TopHat** overrides **–initialize** to initialize graphics that are dependent upon the hat size. If TopHat's **–initialize** does not call **[super initialize]**, George's hat might not fit (see Figure 1.16).

Copying

In Objective-C, all instances have the ability to duplicate themselves (inherited from **Object**). The method **–copy** returns a copy of the receiver, duplicating as much of the entire object graph as seems "reasonable" for objects of the given class. Subclasses override **–copy** to define "reasonable." (**Object**'s default implementation simply returns a copy of the receiver but does not make new copies of any objects referenced by the receiver.)

Suppose the FBI agent wants to send an all-points bulletin out on George for having caused irreparable damage to a juke box (it now plays only "I Want to Be Loved by You, Boop-Boop-Bee-Doo"). This is done by duplicating one of George's views and sending it to all the local law enforcement agencies. In doing so, only the view is sent; the model is neither duplicated nor sent.

Therefore, **RobotView** overrides **–copy** to selectively duplicate its object graph but avoids copying its model:

```
-copy
{
    id aCopy, temp;

    temp = model;
    model = nil;  // Temporarily set the model to nil

    aCopy = [self deepCopy];  // Create a deep copy
    model = temp;  // Reset the model

    return aCopy;
}
```

Thus, what is copied is completely controlled by programmers. If they desire, in this way, programmers can copy both graphics objects *and* application objects.

Memory Deallocation

In Objective-C, programmers must explicitly perform garbage collection by ensuring that all objects are properly freed. This is done by having each class override **–free** to free *owned* instance variables and any dynamically allocated data structures (namely, normal C structures). Each implementation should then invoke **[super free]** to free all inherited instance variables. Given this, each implementation only explicitly frees its instance variables and not those of its superclasses.

Unfortunately for our wayward robot, the intrepid FBI agent received a final tip on George's whereabouts from a spurned telephone answering machine (and yes, in matters of the heart, George was unfortunately quite naive). Consequently, George was unceremoniously captured and briefly placed in jail (Figure 1.17). And, because robots have the same legal rights as toasters, he was returned to the factory for dismantling, where both his views and his model were freed.

```
-free
{
    // Free a robot's views
    [views elementsPerform:@selector(erase)];
    [views elementsPerform:@selector(free)];

    // Free its name
    [name free];

    // Free inherited instance variables
    return [super free];
}
```

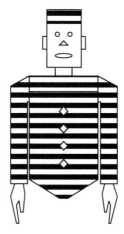

Figure 1.17: George in jail

Storing and Retrieving

All Objective-C objects can be saved on disk using **-storeOn:** and retrieved by using **–readFrom:**. Thus, application objects, as well as graphics objects, can be stored together and exist after the application has terminated. This general purpose implementation of persistency is far more flexible then any conventional graphics package because it will also maintain application-specific context information.

In addition, a framework is built around these methods to allow programmers to optimize object storage files. **–fileOutFor:** allows class designers to prepare instances for storage (passivation), and **–awakeFrom:** allows class designers to initialize instances after being read into an application (reactivation).

Robot overrides **–fileOutFor:** to store only the model data and not its views. This is done by temporarily setting `views` to nil before storing the receiver:

```
-(BOOL) fileOutFor: aFiler
{
    id temp;
    // Set selected instances variables to nil
    temp = views;
    views = nil;
    // Store the receiver
    return_value = [Super fileOutFor: aFiler];
```

```
// Return instance variables to original values
views = temp;

return return_value;
}
```

Similarly, **–awakeFrom:** is overridden to process an instance after it has been read from disk. A default view of George is created after George's model has been instantiated:

```
-awakeFrom: aFiler
{
    id aView;

    aView = [RobotView new];
    [self addDependent:aView];

    return [super awakeFrom: afiler];
}
```

The **Robot** factory maintains an archive of all robots ever made. Because the failure rate for robots is extremely low, the robot factory's quality assurance (QA) manager was very disturbed to hear about George's exploits and eventual demise. Fortunately, the QA manager found that George's Expectation instance variable was set far too high. (Because the factory owners had the philosophical attitude that each robot should be unique, they randomly selected attribute values that defined a given robot's personality.) Thus, like a high-tech necromancer, the QA manager reinstantiated George from factory records but changed George's Expectation instance variable to provide him with *realistic* expectations.

Finally, where is George today? He is now a productive and useful member of society, who lovingly repairs supermarket laser scanners, and who, with his loving wife (a somewhat irascible microwave oven), is raising a family composed of a refurbished video cassette recorder and a once derelict, but now reformed, 8080 microprocessor.

Graphics Kernel Implementation

Because GraphPak was designed as an extension to a preexisting user interface toolkit, much of its foundation for constructing and displaying graphics structures, coordinate systems, and processing events was inherited. Most of our efforts focused on enhancing the API and clipping logic for nonrectangular shapes, on implementing interactive drawing and editing, and, of course, on implementing various primitive classes. This section covers relevant algorithms and implementation details for object-oriented graphics kernel development.

Coordinate Systems

GraphPak's coordinate system is directly inherited from the ICpak 201 user interface toolkit. Each layer has an origin and extent instance variable. **origin** contains a pixel coordinate relative to the system window's origin, and **extent** contains the layer's width and height in pixels. Every layer stores its origin relative to the system window, although the API also allows programmers to set and query the origin relative to the layer's **backLayer**. In fact, programmers commonly define a layer's origin relative to the **backLayer**. When a layer's origin changes, it automatically updates its frontLayers' origins so that they are translated as well. Other than this, there is no formal concept of a world coordinate system as found in most conventional graphics packages. The advantage of this approach is that it frees the programmer from the burden of explicitly managing coordinates.

Displaying

The layer hierarchy used to compose graphics structures also acts as the display list for rendering and distributing events. During a display operation, the layer hierarchy is traversed using the painter's algorithm (backLayers are drawn before frontLayers, and siblings are successively drawn).

Each layer has an instance variable called **frontLayers** that is an ordered collection of arbitrary objects that respond to the **Layer** protocol (they respond to the same messages as the **Layer** class). To support this framework, all layers respond to the **–displayLayer** and **–display** messages.

Each layer overrides **–displayLayer** to draw only itself. The default implementation does nothing; therefore, classes that do not override this method will be transparent (that is, **GraphicLayer** instances are essentially transparent). **–displayLayer** is a private method that is only called by **–display**; it is never called by class consumers.

A layer hierarchy is displayed by sending the **–display** message to the root of the hierarchy. **–display** simply uses recursion to traverse the tree structure, as shown by the pseudocode in Listing 1.10.

```
/* Displaying Layers */
-display
begin
    if not visible
        return self;
    else
        begin
            [self displayLayer];
            send -display to each frontLayer
        end
end
```

Listing 1.10: Implementation of -display

The implementation of **–repaint** is much more complicated because it computes clipping lists for each layer and must account for overlapping layers that may not be part of the receiver's subhierarchy (a sibling may need to be repainted if it is in front of the receiver).

Clipping

It was difficult to enhance the clipping logic in ICpak 201 in support of nonrectangular and semitransparent objects (patterned objects that use a clear background color). In ICpak 201, clipping lists are computed at the time of display, so that only damaged regions of the screen are repaired when layers respond to a **–repaint** message. The clipping implementation assumed that a layer is either rectangular and opaque, or completely transparent. Thus, we had to rewrite the clipping methods to support clipping of nonrectangular shapes, such as circles, lines, and polygons. Unfortunately, because ICpak 201 is a commercial product, we could not change the clipping protocol in **Layer**, and therefore we feel our design was not as "pure" as we would have liked.

However, one of the benefits of having an object-oriented graphics kernel is that changing graphics algorithms has no effect on the API. The clipping methods could easily be replaced at a later time, without impacting the API, to both the GraphPak and ICpak 201 classes, because clipping methods are private methods used only in the internal implementation of **Layer**.

Event Handling

Event handling is initiated by sending the system window, a global variable called **baseLayer**, the **–controlStart** message. In turn, this method runs an event loop:

```
// Start the event processing loop
[baseLayer controlStart];
```

This is done only once within the main() C routine. Whenever an event occurs (for example, the user presses a mouse button) **–processEvent** is sent to **baseLayer** to dispatch the event to the "picked" layer.

All events are handled on a real estate basis; events are sent to the object directly beneath the cursor at the time the event occurred. Each layer can either consume the event or pass it to its backlayer; thus, **backLayer**s only process events that have been ignored by its **frontLayer**s. As shown in Listing 1.11, events are distributed by traversing the layer hierarchy depth first and then using a bounding box check to prune the search path.

Because using a bounding box check is insufficient, an additional check is made to determine if a GraphicLayer is picked. Specifically, each Graph-Pak primitive overrides **–mouseHit** to return YES if a visible portion of the primitive is selected; otherwise NO is returned. For example, in Figure 1.18, point A hits the line, point B hits the circle, and point C hits neither.

Each layer solicits events by simply overriding corresponding event methods. If the event method is implemented to return YES, then no other layer can consume the event. If the method is implemented to return NO, then siblings and backLayers can consume the event. Therefore, class producers only have to accommodate events that are meaningful to the application. This approach considerably simplifies event handling for application programmers.

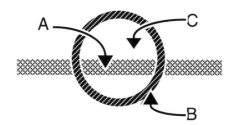

Figure 1.18: Picking graphics

```
/* Dispatching events */
-processEvent
begin
    if I'm visible and the event is within my bounding
        box
    begin
        /*Give frontLayers the first shot at the event */
        for each frontLayer, aLayer
            if [aLayer processEvent] returns YES then
                return YES

        /*At this point, none of the frontLayers consumed
            the event */
        /* Process only if a "visible" portion of myself
            is hit */
        if [self mouseHit] returns YES then
            send my controller the event specific message
            e.g., if the event is a left mouse button down
            then send -leftButtonDown to my controller)
        else
            return NO
    end
end
```

Listing 1.11: Process event method

Drawing and Editing

Drawing and editing of a primitive is initiated by sending a primitive the
–userCreate:whenComplete:do: message:

```
[aCircleLayer userCreate:anEditLayer
    whenComplete:anObject do:aMessage];
```

where **anEditLayer** specifies the drawing surface (an instance of **Layer** or
its subclasses), and **anObject** specifies the object to send **aMessage** to when
the user has either completed or canceled the drawing operation. Note: this
message *does not* block!

The underlying implementation first creates a copy of the primitive and
stores it in the primitive's private **tempLayer** instance variable. Second, an
instance of its corresponding **GraphicCtlr** subclass is created and attached
to the drawing surface (that is, if the primitive is a **CircleLayer**, then a
CircleCtlr instance is attached). **GraphicCtlr** instances are layers that act

as a transparent surface for intercepting events (see class hierarchy, Figure 1.22). Because the temporary layer is part of the layer hierarchy, it receives events in a normal fashion and, like all layers, can be redisplayed and clipped.

Thus, the user can begin editing a primitive, move the cursor outside the edit surface, and then interact with other application objects (for example, scroll the contents of a window). When returning to the edit surface, the user can simply continue the interaction. In fact, the user can simultaneously initiate multiple drawings on different surfaces. Additionally, the associated temporary graphics will properly display and clip themselves if the user rearranges the layers (see Figure 1.19).

After the user finishes drawing, both the temporary copy of the primitive and the **GraphicCtlr** are freed. However, if the user cancels the drawing, then the primitive is returned to its original state using the temporary copy. For example, if the user edits an existing circle, selects a new center, and cancels the interaction without specifying a new radius, the circle is returned to its original state. In this fashion, **–userCreate:whenComplete:do:** accommodates *both* drawing and editing.

Window Systems

Because GraphPak and ICpak 201 were designed for machine- and window-system independence, they use a canonical set of window system procedures collected into an "Earthbase" (see Figure 1.20). Each Earthbase is a window

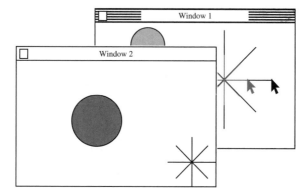

Figure 1.19: Two windows with ongoing interactive graphics

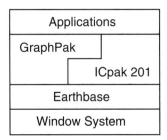

Figure 1.20: GraphPak layered architecture

system-specific library with a uniform API; current Earthbases support X10, X11, and Sun Windows. To support GraphPak's functional requirements, the Earthbase was extended to contain graphic primitive routines to render circles, lines, and polygons. If a window system for a specific Earthbase did not support a particular primitive, then the primitive was implemented in GraphPak using traditional computer graphics techniques (such as digital differential analyzers or flood-fill algorithms).

Extending the Kernel

Careful attention was given to make GraphPak extensible, because we knew early on that we would be adding additional primitives, such as arcs and splines. However, because we also weren't sure if **GraphicLayer**'s API was appropriate to all graphics problems, we provided a lower level interface for rendering objects.

We separated the rendering and the interactive layer objects to allow application programmers to render objects without using layers. Thus, each **GraphicLayer** primitive has an instance variable called **graphicObject** that points to its rendering counterpart, a member of **GraphicObject** (see the GraphicObject class hierarchy in Figure 1.21).

Each **GraphicLayer** primitive has an associated controller that implements the primitive-specific interactive drawing and editing (see the Graphic-Ctlr class hierarchy in Figure 1.22).

Therefore, in order to add a new primitive to GraphPak, we must create a new **GraphicLayer** subclass, a new **GraphicObject** subclass, and a new **GraphicCtlr** subclass. This design allows both users and graphics kernel vendors to easily extend GraphPak's graphics kernel.

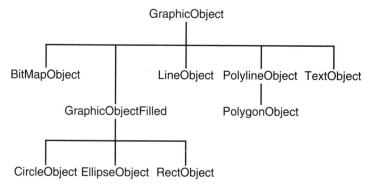

Figure 1.21: GraphicObject class hierarchy

Future Directions

Because we did not have the time and resources to add features like scaling and rotating, and useful primitives like arcs and splines, GraphPak is not a wholly complete 2-D graphics package. Additionally, we felt that ICpak 201's clipping logic and repainting algorithms need to be replaced. However, in all of these instances, there are no technical difficulties in implementing any of these features, only time and budgetary constraints.

Although ICpak 201's developers had the right idea when they created Earthbases to insulate ICpak 201 from window-system specifics, this approach could be improved by encapsulating the window system and device dependencies in a class called **Display**. A **Display** class would define a

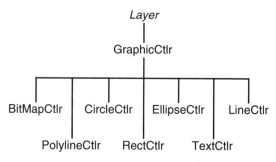

Figure 1.22: GraphicCtlr class hierarchy

generic protocol for a display device, and subclasses would encapsulate device-specific implementations. (For example, there could be a **Display** subclass called **PostScript** that could generate PostScript® files for printing or transmitting GraphPak graphics.) Thus, none of the application and user interface software would be device or window system-dependent, and class producers would greatly benefit from a complete object-oriented implementation.

There are also some exciting ways to enhance the interactive graphics by having programmers easily customize the interactive drawing and editing controllers. For example, if you wanted to show a computed distance while the user is drawing a polyline, you could simply subclass **PolylineCtlr**. Thus, for this application, GraphPak provides a powerful API that hides the low-level rubberbanding implementation.

We found that many API issues can neither be identified nor addressed until we have gained experience in using these kinds of object-oriented graphics tools. For example, we found some unusual problems associated with allowing the user to interactively draw graphics on the screen. If the user places a circle on the screen, he or she expects its center to remain constant even if the border thickness is changed (see Figure 1.23). However, because **–thickness:** adjusts a primitive's extent based upon the thickness value and keeps its origin fixed, we added a method, **–insideThickness:**, that changes the thickness by collapsing or expanding the primitive about its center.

One advantage in conventional graphics packages is the use of a world coordinate system. However, we would prefer an object-oriented variation that supported multiple, or nested, coordinate systems.

Other enhancements we look forward to include extensions to the capabilities of object-oriented programming languages and operating sys-

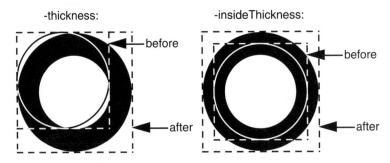

Figure 1.23: Thickness adjustment

tems. These include dynamic loading of class libraries, multi-threads of control, distributed objects, and the notion of a metaclass. These features would be very powerful when used in combination with object-oriented graphics.

Conclusion

Our goal was to develop an easy-to-use and understandable graphics system that allows application programmers to focus their efforts on solving application problems, instead of becoming computer graphics experts. Although GraphPak's current graphics capabilities are not sophisticated, through its object-oriented design, GraphPak provides a better, more intuitive way to program applications. We feel that, though GraphPak's graphics algorithms can be improved and more capabilities added, we can still preserve a simple, yet powerful, object-oriented API.

Unfortunately, the success of object-oriented graphics tools, including GraphPak, is dependent upon the success of object-oriented programming languages. Although much of GraphPak's design is language-independent, we feel that it could *not* have been implemented without proper object-oriented language support. At a minimum, object-oriented programming languages have to provide encapsulation, inheritance, and dynamic binding. Encapsulation hides the implementation, whereas class inheritance facilitates reuse. Dynamic binding (loose typing) provides greater flexibility needed for interactive graphics. A language environment also needs to provide basic frameworks for both application and graphics objects (for example, model-view-controller paradigm and persistent objects). Finally, even if the time comes when most object-oriented programming languages support these features, programmers must continually, and diligently, design for object reuse and extensibility.

References

[Adams 88] Adams, Sam S., "MetaMethods—The MVC Paradigm," *HOOPLA!*, pp. 5-21, July 1988.

[Cox 86] Cox, Brad J., *Object Oriented Programming—An Evolutionary Approach*, Addison-Wesley, Reading, MA, 1986.

[Knolle 89] Knolle, Nancy, "Variations of Model-View-Controller," *Journal of Object-Oriented Programming*, September/October 1989.

[Knolle 90a] Knolle, Nancy T., "Practical Techniques for Memory Management ," *Journal of Object-Oriented Programming*, March/April 1990.

[Knolle 90b] Knolle, Nancy, Martin Fong, and Ruth Lang, "SITMAP: A Case Study in Object-Oriented Design and Object-Oriented Programming," *Applications of Object-Oriented Programming*, Pinson, Lewis J., and Richard S. Wiener, editors, Addison-Wesley, Reading, MA, 1990.

[Krasner 88] Krasner, Glenn E., and Stephen T. Pope, "A Cookbook for Using the Model-View-Controller User Interface Paradigm in Smalltalk-80," *Journal of Object-Oriented Programming*, pp. 26-49, August/September 1988.

[Step 88a] Stepstone Inc., *Objective-C Compiler User Reference Manual*, Sandy Hook, CT, January 1988.

[Step 88b] Stepstone Inc., *ICpak 201 Graphical User Interface User Reference Manual*, Sandy Hook, CT, January 1988.

Chapter 2

ObjectGraphics

Robert Howard
Frank Zinghini

There is a perception among software developers that graphic applications are among the most difficult to write because of their complexity and diversity, and because of the sheer volume of work involved in implementation. The reason for this difficulty is that typical graphics development libraries consist of a vast array of procedures needed to create and manipulate visual effects. Unfortunately, these procedures provide only extremely low level graphics support. Although these libraries will effectively render images onto a screen, the application programmer must perform a significant amount of bookkeeping to coordinate graphic images with application-specific information. Thus, one unfortunate consequence is that an application is typically dominated by its graphics code, both in its design and its implementation.

The problem lies in the design philosophy behind most graphics libraries, specifically their application programming interface (API). Although these libraries are extremely powerful, they require a tremendous amount of guidance to perform relatively simple tasks: For example, drawing a box requires knowing where it should be placed, what it looks like, how big it is, how to render it, and so on. All of this information must be supplied *in addition to* whatever the box represents in the application. A simpler but less traditional interface would allow you to *make* a box, specify what it looks like, and then let it take care of itself.

This latter view of the graphic element as an *intelligent entity* demonstrates how an object-oriented approach to computer graphics can substantially reduce software development costs. Graphic elements can now become active objects that "know" how to perform graphics-related tasks, allowing you to simply use them without becoming unnecessarily burdened by details.

ObjectGraphics

ObjectGraphics™, a commercially available class library for the Actor development environment, supports such an object-oriented approach to computer graphics programming. (Actor, a product of The Whitewater Group℠, is a complete object-oriented programming language and environment for developing applications under Microsoft® Windows™.) ObjectGraphics extends the Actor system to include a comprehensive set of graphic objects for use in Actor applications. Although ObjectGraphics was implemented in Actor, versions are also available for C++ and Turbo Pascal®.

ObjectGraphics was developed with two goals: first, to provide an object-oriented graphics programming environment for Actor, bringing the benefits of object-oriented technology to the development of graphic applications under Microsoft Windows, and second, to be easily ported to a variety of graphics platforms, such as Macintosh and the X Window System™, and programming languages, such as Object Pascal and C++.

Actor Language Overview

Actor is both a pure object-oriented language and an interactive development environment that runs under Microsoft Windows, used to create Microsoft Windows applications. Actor is a "pure" object-oriented language because, like its ancestor, Smalltalk, all program entities are objects. This includes integers, real numbers, and strings, and even the compiler and all of the development tools! In contrast, hybrid object-oriented languages, such as Objective-C, support both objects and data types as distinct entities. However, like Objective-C, Actor allows the programmer to choose between early and late message binding. This allows programmers to choose between implementation convenience and speed.

Message Sending

The format of a message send in Actor is similar to a procedure call in C. For example, the statement:

```
print(aNumber);
```

sends the message **print** to the object named **aNumber**. However, because the result depends on what kind of object **aNumber** actually represents, **print** is actually a generic function. In addition, these generic functions, or methods, may also accept parameters. The statement:

```
show(aWindow, visualState);
```

causes the **show** message to be sent to the **aWindow** with the **visualState** object as a parameter.

Garbage Collection

One of Actor's features that greatly simplified ObjectGraphics' design is automatic garbage collection. Once an object is no longer referenced, it is magically and transparently destroyed. This mechanism is particularly helpful in graphics programs in which an extremely large number of graphic elements are being continuously created and destroyed. By managing the allocation and disposal of these objects automatically, Actor removes a substantial burden from the developer. In addition, as most programmers know all too well, mismanagement of memory allocation is almost always catastrophic; luckily, automatic garbage collection significantly reduces the likelihood of this problem.

Object-Oriented Graphics

The term *object-oriented* is often misapplied in computer graphics. Although most graphics libraries claim to be object-oriented, in reality their procedures only manipulate graphics as logical shapes as opposed to arrays of dots on a screen. Therefore, the mechanisms for actually performing those manipulations are still procedural and are still difficult to use.

In contrast, object-oriented graphics present a uniform model for both end-users and programmers. Thus, ObjectGraphics provides a simple, coherent set of graphic objects that not only draw themselves, but that provide a wide range of graphic behavior that is traditionally the responsibility of the application. Because these graphic objects manage themselves, programmers can concentrate on developing the application code rather than graphics code.

To illustrate the difference between this approach and traditional procedural libraries, consider drawing a rectangle using the Windows graphic device interface (GDI) library and conventional C programming techniques as shown in Listing 2.1.

A better design would be to group the rectangle's attributes into a logical structure; however, the application would still have to manage the rectangle's data and would still be responsible for allocating, deallocating, and maintaining the data.

On the other hand, when using ObjectGraphics, the application would only need to instantiate and attribute a graphic object. The application never manages the object's data: If it needs to change an object's attribute, it requests the object to change it. This enforced encapsulation automatically provides a cleaner and more easily maintained design. Thus, using ObjectGraphics, the following code creates and draws a blue rectangle:

```
aRect := build(Rectangle, 0@0, 100@100);
setColor(brush(aRect), primary(Color, #blue));
draw(aRect, aPort);
```

This creates a rectangle with the top-left corner at (0, 0) and the bottom-right

---

```
void drawRectangle(HDC hDC; int x0, y0, x1, y1)
{
    LOGBRUSH lBrush;
    HPEN     hPen;
    HBRUSH   hBrush;
/* Set a new pen in the display context and destroy the
   old one
*/
    hPen := CreatePen(PS_DOT, 2, RGB(0,0,0));
    DeleteObject(SelectObject(hDC, hPen));
/* Set the logical operator to copy */
    SetROP2(hDC, R2_COPYPEN);
/* Set the background mode to transparent so that the
   gaps in lines are not colored
*/
    SetBkMode(hDC, TRANSPARENT);
/* Set a new brush in the display context and destroy
   the old one
*/
    lBrush.lbStyle := BS_SOLID;
    lBrush.lbColor := RGB(255,255,255);
    hBrush := CreateBrushIndirect(lBrush);
    DeleteObject(SelectObject(hDC, hBrush));
/* Draw the rectangle in the display context */
    Rectangle(hDC, x0, y0, x1, y1)
}
```

Listing 2.1: Drawing a rectangle in Windows with C

at (100, 100), sets the rectangle's brush color (which determines the interior color) to blue, and then directs the rectangle to draw itself in a display port. As this example shows, the low-level graphics modeling and rendering details are encapsulated in ObjectGraphics' **Rectangle**, **Brush**, and **Port** objects, which in turn simplifies the task of the applications programmer. However, any application using ObjectGraphics manipulates objects using predefined, high-level protocols. Thus, ObjectGraphics implements a wide selection of objects and behaviors that address the needs of most graphics applications. By having these objects cooperate among themselves, ObjectGraphics addresses all of the lower-level details needed to create and manipulate graphic images. Further, ObjectGraphics' object-oriented architecture allows users to extend ObjectGraphics to satisfy the requirements of their particular application by subclassing preexisting ObjectGraphics classes.

Overview of ObjectGraphics

The ObjectGraphics package comes with a graphics class library containing over 30 classes. This section provides a short introduction to the library's architecture. All of the classes defined by the ObjectGraphics standard are divided into three categories: rendering tools, platform filters, and graphics and shapes.

Rendering Tools

Defining the appearance of a graphical shape is usually modeled on our real-world experience with drawing. If we were to use a drafting template, we would select the pen or pencil that gave us the line color and thickness we wanted and then trace the outline of the shape with that tool. If you want a dotted or dashed line, you do that by hand as you trace the shape. Once the shape is drawn, a marker or paint brush fills in the shape with color.

In ObjectGraphics, a shape's appearance is governed by its *framing* (the outline) and *filling* (the interior) characteristics. These attributes are represented by pen and brush objects that define the framing and filling characteristics, respectively. When a shape is told to draw itself, it uses its pen to define the appearance of the lines that form it and, if it is a closed shape, its brush to define the appearance of its interior.

The term *rendering tools* describes classes of objects that organize conceptually related graphic attributes into conveniently manipulated packages. The rendering tools supplied with ObjectGraphics are **Pens**, **Brushes**, **TextPens**, and **GraphSpaces**. The appearance of any drawn graphic, with the exception of its actual shape, is controlled entirely by these tools. **Pens** control the appearance of lines, and **Brushes** the appearance of filled regions. **TextPens** define the appearance of text, including both font selection and style elements, and **GraphSpaces** control the coordinate system, measurement units, direction of axes, scaling, panning, and gridding.

Platform Filters

Platform filters are classes that hide the API set and technical details of the underlying graphics engines from the ObjectGraphics programmer. They allow graphics code to be fully portable across all windowing environments to which the class library is ported. Filter classes include **Port**, **PhysicalPort**, **Bitmap**, and **Color** classes. Ports represent generic output devices on which all graphics draw themselves. The **Output Device** classes can also be considered platform filters; **Bitmap**, **Window**, and **Printer** all subscribe to the common output device protocol. The code that draws your graphics will not require any changes, whether drawing on a window, bitmap, or printer.

Graphics and Shapes

Graphics are classes of objects that can be asked to render themselves in a port. A graphic owns rendering tools to implement its color, size, and other characteristics. It is in this part of the class tree that inheritance is most fully exploited; graphics support a rich, common protocol useful in both interactive and noninteractive graphics applications.

A Sample Drawing Application

Now that you have some idea of the features of the ObjectGraphics class library, we present an example of a simple, interactive application, after some necessary background on graphic applications and their construction under windowed environments. In the present context, a line drawing application might be considered the interactive graphics equivalent of "Hello, world." A sample screen is shown in Figure 2.1.

Elements of Graphic Applications

Generally, a graphic application handles its rendering in one of two ways: painting or drawing. In the painting model, the user of the application is presented with a drawing area that represents a canvas and is allowed to draw. Just as in real life, anything that is drawn becomes a part of the canvas and can never be changed; it can be painted over, or cut out and pasted down elsewhere, but a square on the page loses its identity as a square once drawn. The strong point of this model is that it allows for manipulation of the image at the pixel level, allowing an artist to create intricately detailed images.

The drawing model, often referred to (incorrectly) as object-oriented drawing, contrasts sharply with this metaphor. In this model, a shape retains its identity when drawn, giving us the option of going back later and either moving or changing it. Since the square is always a square, and not just some dots on a screen, it can be resized, recolored, and generally messed around with until we're happy with it. This is the model adapted by most computer-aided design (CAD) and illustration systems.

In the painting model, the current state of the canvas is all we must

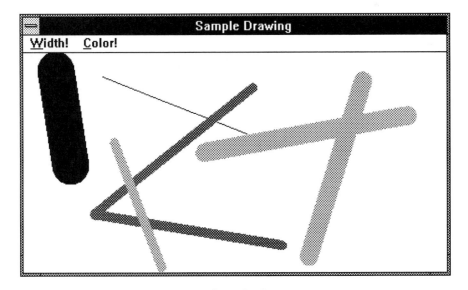

Figure 2.1: Sample draw screen

remember in order to reproduce the image. This is generally held in a bitmap that represents the drawing area of the screen. In order to save the picture, all we need to do is save the bitmap.

This is not the case with the drawing model. First, we need to remember the identity and characteristics of every single graphic element in the picture, so that we can not only reproduce the image, but we can later modify its elements as well. We also need to keep track of the order in which the elements were placed in the picture, so that we can properly reproduce the stacking and overlapping of shapes. What we need is a list of everything that makes up a display, or a "display list."

Given the ability to render a display list onto an output device, developing many graphic applications reduces to the twin tasks of manipulating the list's elements and drawing the list. If, in addition, the application must support the interactive creation of those graphic objects, there is actually one more task to cover. Let's examine the basic structure of all interactive graphic applications in terms of these three jobs.

Basic Framework for Windowed Graphic Applications

Implementing applications in a windowing environment imposes a number of contrasting requirements. We must be able to interact smoothly with a user, and we must also give the underlying windowing environment the support it needs to maintain its display. This section provides a basic understanding of these requirements, providing the rationale for the sample application's design.

Window Repair Responsibilities

One of the most important functions of the windowing environment is to keep the screen image in good shape. As windows are moved around, covering and uncovering other windows or popping up new ones, the window manager must shift images around and fill newly vacated spaces. Just moving a window from one place to another is fairly easy: The bitmap that represents the window can be moved to another area in the display memory with a bit-block transfer, or *bitblt*. This gets complicated when the window you moved was covering part of another window. The newly uncovered window is considered damaged by the action and must be repaired.

The window manager could keep bitmap copies of all of the windows laying around and use those to repair the damages. This would require a great deal of memory, though, and it still wouldn't address the need for the first-time drawing of the window. Thus, the window manager relies on the applications owning the window to do their own repair work on demand.

When the window manager decides that it needs a window to fix itself, it sends that window a message to that effect. This message, generally referred to as the **Paint** message, tells the application to redraw the part of the window that was damaged and identifies the damaged area as a rectangle. Thus, any application running in this environment must be able to redraw its image at a moment's notice.

User Interaction Responsibilities

The other events likely to cause a change in the appearance of the window are the result of mouse (or other pointer) activity. It's very common for interactive programs to use the mouse for creating and modifying graphic shapes. The simplest case of this is an interactive drawing program, where the mouse is used to plant and stretch out shapes such as squares and circles.

Mouse activity is expressed in terms of clicking and dragging. To a graphics program, the three mouse events of interest are generally these:

beginDrag   The first click of the mouse, which often signals the start of a new shape.

drag   Movement of the mouse with the button held down, which usually extends the shape to follow the mouse.

endDrag   Releasing the mouse button, signaling the end of the shape definition.

What makes this interesting is the graphic requirements imposed by these actions. For applications implementing dynamic shape creation, we must be able to draw the shapes in real time, in addition to drawing them on system request, in the repaint or repair messages. We must also be able to animate the creation or movement of shapes. The basic flow of this process is as follows:

beginDrag   Initialize the shape object to be animated, and draw it once, with the **xor** drawing mode set. This will allow us to erase it, in subsequent animation frames, without damaging the rest of the display.

drag   Draw the shape in its current position, which erases it. Then, update the shape (resize it, move it, or whatever) and draw it again.

endDrag   Draw the shape one last time with the combination mode set to **copy** and add it to a display list so it can be easily rendered in service of a repainting message.

As long as we drag the mouse, we will be erasing, updating, and redrawing the shape. When we finally release the mouse button, the shape becomes permanent.

So, we come at last to a small sample of the ease with which we can implement these functions using ObjectGraphics.

SampleDraw Requirements

The SampleDraw application is a very simple drawing tool that illustrates the fundamental behavior of any interactive graphics program. It will let you use a mouse to draw straight, solid lines in any color or width, and it will keep track of all the lines you've drawn so it can properly recreate them whenever window area needs to be reconstructed. In the previous section we described a framework that divided a program's graphical responsibilities into two categories: repainting and dragging. In this example you will see how easy it is to meet these requirements when your graphic objects know how to take care of themselves.

To satisfy the repainting requirement, the application will maintain a **Picture** object into which all newly created **Line** objects are added. Pictures are objects that contain a collection of other graphic objects, and that allow you to treat that collection as a single entity. When the windowing environment instructs the SampleDraw window to repaint itself for any reason, SampleDraw will respond by telling the **Picture** to draw its collection of graphics. To meet the needs of the dragging behaviors we will define **beginDrag**, **drag** and **endDrag** methods for the window, which will use a **Line** object to construct and manipulate a line in response to mouse movements. Finally, we will add two dialogs to control the width and color of the drawn lines.

Creating and Saving Lines

SampleDraw will provide a dragging behavior that allows the interactive creation of lines, which are then saved into its **Picture** object. This requires us to implement the three dragging methods discussed earlier. The implementation of these methods is as follows.

beginDrag: When the SampleDraw window receives a **beginDrag** message, it creates a new **Line** object and specifies its **Pen** as one that draws a solid, black, one-pixel-wide line, with a combination mode of **#nxor** so that it can be animated against the white window background. Then, the application associates the port with the SampleDraw window, signaling ObjectGraphics to prepare it for drawing by performing any platform-specific attribute setting. Finally, we send a **Draw** message to the **Line**, which will cause it to set its **Pen** attributes and then draw itself in the port:

```
Def beginDrag(self, keyStates, aPoint)
{ theLine := build(Line, aPoint, aPoint);
   setPen(theLine, build(Pen, nil, #solid, 1, #nxor,
          #opaque));
   associate(port, self);
   draw(theLine, port);
}
```

By drawing the line once as one single point (it starts and ends at the same place, **aPoint**), and giving it a **Pen** that will cause it to draw in black with a combination mode (**nxor**, for "not-exclusive-or"), we are ready to begin animating the drawing process. Exclusive-or drawing will cause the line to draw by inverting whatever is already on the screen; this way it will draw in black wherever there is white, and will draw in white where there is black. Notice that if the line is drawn in the same place twice, it erases itself.

drag: When the SampleDraw window receives a **drag** message, it redraws the **Line** in its most recent position, erasing it. It then changes its size and position based on the current mouse location, and draws it in its new place.

```
Def drag(self, keyStates, aPoint)
{ fastDraw(theLine, port);
  setCorner(theLine, aPoint);
  fastDraw(theLine, port);
}
```

We took a small optimization by using **fastDraw** messages. Since the **Line** already set its **Pen** into the port in the **beginDrag** method, and since we want the **Line** to stay the same color during rubberbanding, we don't need to set its **Pen** again. Because **fastDraw** skips **Pen** setting, it speeds things up.

endDrag: When the mouse button is released and the **endDrag** message is received, we want to set the **Line**'s attributes to their intended values. We do so by taking a copy of our current **Pen** and giving it to the **Line**, and then telling the **Line** to draw itself in its final location. Then we dissociate the port from the **Window**, signaling ObjectGraphics to perform any platform-specific cleanup that has become necessary. The new **Line** is finally added to the **picture**, ensuring its automatic drawing during repainting.

```
Def endDrag(self, keyStates, aPoint)
{ setPen(theLine, copy(currentPen));
  draw(theLine, port);
  dissociate(port);
  add(picture, theLine);
}
```

Notice that we simply draw the line on top of the last rubberbanding line. We make sure that **currentPen** has a combination mode of **copy**, causing it to write over whatever is on the screen at that point.

Selecting Colors and Widths

In the dragging examples we alluded to the existence of **currentPen**, which represented the most recent user selections for line style and color in the drawing program. Now we'll look at how that **Pen** object works with us to obtain and remember those selections.

For the purpose of this example, we can assume that we have two objects that implement dialog boxes for specifying colors and line widths. Sending a **getWidth** message to the **widthDialog** will prompt the user for a width and will return the width that is entered. **RGBDialog** will do the same thing for a color: the user enters red, green, and blue values for the color, and the dialog constructs and returns a **Color** object that contains those values. We would then execute the following methods in response to menu selections:

```
Def chooseColor(self)
{  setColor(currentPen, getColor(RGBDialog));
}
Def chooseWidth(self)
{ setWidth(currentPen, getWidth(WidthDialog));
}
```

The key to this process is to maintain the **currentPen** object in the state that represents the most recent operator selections. Then all we need to do is to give a copy of that pen to any new line to have it draw as requested.

Redrawing the Picture

Since the application's **picture** instance variable contains the current image, we must redraw that picture when requested. ObjectGraphics sends the application a **gPaint** message whenever the window needs to be repainted, so we define the following method in the class **SampleDraw**:

```
Def gPaint(self, aPort, invalidRect)
{ draw(picture, aPort);
}
```

ObjectGraphics sets up the **Port** parameter for us, so all we need to do is draw in it. The **invalidRect** parameter indicates the actual area of the window that needs to be repainted, but we can safely ignore this here since ObjectGraphics will automatically discard attempts to draw outside this area. We then tell the picture to draw itself in the port. The picture runs through its collection of graphic objects, telling each one in turn to draw itself in the port. The result is that all of the lines in the picture are drawn in the window.

A Deeper Look at ObjectGraphics

Now that you have an idea of the concepts and style of ObjectGraphics, we can take a closer look at some of its more interesting features. We'll explore objects that provide behaviors common to many graphics applications, and then we'll expand on our drawing tool to take advantage of these objects and illustrate their value.

Drawable Objects

The raw materials of graphics programming are, for the most part, the fundamental shapes from geometry: lines, rectangles, ellipses, polygons, arcs, and curves. If you were to look inside even the most sophisticated graphic application you would find manipulations of these simple shapes. Working with shapes in software is not much different from using traditional mechanical drawing tools; it's a process of determining a position and size for the new shape, choosing a tool (like a pen or pencil) to draw it with, and drawing it. Although the specifics of these actions vary considerably among different graphics libraries and environments, the basic concepts still hold true.

So we now come to the heart of the matter, the graphic objects themselves (see Figure 2.2). ObjectGraphics provides a rich protocol for manipu-

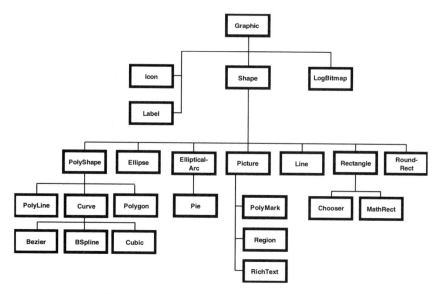

Figure 2.2: Graphic hierarchy diagram

lating those components of your model that require graphic representation. The behaviors discussed in the following section hold true for all graphic classes, regardless of their type or of any platform-imposed differences in the way they must be handled.

Common Protocols

In this section we describe message protocols that are common to all drawable objects. One of the dominant themes of object-oriented graphics is the uniformity of the graphic manipulation protocol. This allows applications the freedom to deal with their graphic portions at a much higher level of abstraction. Rather than dealing primarily with the storage and manipulation of primitive display information, the applications' code is free to address application-specific problems while ObjectGraphics addresses graphical ones.

Drawing: All descendants of **Graphic** class, (rectangles, bitmaps, or whatever) are drawn by sending them the draw message. The draw message, with a port object as a parameter, causes the graphic to set optionally its rendering tools in the port and draw itself on the output device. Because each graphic knows its shape and position within the port's **GraphSpace**, and because it knows its display attributes through the ownership of rendering tools, this simple draw message is sufficient to render even complex objects.

Positioning: All graphic objects support a rich, uniform positioning protocol. The simplest message, **positionAt**, moves the graphic so that its upper left-hand corner coincides with the supplied point object. A minor variation, **centerAt**, positions the graphic so that its center aligns with the supplied point, instead. The **offset** message treats the passed point object as an *x* and *y* offset and moves the receiver graphic accordingly.

Two messages, **setOrigin** and **setCorner**, are not quite uniform in the behavior they invoke from various classes of graphic objects. For many graphics (rectangles, ellipses, lines, bitmaps, round-cornered rectangles), they will reposition the origin and corner points of the graphic to the supplied point. Although these are very useful messages (it would be difficult to rubberband these shapes without them), they could cause trouble with more complex shapes (such as polygons, curves, polylines, and pictures), which must calculate their own origin and corner points based on internal considerations. For these descendants of **Graphic**, **setOrigin** and **setCorner** have no effect.

If you need to resize a graphic, the **scale** message can be sent. The point object that accompanies it is interpreted as percentages of growth in *x* and *y* directions. This allows nonproportional scaling. The message works equally well on simple shapes and deeply nested picture objects.

Informational: As with all objects, drawables know how to report an array of information about themselves. In addition to the obvious things such as their origin, corner, width, height, and so on, these objects can perform fairly complex operations on themselves that result in a simple piece of information. For example, any object can give back a rectangle that completely encloses itself (known as a bounding rectangle). The determination of this rectangle is obviously highly dependent on the characteristics of the shape: It's easier to determine the **boundsRect** of a circle than of a polygon. However, the object knows about the differences and handles them naturally. All the application ever needs to know is that the result of the request is a proper bounding rectangle. Once again, we can treat all graphic objects in a consistent way.

A simple, yet powerful protocol is named **asBitmap**. This message, understood by all graphics including pictures, causes the graphic to create a monochrome or color bitmap rendition of itself. This mechanism can be used to provide improved positioning feedback during drag operations, creating "thumbnail" icons of complicated graphics, and the like.

All rendering tools, color objects, and graphics can write themselves *to* and read themselves *from* files, regardless of their complexity. The scheme is easily extensible by the user, so accommodating newly derived graphic classes is quite simple.

Shapes

The largest branch within the graphic class hierarchy descends from class **Shape**, as shown in Figure 2.3. The formal **Shape** class unites all graphic objects that draw themselves by outlining (framing) with a **Pen** object and filling their interiors, if any, with a **Brush** object. From this class descend graphic objects as diverse as lines, rectangles, polygons, curves, pictures, and more.

To manipulate the appearance of a shape-descended object, you ask it for its rendering tool, and then modify that tool. For example, to change the color of an an ellipse's brush without affecting its other attributes, send

```
setColor(brush(anEllipse), RGB(Color,255,128,128));
```

Another major branch within the **Shape** class hierarchy is class **Poly-Shape** and its descendants such as **Polygon** and **Curve**. This formal class unites all graphics that define their appearance through the manipulation of a collection of **Point** objects. The **Curve** class descends from **PolyShape** because curves need to manipulate internal collections of **Point** objects in much the same way as other PolyShapes. With Polygons and Polylines, the points represent vertices that are connected with lines. In **Curve** objects, those points represent control points, not vertices, and don't necessarily lie on the curve itself.

The manner in which the control points' positions affect the curve's shape is specified differently by each descendant of **Curve**. If you created a descendant of **Curve** called **Parabola**, for example, the only difference

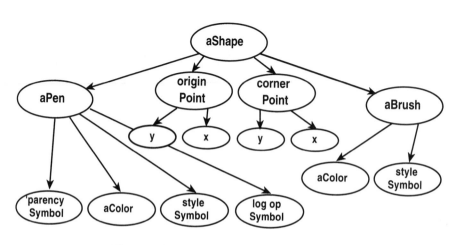

Figure 2.3: Shape part-whole diagram

between a **Parabola** object and a **Bspline** object would be the unique way in which each one would calculate its shape in relation to its control points' positions.

Pictures

The **Picture** class is probably the most important descendant of the **Shape** class. Picture objects provide a means of creating and manipulating graphic collections. **Picture**, and its descendants **Region**, **RichText**, and **Poly-Mark**, implement intelligent collections of graphic objects. Of all ObjectGraphics classes, **Picture** supports the richest set of protocols, inheriting from classes **Shape** and **Graphic**. From **Graphic**, graphic objects inherit all of the behaviors of graphic objects and extend them to entire collections of these objects. From **Shape**, they inherit pen and brush manipulation behaviors and use those rendering tools to default the appearance of their owned **Graphic** objects. From the Actor **Collection** class they borrow most of the protocol that makes descendants of that class so powerful: the ability to construct and manage a heterogeneous collection of objects in a consistent way. Adept manipulation of these nestable graphic collections provides the "meat" of any complex, interactive graphics application.

Text

Labels are the graphics that draw themselves as attributed text with attributes like font, style, and combination mode. Objects of class **Label** hold this text as a **String** object in an instance variable named *string*. They inherit all of the general protocols of **Graphic** class. They also follow a rendering model similar to that of **Shape** class. When asked to draw themselves, labels merge their pens with an equivalent port-owned rendering tool. Then they draw their **String** objects on the port's output device. The difference between a label and a shape is that **Label** objects own neither pens nor brushes; they own **TextPen** objects instead.

The **RichText** class creates and manages collections of attributed text. Strings that contain mixtures of text styles know how to draw and edit themselves. A **RichText** is useful in any application that requires items of attributed text to be treated as a unit or group, such as a WYSIWYG word processing or publishing system. Note that **RichText** derives much of its collection handling behavior from the **Picture** class, from which it descends. In general, pictures own a pen, a brush, and a collection of mixed graphics. They allow you to manipulate groups of graphics as if they were ordinary collection objects. **RichText** objects are picture-type collections that allow only **Label** or other **RichText** objects as members, and that also know how to do some text-oriented functions on themselves.

Coordinate Systems: The GraphSpace Object

One big difference between drawing by hand with tools and doing it in software is the way you position and size a shape. If you have ever used a drawing template, then you are probably accustomed to picking a shape size that looks about right, positioning it on the paper, and drawing it. In a program, this process is more mathematically specific: Everything is expressed in terms of precise coordinates and dimensions, rather than approximate sizes and positions.

Coordinate Systems

Coordinates are the positions (x, y) of points in a two-dimensional Cartesian coordinate space, and these points define shapes. Spaces can vary in many ways: The directionality of the space may be different (negative could go to the right instead of to the left), its coordinates could be spaced closer together, or its origin could be to the side or in one of the corners of the space. Examples of different coordinate systems are shown in Figure 2.4.

There are times when each of these different types of spaces may be useful. If, for example, we are modeling something that does not allow negative values, then it makes sense to use a coordinate system that only has positive coordinates. One common use of such a space is to model the physical structure of a graphic display device, which is known as a device space. This device space treats the grid of pixels as a coordinate system with its origin at the lower-left corner of the screen, and coordinates increasing positively out from the origin, x to the right, and y moving upward. Each (x, y) coordinate pair represents a different pixel on the display. We will talk about different types of coordinate systems later, including those with real-world measurements, but for now we will use simple device space as our example.

The GraphSpace Object

The ObjectGraphics object that embodies the coordinate space is the **Graph-Space**. This is the first instance in this discussion of an object that does not have a concrete real-world counterpart.

A port always contains a graph space, and all drawing done to that port is done relative to that space. The port's space controls how a piece of the application's conceptual world is mapped onto the physical display device, and thus how the final image appears. A graph space is a rendering tool because it bundles diverse visual attributes into a conceptual package. It might help to think of a graph space as a brush with which you can paint the *dimensionality* of your graphic objects.

To model this process, a graph space contains three rectangles: the

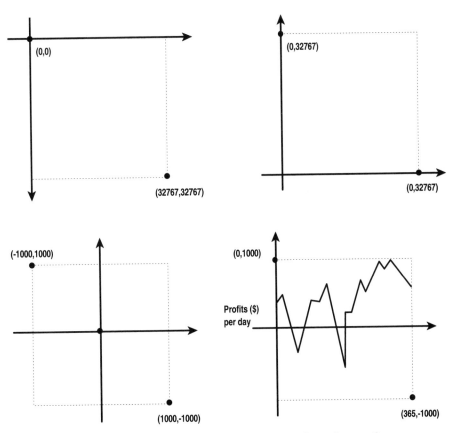

Figure 2.4: Three coordinate axes showing alternatives

world rectangle defines the world represented by the space, the *mapping rectangle* defines the part of that world that is to be mapped onto the display, and the *display rectangle* defines the relative size and shape of the resulting image. The mapping rectangle defines the portion of the world that is viewed. The display rectangle defines the area of the output device in which that view appears. The relationship between these rectangles is depicted in Figure 2.5.

Coordinates within the space defined by the world rectangle are known as *world coordinates*. These represent real measurements, and are expressed in the units of the space, such as inches, feet, or miles. The coordinates of the mapping rectangle are also world coordinates, which position the mapping rectangle within the world. The display rectangle, however, is expressed in *device coordinates*, or *pixels*, that correspond to the output device that will eventually display the image. In the example of Figure 2.5, the world rectangle is defined to be of sufficient size to enclose the entire jet, say 100 feet by 80 feet. The mapping rectangle encloses some portion of that, measured in the same units. The display rectangle is computed to cause the area covered by the mapping rectangle to appear in a selected area of the display.

Every **GraphSpace** object owns and maintains three rectangle objects, one each for its world, mapping, and display rectangles. Working with GraphSpace objects generally boils down to defining and manipulating these rectangles.

Defining a GraphSpace

A **GraphSpace** is created by defining its world rectangle. The origin of this rectangle becomes the top-left corner of the world, and the corner of the rectangle is the bottom-right corner of the world. The world rectangle defines both the allowed ranges for coordinates used in drawing with the space and the directionality of the space.

Recall that directionality of the space is an indication of whether coordinates increase or decrease moving to the right and down. Table 2.1 shows some examples of world rectangle definitions and the spaces that result.

Once a world is defined, the real work is in defining how a piece of that world is to appear on the physical display device. This process, known as *display mapping*, involves positioning a rectangle in the world, and then defining an equivalent rectangle in the device into which that piece of the world is to be mapped.

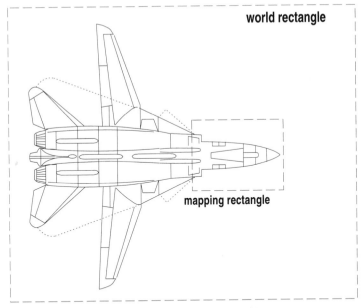

The mapping rectangle defines the portion of the world that
is viewed.

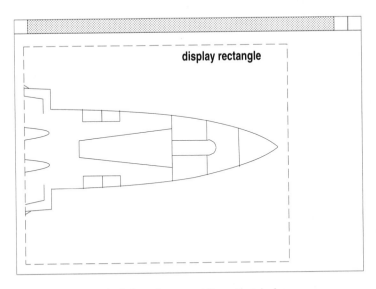

The display rectangle defines the area of the output device
in which that view appears.

**Figure 2.5: The relationship between the world, mapping, and display
rectangles**

Origin (top left)	Corner (bottom right)	Resulting Space
(0, 0)	(32767, 32767)	The range of positive integers, with the y axis directed downward.
(0, 32767)	(32767, 0)	Same range, with the y axis directed upward.
(−1000, 1000)	(1000, −1000)	A traditional four-quadrant space, with (0, 0) in the center, and an upward-directed y-axis.

Table 2.1: World rectangle definitions and resulting spaces

Display Mapping

The mapping rectangle is a window into a world, something like a periscope, microscope, or a pair of binoculars. By moving it around, you can change what is mapped onto the display; by changing its size, you can shrink or enlarge the image on the display. These are all operations common to graphics applications. The following sections examine the specific operations of display mapping: scrolling, zooming, and changing the aspect ratio.

Scrolling

Moving the window around inside the world is generally known as *scrolling* (it also goes by the names *panning* and *roaming*). Since the position of the top-left corner of the mapping rectangle is expressed in relation to the top-left corner of the display window, repositioning the mapping rectangle is all that is required to achieve scrolling. The **GraphSpace** will make whatever internal adjustments are necessary, including constraining the movement to stay within the world.

Zooming

To zoom the image (make it smaller or bigger), change the relationship between the mapping rectangle and the display rectangle. If they are the same size (taking unit conversions into account), the image is actual size, represented by a zoom factor of 100 percent, or one-to-one. To zoom in or enlarge a part of the picture, make the mapping rectangle smaller relative to the display rectangle, forcing a smaller piece of the world to be displayed in the same display rectangle. This corresponds to a zoom factor of greater than 100 percent. The reverse process, making the mapping rectangle bigger than the display rectangle, gives the effect of backing away from the image. More of the world is displayed in the same space, corresponding to zoom factors less than 100 percent. Similar effects can be achieved by manipulating the display rectangle rather than the mapping rectangle.

Take, for example, a drafting program. By defining a mapping rectangle in world coordinates that encloses a 4-foot square, and mapping it onto a corresponding display rectangle that encloses a 4-inch square on the screen, a view is created that maps 1 foot in world coordinates to 1 inch in display coordinates. In this case, the zoom factor is 4 inches divided by 4 feet, or 8.33 percent. The resulting image is much smaller on the screen than it is in the world.

Support for this type of precise mapping is provided directly by the **GraphSpace**, shielding the application from these device-specific calculations. In fact, applications never directly specify a display rectangle. **Graph-Space** provides two mechanisms for achieving these effects. First is the request to set the zoom level to a specific percentage:

```
setZoom(aGraphSpace, zoomPt);
```

where **zoomPt** is a **Point** containing the zoom percentage in the x and y directions (this uses a **Point** as a convenient way to hold an x and y value). Notice that this lets you apply a different zoom in each direction. You would only need to do this if you wanted the output to be stretched or squashed to fit a specific display rectangle. **GraphSpace** does this for you with the following message:

```
fitToRectangle(aGraphSpace, dispRect);
```

This tells the **GraphSpace** to compute a set of zoom factors to cause the current mapping rectangle to fit the given display rectangle. This is not quite the same as simply setting the display rectangle of the space, because of an additional consideration here that may prevent the image from fitting the given rectangle perfectly: the aspect ratio lock, described in the next section.

Aspect Ratio

The *aspect ratio* of an image is the ratio of its height to its width. Consider what would happen if the aspect ratios of the mapping and display rectangles were different: The resulting image would be stretched or squashed to match the aspect ratio of the display rectangle. To keep you from having to maintain aspect ratio correspondence, **GraphSpace** objects provide a mechanism for enforcing a proper aspect ratio on the display rectangle, and alternately for allowing the image to be distorted. This is known as aspect ratio locking.

This is represented in the **GraphSpace** by the **aspect** attribute, which can take on one of two symbolic values: **#locked** and **#unlocked**. This is set as follows:

```
setAspectLock(aGraphSpace, aspectSymbol);
```

GraphSpace objects are normally **#locked**, making sure that the proper aspect ratio is maintained by effectively modifying the display rectangle. This is the most common way to use a **GraphSpace**, but there is often a need to **#unlock** it. One example is the "fit-to-window" view that most drawing packages, including ObjectDraw, offer.

Measurements

Since such a large number of graphic applications deal in real-world measurements, ObjectGraphics provides support for coordinate spaces that define these measurements. **GraphSpace** objects include a units attribute that tells ObjectGraphics what units of measurement are represented by the world coordinates. As with all non-numeric drawing attributes, they are represented with symbols. ObjectGraphics recognizes **#inches, #centimeters, #picas, #points**, and **#device**. The **#device** units are pixels on a computer screen.

Measurement is also determined by a **GraphSpace** object's granularity, which defines how many world coordinate increments represent one of those units. Thus, a space in units of **#inches** and a granularity of 16 represents a world of $\frac{1}{16}$-inch measurements.

If the space's zoom factor is set to 100 percent, ObjectGraphics makes every attempt to map these real-world measurements onto the display device such that the image appears full size. This is not always possible, because this process is based on assumptions about the physical size of the display. What might appear as 1 inch on a 12-inch diagonal monitor appears considerably larger on a 19-inch monitor. This doesn't apply to **#device** units, since they represent physical pixels on the display device and not real-world measurements. The only way to guarantee the outcome is to specify the display hardware and test it out yourself. Units are defined by the following message:

```
setUnits(aGraphSpace, unitsSymbol, granularity);
```

Grids

It's often useful, particularly in interactive drawing programs, to constrain the placement of points to a grid. **GraphSpace** objects support this by maintaining a grid definition as an (x, y) pair that defines the increments of the grid in the two dimensions. For example, a grid definition of $(10, 20)$ will constrain x coordinates to be only multiples of 10, and y coordinates to multiples of 20.

A **GraphSpace** object's grid is expressed in a **Point** object (a convenient way to hold an x and y pair) as the number of grains per grid unit. For example, using a **GraphSpace** with units of **#inches** and a granularity of 100, set its grid to $(25, 25)$ to obtain $\frac{1}{4}$-inch spacing of objects, like this:

```
setGrid(aGraphSpace, 25@25);
```

Grids don't actually impose themselves on the space, but can be used whenever you want to. You do this by asking a **GraphSpace** to adjust a point the nearest grid point, like this:

```
snapToGrid(aGraphSpace, aPoint);
```

This actually modifies the given point's (x, y) values to place it at the nearest grid crossing.

Coordinate Conversions

One of the more useful facilities provided by a **GraphSpace** object is the ability to convert coordinates from one system to another. This is often necessary when dealing with multiple views of an image. An example of this would be a design package that displays multiple views of a drawing at different scales. A more common example of a coordinate conversion is translating pixel positions on the screen (which are, after all, just points in a **#device** space) into world coordinates of the graphic model being displayed. For example, ObjectGraphics uses this mechanism to provide the mouse position in terms of world coordinates.

GraphSpace provides two forms of conversion. The more generic form will convert a given point from the space's coordinate system to that of another space:

```
convertPoint(aGraphSpace, aPoint, destSpace);
```

This method returns a **Point** that is equivalent, in **destSpace**, to the given point in **aGraphSpace**. Equivalence is based on relative position: If **aPoint** is dead center in the world of **aGraphSpace**, then the returned point will be the center of the world of **destSpace**. The second set of conversions allow you to convert points between display coordinates and your current graph space. Thus, **GraphSpace** provides a more specialized set of behaviors for that purpose:

```
displayToWorld(aGraphSpace, aPoint);
worldToDisplay(aGraphSpace, aPoint);
```

These convert the given **Point** between the space's world coordinates and display coordinates. This conversion takes into account all of the zooming and scrolling that could take place, so that the display and world points will always coincide. For example, if you are looking at a zoomed up piece of the image, converting a pixel coordinate in that display to the image's world finds the same point as it would if the image were not zoomed.

Sample Application: Part II

Now that we've looked a little deeper into the features of ObjectGraphics, we will expand on our earlier example of a simple drawing tool.

Dragging

First, consider what it would take to generalize the tool to draw any graphic object, rather than just a line. Because all graphic objects follow a common set of protocols, we can use our original dragging model almost unchanged. All we need to add is code that relates, in some way, a menu selection to the name of one of the graphic classes. In Actor, we would use a **Dictionary** that maps the integers, given to us by Windows to indicate menu selections, onto class names:

```
$Tools := static(%Dictionary(710->Chooser 711->Line
        712->Rectangle 719->RoundRect 713->Ellipse));
```

We get a graphic class from this dictionary based on a menu choice, create and initialize an instance of that class, and the rest of our dragging behavior would be the same. The result is shown in Listing 2.2.

This is limited, because it only works with rectangularly defined objects such as rectangles, ellipses, and lines. More complicated shapes such as polylines or curves would take some special handling, but not much. The general concept of initializing, growing, and then saving an instance of a graphic object is common to all possible shapes.

Zooming and Scrolling

Coordinate space manipulation is usually one of the more complex aspects of any graphic application. This is particularly true of the common functions of zooming and scrolling an image: The application must keep track of the current state of the display so that it can properly manage the correspondence between screen locations and positions within the world. In this section, we'll see how the **GraphSpace** object discussed earlier can be put to use in meeting these requirements.

We have already encountered one application of the **GraphSpace** without even knowing it. You may have noticed that the point parameter (**aPoint**) to the dragging methods shown earlier is provided in world coordinates, in spite of the fact that the Windows cursor handler only knows about screen (device coordinate) positions. This conversion is done automatically by the ObjectGraphics **Window** object, from which any application would descend. The window owns a **GraphSpace**, held in the instance variable **space**, that defines the current state of the window's coordinate system.

```
Def beginDrag(self, keyStates, aPoint)
  { aGraphic :=
      build(Classes[$Tools[menuID]], aPoint, aPoint);
    setPen(aGraphic,
      build(Pen, nil, #solid, 1, #nxor, #opaque));
    associate(port, self);
    draw(aGraphic, port);
  }

Def drag(self, keyStates, aPoint)
  { fastDraw(aGraphic, port);
    setCorner(aGraphic, aPoint);
    fastDraw(aGraphic, port);
  }

Def endDrag(self, keyStates, aPoint)
  { setPen(aGraphic, copy(currentPen));
    draw(aGraphic, port);
    dissociate(port);
    add(picture, aGraphic);
  }
```

Listing 2.2: Dragging behavior

When mouse activity is received from Windows, the mouse position is converted from screen coordinates to the corresponding world coordinates. Regardless of any scrolling or zooming that has been applied to the space, the conversion properly maps the mouse position into the world.

As we discussed earlier, the zoom and scroll functions are achieved through manipulation of the mapping and display rectangles of the **Graph-Space**. For an interactive drawing tool, the most intuitive way of selecting a zoom is to stretch a box around an area of interest, causing the contents of that box to fill the window. Assuming that our application sets **aGraphic** to be a **Rectangle** when Zoom is selected, we would use that rectangle in conjunction with the **displayRect** request to the application window (which returns a rectangle representing the drawing area of the window) to redefine our **endDrag** behavior as follows:

```
Def endDrag(self, keyStates, aPoint)
{ if (selectedTool = #zoom) then
    setMappingRect(space, aGraphic);
    fitToRectangle(space, displayRect(self));
  else
    setPen(aGraphic, copy(currentPen));
    ... same as before ...
    add(picture, aGraphic);
  endif;
}
```

We first use **aGraphic** to select the area of interest, and then use **fitToRectangle** to instruct the **GraphSpace** to map that area of interest into the window's drawing area.

To scroll an image, move the mapping rectangle to the new area of interest and the image follows. This actually requires two steps: First we update the **GraphSpace** to reflect the movement of the **MappingRect**, then we ask the **port** to perform the scroll on the screen. If we presume that we can translate scroll bar activity into an (x, y) point representing the distance by which we are to move, a scroll method would look like this:

```
Def scrollBy(self, offsetPt | newOrigin)
{ newOrigin := origin(mappingRect(space))+offsetPt;
  moveMappingRect(space, newOrigin);
  scrollPort(port, newOrigin, self);
}
```

These are just a few examples of the kind of high-level application support embedded in the standard ObjectGraphics objects. Before we close, we'll take a deeper look into the internal structure of ObjectGraphics.

Behind the Scenes: ObjectGraphics Internals

Platform Encapsulators

The classes termed *Platform Filters* provide a translation layer between an application's usage of generic graphic manipulations, objects, and attributes, and each target windowing environment's specific function calls, data structures, and attribute identifiers. These are the classes that allow ObjectGraphics application code to run unchanged under each target it supports.

Platform filters also hide some windowing environments' design flaws. A case in point is Microsoft Windows, which makes it the responsibility of individual applications, rather than the environment, to manage both persistent GDI "objects" and Display Contexts. Mismanagement of these entities is very common and is usually catastrophic. Therefore, the Windows version of **PhysicalPort** takes on the burden of managing these items in a fashion that is transparent. ObjectGraphics users never manipulate either Display Contexts or GDI objects, so they can't accidentally be mismanaged.

Ports and Physical Ports

The heart of ObjectGraphics' platform insulation scheme is the partnership between the class **Port** and its descendant, **PhysicalPort**. From the developer's viewpoint, Ports are display-independent, virtual output devices on which they draw graphics, similar to Display Contexts, Presentation Spaces, GraphPorts and Graphics Ports under Microsoft Windows, Presentation Manager, Macintosh and the X Window System, respectively. Because Ports fully encapsulate these diverse, platform-dependent entities, developers need not concern themselves with the details of graphical output under each environment.

Ports and PhysicalPorts divide their duties along very clearly defined bounds. If an intended Port behavior or data structure deals exclusively with ObjectGraphics objects and methods, it is assigned to **Port**. If it is dependent on a specific environment, it is assigned to **PhysicalPort**. In fact, **PhysicalPort**, **Color**, and **Bitmap** are the only classes that ever call a graphics kernel function. When a Port method necessarily involves both platform-independent, conceptual manipulation of graphic objects and lower level, platform-specific manipulation of an environment's data structures and/or function calls, the method is divided into two parts.

Association and Dissociation: Port objects support few public protocols; most of the messages they receive are sent by graphic objects when they need low level, platform-specific services. The most important public protocols, however, are associate and dissociate. The associate message, sent to a port object with a window, printer, or bitmap object as a parameter, connects the output device to the port and prepares it for output. Subsequent drawing messages, sent to graphic objects with the port as a parameter, cause changes on the display surface of the output device. The port hides the kernel-imposed API variations caused by both graphic type and output destination. The dissociate message disconnects the port from an output device and performs any environment-specific cleanup that may be necessary at that time.

Color Objects

Numerous schemes have evolved to model the concept of color in various industries and graphics systems. From graphics hardware comes the RGB model, which corresponds to the three electron guns in a color monitor. From the publishing industry comes the CMY or CMYK model, which corresponds to the colors of ink used in the process of color separation. From the world of art, the hue-saturation-lightness (HSL) model (which has more aliases than we can count) models color in a way that is somewhat more comfortable for graphic artists. Within each of these models, there is considerable variation in the numeric ranges used to express the component color attributes. Consequently, different graphics environments model color in their own ways. In order to bridge this confusion with a consistent standard, ObjectGraphics defines the platform filter known as **Color**.

The objects created by **Color** class conform to a modified RGB color model. In the standard model, colors are specified by three real values in the range of 0.0 to 1.0, which correspond to intensities of red, green, and blue. ObjectGraphics utilizes three values for these primaries as well, but their range is represented by integers with values from 0 to 255. Thus, color objects can handle up to 24-bit color displays.

The library provides two principle ways to specify color. **Color** defines the class method **RGB**, which takes three integers representing intensities of red, green, and blue as parameters. This allows the custom mixing of any color. The class method **primary** allows the symbolic specification of one of the defined primary colors. As shipped, ObjectGraphics recognizes the three RGB primaries plus the three CMY primaries plus black and white as primary colors. Color class implements the **addSymColor** method to extend the primary color dictionary to include any color that the user wishes to specify symbolically.

Any color object may be queried as to its component colors with the **red**, **green**, and **blue** messages, each of which will return a value in the range of 0 to 255. Also, as a convenience, a color's components may be queried according to the CMY model with the **cyan**, **magenta**, and **yellow** messages.

Files and Streams

We mentioned earlier that all ObjectGraphics objects know how to transfer themselves into and out of a file. The underlying mechanism by which this is achieved is the **OGXStream** object. This object implements a conceptual stream of data that understands the structure of objects and can direct the movement of object data into and out of itself. In order to get that data on and off a disk, the stream is associated with an instance of **OGXFile**, which is a descendant of the standard Actor **File** class. OGXFiles know the details of opening, writing, reading, and closing MS/DOS files.

An interesting benefit of this structure involves support for clipboards. The Windows clipboard is a medium for the exchange of information among applications. The format of this information is fairly open and allows for application-specific data. The most common use for application-specific data formats is for the traditional cut-and-paste operations within an application. For ObjectGraphics applications, the application-specific clipboard format comes almost free: because OGXStreams can be associated with a piece of memory just as easily as with a disk file, the clipboard can be supported by writing the objects to a memory stream just as if it were to a file. That memory can then be installed in the clipboard and used either within the same application, or by another ObjectGraphics application.

Conclusion

Although we've only highlighted some of the ObjectGraphics features, ObjectGraphics has a wide range of useful and interesting capabilities that can be used for a variety of graphics applications. However, even given this, these graphics objects can be further refined through subclassing to support application-specific requirements and further lighten the load on the application developer. Thus, we feel that ObjectGraphics, and similar object-oriented graphics libraries, are needed to make the task of creating graphics applications both easier and more rewarding.

Chapter 3

Implementing GEO++ in Smalltalk-80

Peter Wisskirchen

The GEO++ graphics system was introduced as a system to build up, display, and modify graphics object hierarchies. The description in Wisskirchen [1990] serves mainly as an abstract specification to reach a new definition of a graphics system supporting part hierarchies. The GEO++ functionality was compared with PHIGS as far as the construction and editing of graphics object hierarchies were concerned.

This chapter describes our first experiences in integrating GEO++ into the Smalltalk-80 environment. It shows how GEO++ was integrated into the Smalltalk-80 window management, how an optimal use of the model-view-controller (MVC) metaphor could be achieved, and how the high-level graphics functionality of GEO++ could be combined with the predefined graphics kernel already existing in the environment. In addition, it discusses how the potential of object-oriented programming can be used to specialize and modify the behavior of a predefined graphics application, in this case, a simple graphics editor.

GEO++

GEO++ provides a class library to support the following tasks:
* Definition, modification, and display of a graphics object hierarchy (Wisskirchen [1989]).

The author thanks Klaus Kansy for many suggestions and Rüdiger Kolb for realizing a first version of the editor.

- Integration of its predefined functionality into an application system by means of object-oriented programming techniques.

GEO++ draws extensively on the tradition of graphics standards such as GKS (ISO [1985]) and PHIGS (ISO [1989]) concerning its overall model. Besides this, GEO++ is influenced by object-oriented techniques provided by different object-oriented graphics kernels.

Traditional Sources

GEO++ constitutes a workstation-independent (and to a high degree, language-independent) functional specification with hidden implementation and with a functionality to support graphics part hierarchies.

GEO++ is presented as a predefined kernel. The kernel's internal implementation is supposed to remain hidden. An application programmer should not modify the internal implementation code, even if it is technically possible (as in the Smalltalk-80 environment). Otherwise, the modifications would restrict portability of the application. The principle of a *hidden* kernel has the advantage that the manufacturer of the kernel system may implement the internal components according to his own notions, including the effective implementation of time-critical operations in hardware (Enderle et al. [1987]). Here the principles of GKS and PHIGS are still valid.

The tradition of graphics systems is strongly influenced by the semantics of a part hierarchy. Multilevel systems support the concept of building composites from smaller units and handling them as new entities that may be treated as higher-level graphics primitives. In these characteristic aspects GEO++ aims to support part hierarchies as well as PHIGS does. Compared to PHIGS, however, GEO++ enables the management of a multilevel part hierarchy to allow access to individual parts as well as to geometrical descriptions shared by several parts. In addition, the naming concept of GEO++ differs quite extensively from PHIGS.

Advantages of an Object-Oriented Design

Many aspects of GEO++ were stimulated by the general object-oriented design philosophy and by the graphics kernels incorporated in existing object-oriented programming environments.

Being forced to think in terms of objects leads to a natural description of the functionality of graphics systems. It entails the following:

- Direct naming of items that can be visualized.
- The treatment of objects' attributes and behavior as inherent information of these objects.
- Viewing different objects with equal behavior as instances of a common class.

In GEO++, all visible graphics units exist as objects in the sense of object-oriented programming; that is, they can be addressed by name, they carry their own information (attributes), and they keep methods for the assignment and inquiry of this information. To a much higher degree than in traditional graphics systems, the construction and update of graphics structures therefore can be described as the applications programmer "feels" them: as the construction and update of displayable objects. Programming becomes easier and unwanted side effects are avoided.

Inheritance can be employed in a graphics system in a multitude of applications. The implementer of a graphics kernel uses inheritance to organize the class hierarchy so that common behavior of instances of different classes can be shared by a superclass of these classes, as will be shown in Figure 3.2. The application programmer uses inheritance mainly as a programming technique to customize a predefined graphics kernel for specific needs. Inheritance allows the *integration* of application-specific knowledge into graphics objects by extending their functionality, as will be shown in the discussion of the Graph model. In many cases, subclassing is a much more natural structuring aid than yet another layer above a predefined graphics kernel, as is required if traditional procedure-oriented systems such as GKS and PHIGS are extended. The latter may achieve combination, but suffers in integration.

GEO++ in Smalltalk-80

The specification of GEO++ was motivated by the goal to build a bridge between traditional approaches and object-oriented systems. To achieve this, a pure specification as worked out in Wisskirchen [1990] is not sufficient and has to be supplemented by an implementation.

GEO++ was implemented in Smalltalk-80 mainly to get experience for the author's work in standardization (Kansy & Wisskirchen [1989]). We do not intend to develop "GEO++ in Smalltalk-80" as a product. Thus, the implementation serves as a research tool and a personal experiment.

At present, the implemented GEO++ functionality supports mainly one-level graphics hierarchies. This is the functionality required to realize the simple editor described below. We started with such a simple system to get experience, as quickly as possible, about how to integrate a kernel with hidden internal implementation into the window system and the MVC concept. In addition we wished to get answers about the integration of modern input techniques as classified by Myers [1990], because mouse input with state-of-the-art interaction feedback techniques had not been considered in existing standards and had not been studied in the previous specification.

Why Smalltalk-80?

There are good reasons to implement GEO++ in Smalltalk-80:
*   The Smalltalk-80 language is widely recognized as the most stringent implementation of the object-oriented paradigm, simply because it is a pure object-oriented language. We have chosen Smalltalk-80 with Xerox Parc's programming environment, which is well known, widely available, and excellently documented in the books by Goldberg and Robson [1983] and Goldberg [1984].
*   The process of programming differs from a conventional system because of the great number of predefined classes and methods, the comfortable editor, and especially the possibilities provided by inheritance: taking over predefined functionality and modifying it to fit current needs. In particular, the collection classes in Smalltalk-80 make it easy to build up graphics part hierarchies.
*   The direct support of graphics functionality. The Smalltalk-80 graphics kernel with editable primitives could be used advantageously to implement the GEO++ output primitive classes.
*   The predefined functionality to write window-oriented interactive applications assisted by the predefined *view* and *controller* classes. Note that in Smalltalk-80 a drawing area with a frame as boundary (often called window) is an instance of class **View** or one of its subclasses, that is, a *view*.

The GEO++ Class Library

The GEO++ implementation in Smalltalk-80 consists of a class library and is organized as one category of the environment. GEO++ will be used by the application programmer by passing messages that are declared as part of the application programming interface (API). In addition, subclasses of the pre-defined (transparent) GEO++ classes can be defined to extend the inherited functionality and to override methods that are declared as part of the API.

Besides GEO++, the application programmer will of course also use the functionality of the many predefined classes of the Smalltalk-80 environment. To avoid an unsystematic approach to the design of computer graphics software, we propose (and provide) a well-defined division of labor between GEO++ and the Smalltalk-80 window and menu system.

In GEO++, a graphics object hierarchy is represented as a tree. A tree is defined as an object of the class **Group**. To model our graphics editor one specific instance of group is created. This object is called **root** and it contains all visual graphics items edited by the user. These items, which are the subnodes of the tree, are named parts representing the visual objects of the respective subhierarchy of the given hierarchy. Each part consists of two main components, a geometrical description, the *content,* and a set of *part attributes.* In general, the content of a part may be a group itself, that is, a part hierarchy in its own right, or it may be an output primitive. Contents of a part are described by groups only if multilevel hierarchies are to be manipulated (Wisskirchen [1990]). The simple graphics editor described here can do without multilevel operations so that the parts of the editor are always *end-parts,* that is, parts with an output primitive as content.

Different parts may share one and the same content, whereas a part's attribute can be seen as the part's own individual information. Parts sharing the same content are called *equivalent.* In our editor, equivalent parts are generated by the copy operation provided as a menu option. Changing an attribute such as linestyle or linewidth, or transforming a part will not affect its content and its equivalence relations with other parts. Editing a part, however, will replace the content of a part and thus destroy equivalence relations with other parts, as will be discussed in the next section.

In this chapter, we focus on those GEO++ classes that are important for the graphics editor described in the following paragraphs. The GEO++ classes can be divided into classes that manage the graphics hierarchy and classes that define input and output devices. The main classes to build up hierarchies are **Group**, **Parts**, and classes that describe the end-nodes of a hierarchy, that is, parts containing output primitives as content. Note that there is no class **Part** to model one single part; single parts are described by end-parts. **Parts** is defined as a subclass of the Smalltalk-80 class **Ordered-Collection** (an ordered set of key-value pairs with integer type keys) to model the complete part hierarchy of a group (in our single-level case); it is

used to define an instance variable **myParts** of **Group**. The ordering relation inherited from **OrderedCollection** is used to define priority rules
between overlapping parts (display priority). Output primitives in GEO++,
organized as subclasses of **GEOPrimitive**, differ slightly from the Small-
talk-80 classes. Their coordinates are defined as world coordinates; in
addition, these primitives know that they are components of the graphics
system and they inform it when their coordinates or attributes have changed
due to editing operations in order to restore the display.

Figure 3.1 shows a part hierarchy (corresponding to Figure 3.3a) with
three equivalent end-parts of class **PolylinePart** and two equivalent end-
parts of class **RectanglePart**. Note that all five parts carry different attributes, namely different transformations. **Parts** allows the same editing methods as GEO++ primitives, which themselves provide the same editing
operations as the Smalltalk-80 primitives in the environment. Figure 3.2
shows a part of the class hierarchy of the output-oriented GEO++ classes (a
subset of the different output primitive classes). The class **Object** is the root
of the complete Smalltalk-80 inheritance tree.

Note that the Smalltalk-80 primitives **Arc**, **Circle**, **Quadrangle**, and
LinearFit are not part of the GEO++ hierarchy, but each GEO++ primitive
has access to a corresponding Smalltalk-80 primitive through an instance
variable. Defining the GEO++ output primitives as well as subclasses of the
Smalltalk-80 primitives would have required multiple inheritance, which is
not provided by Smalltalk-80.

Main Output Methods

A new end-part is created by informing its class about the root of the
hierarchy and by the primitive to be used as content. Usually, a third
parameter denoting an attribute is applied. Thus, for example, a new part of

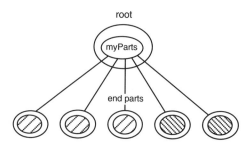

Figure 3.1: Part hierarchy spanned by the root of the editor

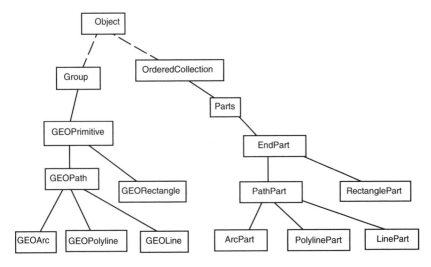

Figure 3.2: Class hierarchy of the GEO++ output classes

class **PolyLinePart** is generated for the hierarchy **root** by using **aPolyLine**, an instance of **GEOPolyline**, as content and applying an attribute:

```
aPart ← PolyLinePart for:root content:aPolyLine
          attribute:anAttribute
```

For special attribute types, such as a translation, a part can be created by:

```
aPart ← PolyLinePart for:root content:aPolyLine
          moveBy:aDeltaPoint
```

where **aDeltaPoint** is a two-dimensional point describing the amount of the translation. By using this method the Σ-shaped polyline displayed in the top-left area of Figure 3.3a was created.

An empty part can be created and then instantiated as part of a hierarchy by the following two statements:

```
aPart ← PolyLinePart new
aPart for:root content:aPolyLine moveBy:aDeltaPoint
```

A *copy* of a part will result in a new part sharing the identical content with the original part:

```
aPartCopy ← aPart copy.
```

By copying parts (and by applying then an additional transformation) the other two polyline parts were created, resulting in three equivalent parts (Figure 3.3a).

As mentioned above, a part can be *edited* with the effect that exactly one visual object on the screen will change. As a result, the part in question will be provided by a new content. In our example, the fourth coordinate of the picked part was changed (in the local editing mode of the editor) as shown in Figure 3.3b by:

```
aPart at:4 put:aNewPoint.
```

After this operation, the only Σ-shaped polyline parts still equivalent are the two remaining objects.

To demonstrate *content editing* the user selects the menu option *global* and picks one of the equivalent objects with the mouse, resulting in Figure 3.3c showing all control points of the selected part and those of its equivalent partners. Then the fourth control point of one of these selected parts is picked and moved. These user actions are handled internally by the following: detecting the picked part **myPart**, inquiring its content **pickedContent**, sending the edit feedback message to it for showing the control points, evaluating the second pick resulting in the coordinate number **anInteger**, and replacing it by the new point **aNewPoint** delivered by the locator when the mouse button is released. Then

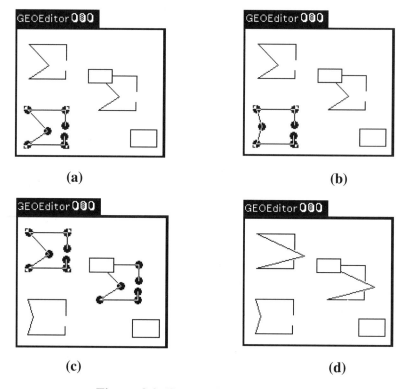

Figure 3.3: Part and content editing

```
pickedContent at:4 put:aNewPoint
```

will change the content and restore the drawing resulting in Figure 3.3d. Thus all equivalent parts referring to the identical content are redisplayed by GEO++ accordingly.

Attributes for Parts

The attributes used for our editor, as far as it is described here, are **highlightingOn**, **highlightingOff**, a translation (move) of a part, and methods to change the display priority, reordering the collection of parts:

```
aPart highlightingOn
aPart moveBy:(4@5)
aPart highestDisplayPriority
aPart displayPriority:5.
```

Input and Interaction Feedback

The Garnet system offers a framework with seven different types of interactors to handle almost all the kinds of interactions found in graphical direct manipulation interfaces (Myers [1990]). In our view it is still an open question how the ideal set of input and interaction tools should be defined, particularly for future standard packages. At present, GEO++ supports only a limited set of interaction techniques, mainly to control mouse interaction for the editor application. With our approach we have tried to extend the GKS and PHIGS input devices *locator* and *pick* by introducing special classes **Locator** and **MousePick**, supplemented by classes providing interaction feedback (**RubberBand** and **Dragger**). The methods controlling these input devices are similar to those provided by the Smalltalk-80 class for the mouse.

The ideal Smalltalk-80 mouse supports graphics interaction with three buttons colored red (left), yellow (middle), and blue (right). Many Smalltalk-80 implementations simulate the ideal mouse by a one-button mouse. Here, the three colored buttons are virtual buttons which are mapped to the one mouse button plus the two keys, Option and Command. The red button is mapped to the single button, while the yellow and blue buttons are mapped to the single button on the mouse plus the Option and Command keys, respectively. In our implementation, mouse operation inside a view, that is, handled under control of GEO++, is provided by the class

MouseLocator, delivering coordinates in world coordinates. **MouseLocator** is defined as a subclass of the predefined class **InputSensor** (the class for the Smalltalk-80 mouse with three buttons). To give some examples, for a locator defined by

```
aLocator ← MouseLocator new
```

the statement

```
aLocation ← aLocator mousePoint
```

gives the current mouse position, whereas

```
aLocation ← aLocator waitButton
```

waits for the user to press any button.

```
aLocator redButtonPressed
```

answers (with **true** or **false**) whether the red button is being pressed.

A *pick device* delivers the picked part of the object hierarchy (or *nil*). As mentioned, in GKS and PHIGS the user interface of a pick operation is not precisely defined by the application programming interface. The concept of a mouse pick device is introduced to define precisely how the user may pick an object, allowing the definition of the various interaction styles used for selection shown by the following examples. For a mouse pick defined by

```
pick ← MousePick new
```

the statement

```
aPart ← pick waitButton
```

waits for the user to press any button and uses the position to select.

```
aPart ← pick location:aPoint
```

provides the pick device with a location (already known by the application) to select the picked part.

A *dragger* provides dragging of a part with interaction feedback (see Figure 3.6 later in the chapter). With

```
aDeltaPoint ← aDragger dragPart:aPart
   from:startPosition
```

the outline of **aPart** is displayed at the mouse position until the mouse button is released, then the difference **aDeltaPoint** between the new position and **startPosition** is delivered back. Note that dragging only provides the user with feedback. If dragging should result in a translation of the part, the additional operation **moveBy:** to move a part is required.

A *rubberband* also defines a pure interaction feedback. It is provided with a location of the origin of the band and echoes a line from it to the current position of the pressed mouse. When the mouse button is released, the end position will be delivered as the result

```
endPoint ← aRubberBand from:beginPoint.
```

The Abstract Workstation View Device

The abstract workstation called *view device,* which will be described in the section on the integration of GEO++ with MVC, provides many methods inherited by the Smalltalk-80 environment because it is realized as a subclass of the predefined class **StandardSystemView**. In addition, this device provides methods realized by GEO++ that are similar to the PHIGS or GKS access methods to the workstation description table. In particular, the above-mentioned input and interaction feedback can be associated to a view device by special methods.

MVC

The model-view-controller (MVC) metaphor is one of the most important concepts in the Smalltalk-80 programming environment (Krasner and Pope [1989]). One of the objectives pursued by the MVC concept is a modularization of the system components—application, interaction, and output. The MVC concept supports a strong separation between these three components, especially for creating different versions of user interfaces for one application. The MVC concept is more than a pure concept. Because of its many predefined classes it may be regarded as a elegant toolbox for interface design.

If the code of a typical interactive graphics application program is analyzed, three types of code may be distinguished:

1. Code that handles the internal data and operations of the "actual" application, isolated from any display operations on the screen.
2. Code that is directly concerned with graphics output or input, such as the direct calls of a graphics kernel's functionality.
3. Code for mediating between the internal application and the graphical output and input.

The basic concept of MVC is the construction of a triad consisting of three different objects:

- An application object, called *model.*
- A presentation object, called *view.*

• An object for providing the interface between model and view, called *controller*.

The Smalltalk-80 environment provides much support for establishing the MVC triad.

Predefined Classes

The class **View** is predefined in the environment with many useful subclasses to provide everything required for constructing windows with specific types of content, such as text views, form views, and list views. The class **Controller** with many subclasses provides all input devices, such as mouse, keyboard, and menus. The Controller classes are correlated to the View subclasses in the sense that they provide the style of interaction to control the corresponding views. For example, the class **TextController** supports text editing for **TextView**. To avoid any confusion for the application programmer looking for a class **Model**, Smalltalk-80 does not provide any predefined class for the model, because the model is completely application-dependent and must therefore be implemented by the application programmer. The predefined functionality of the view-controller pairs makes it easy for the application programmer to achieve a modularization of methods that correlates with the three types of code mentioned above. In particular, it is possible to describe the internal application completely independently from its concrete realization of its interface, making it easy to change and improve a user interface for a given implementation (see the description of the Graph model later in this chapter).

Smalltalk-80 provides its own view management system. There is a predefined functionality for switching between different views and different processes associated with them. Resizing, collapsing, and moving windows is also to a high degree inherited by the predefined Smalltalk-80 classes **StandardSystemView** and **StandardSystemController**.

Setting Up the Triad

In a typical application, the application programmer defines subclasses of a predefined controller class and view class by selecting a controller-view pair that embodies the best predefined functionality for the anticipated application. Then three instances, one of the model class, one of the controller class (a subclass of a predefined controller class), and one of the view class (a subclass of a predefined view class) are defined. These instances will be correlated by a special message, which establishes the triad. Suppose that the objects **aModel**, **aView**, and **aController** describe the model, the view, and the controller, respectively. Then the correlation is established by:

```
aView model:aModel controller:aController.
```

This statement has the effect that a predefined instance variable **view** in **aModel** is instantiated to **aView**, a predefined instance variable **controller** in **aView** is instantiated to **aController**, and both the controller and view own a instance variable model, instantiated to **aModel**. This is the basic requirement for communicating between the components by message passing. Note that the model has no direct access to the view and the controller, but the above coordination message establishes a dependency relation between the model and the view, a special mechanism to allow indirect communication between the model and the view.

Standard Control Sequence

Once the triad has been established, the view is automatically integrated into the *standard control sequence* (sometimes called *main event loop*). A mouse down request inside the view will activate the view and an event message is sent to its controller. The controller analyzes the event (in the default case) by checking whether the red, yellow, or blue mouse button was pressed. Associated messages (**redButtonActivity**, **blueButtonActivity**, **yellowButtonActivity**) are defined by the environment, and are sent to the controller itself. All control messages can be modified by the user by overriding the predefined methods. Our graphics applications are typical window-oriented applications; the application-dependent controllers and views defined below are always subclasses of the classes **StandardSystemController** and **StandardSystemView**. Thus the blue button activity will activate a menu with predefined menu messages (*new label, under, move, frame, collapse, close*) for the window management and will therefore not be changed by the programmer. The window operations activated by use of the blue button menu often require a redisplay of the view's content. To do this, the predefined method **displayView** must be extended by the application programmer to fill the inside display box of the view with the application-dependent information. The yellow button will activate a menu that is defined by the application programmer, as illustrated in the Graph Editor example. If the red button activity offers a value inside a view, this event is normally used as a pointing device to maintain the user interaction inside the view.

Integration of GEO++ into the MVC Triad

GEO++ will be used as a high-level graphics system aimed to support graphics interaction inside a view. Due to the predefined graphics-oriented programming environment of the Smalltalk-80 system, it is not sensible to realize graphics functionality "outside" a view (graphical menus, window management, and the like) using GEO++. Rather, it is preferable to use all the advantages of the predefined functionality of the MVC metaphor. In this sense, GEO++ in Smalltalk-80 cannot be considered as a general purpose graphics system to support all graphics tasks in a system.

While using predefined functionality "besides" GEO++, it is highly desirable to provide the application programmer with a consistent model for the task that avoids any confusion and mixture between GEO++ operations and low-level graphics operations supported by the Smalltalk-80 graphics kernel. The use of a high-level system should allow graphics programming in a device-independent manner based on graphics objects modeled in world coordinates. To support this we have integrated the GEO++ functionality into the MVC model in such a way that (1) display and interaction inside a graphics view is completely supported by the GEO++ functionality (and not by any Smalltalk-80 output primitive or input device); and (2) interaction outside a graphics view, including menu handling, is completely supported by the tools provided by the predefined Smalltalk-80 environment (and not by GEO++). To support this concept, we introduce a workstation (view device) for interactive graphics applications. Seen through the traditional lens, the view device constitutes an abstract workstation, similar to the PHIGS workstation concept, with a display surface described in normalized device coordinates, and with associated input devices seen as abstractions of physical devices. In contrast to PHIGS, however, our device has a flexible display surface of variable size. From the object-oriented standpoint, the workstation is realized as a view-controller pair, that is, the two classes **ViewDevice** and **ViewController**, defined as subclasses of **StandardSystemView** and **StandardSystemController** (see next section).

The two classes, **ViewDevice** and **ViewController**, are part of the predefined GEO++ functionality, and their internal implementation is hidden. The devices can be activated and inquired. Inquiry delivers what is traditionally called a workstation description table. In particular, the actual size of the view that can be changed by user actions and that is controlled by the view management system (and not by GEO++) can be inquired at any time. In addition to this, different classes of input and echo devices are supported for the view device. Examples of these classes are the above-mentioned classes **MouseLocator**, **MousePick**, **Dragger**, and **RubberBand** for input devices or echo devices.

As is common in object-oriented systems, the activation of devices will be described by the standard class message **new**, delivering an activated device as an instance of its device class. The messages **locator:** and **pick:** allow the input devices to be associated with the view device. The associated input devices can be inquired from the view by inquiry messages defined for **ViewDevice**, as shown in the examples. The same is true for the classes supporting interaction feedback, such as the **open** method in Listing 3.2.

ViewDevice and ViewController

The two classes **ViewDevice** and **ViewController** are realized by the internal GEO++ implementation in such a way that they incorporate the default behavior of a graphics device. So, for example, the **displayView** method is implemented to redisplay all roots that are defined as posted for the view device. Therefore, the application programmer need not care about the regeneration of views due to operations of the window system.

Because we use a Macintosh computer with a one-button mouse, the style of interaction for the standard control sequence was slightly changed. We have used a software goody often used in the Smalltalk-80 community to add a third area: the *yellow menu area* (displayed by three buttons emphasizing the yellow one of the original Smalltalk-80 mouse) on top of the view and right from the so-called blue-button menu area, where the view's label is displayed as was shown in Figure 3.3. Depending on the area where the mouse button is pressed, the controller will send one of the messages **yellowButtonActivity**, **blueButtonActivity**, or **insideViewActivity** to itself as will be shown in Figure 3.4.

In addition, an instance variable **eventPosition** is introduced for the controller to store the position of the mouse in world coordinates for GEO++ at the time when it was detected by the control loop. This value is used to support the pick operation.

Up to this point we have described the GEO++ functionality as it is given in the hands of the application programmer. To summarize: The application programmer can use the predefined GEO++ methods and can define subclasses of these classes including the abstract device classes **ViewDevice** and **ViewController**. The steps described in the next paragraphs are completely within the responsibility of the application programmer.

A Small Graphics Editor

The complete application for the simple editor is realized by methods of **EditView** and **EditController**, which are defined as subclasses of the classes **ViewDevice** and **ViewController**, respectively.

Message Flow

Depending on the area selected by the user, one of the three messages **blueButtonActivity**, **yellowButtonActivity**, or **insideViewActivity** is sent from the controller to itself. In the first two cases the blue or yellow button menu will be displayed, giving the user the choice to select one of the menu options. Then the menu message corresponding to the selected option is sent to the controller. In the case of the blue button menu, the selected option performs the corresponding application-independent menu message inherited from the system. When a yellow button menu option is selected, the corresponding message will use GEO++ to create parts of the hierarchy, change, edit, or delete them. The third case is most useful if a nonempty part hierarchy already exists and the user wishes to select, deselect, drag, or edit a part. In this case, the method **insideViewActivity** inquires the value of the location of **eventPosition** from the controller and supports the pick device with this value to get the object to be manipulated (selected, moved). Note that all methods defined by the application programmer are subordinated to these three control activities in the sense that they are called by them. Consequently control is given back to the controller after one of these three methods has been executed, as shown in Figure 3.4.

Initializing the Controller

How can the association between menu options and menu messages be defined by the application programmer? Due to the predefined functionality of the controller's superclasses, the application programmer has only to describe the menu entries and the associated messages, shown in Listing 3.1, as parameters of the method **yellowButtonMenu:yellowButtonMessages:**. In our case we have used the same names for the menu entries and the corresponding messages.

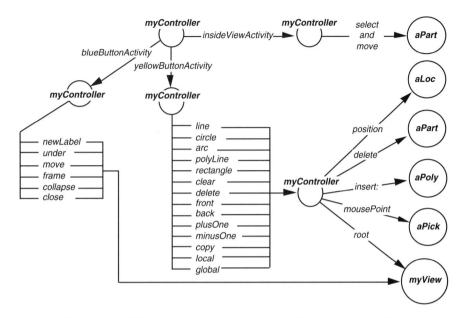

Figure 3.4: Message flow diagram for the graphics editor

The Editor's View

The complete application is started by evaluating the expression **EditView open**. This type of activation is very typical for starting MVC applications in Smalltalk-80. After having associated the input devices, the controller is created by **new** (which calls **initialize** of Listing 3.1 internally to define the menu). Then, in the general case, the components of the triad would be established by using the message **controller:model:**. In the simpler case of a pure graphics editor, one can do without the specification of a (nongraphical) model. The whole "model" coincides with the graphics part hierarchy (the instance variable **root** in **EditView**) describing the state of the objects generated by the user at any time. The activation of the system is therefore slightly different in the sense that no triad but simply a view-controller *pair* has to be established. To do this, Smalltalk-80 provides the method **controller:** to combine a controller with its view.

As mentioned above, the objects generated by the user are defined as parts of a single object hierarchy, described by a GEO++ group. This group is created with the method **init** and stored as a instance variable **root**, which is accessible by an inquiring method. In addition, a variable to store and give

EditController	*Menu Definitions*
class name	**EditController**
superclass	ViewController
instance methods	

initialize	"Initialize yellow button menu"
super initialize.	"Use first inherited initialize message for blue button menu"
self yellowButtonMenu:	"menu entries and messages:"

(PopUpMenu labels:
'line circle arc polyLine rectangle clear delete front back plusOne minusOne copy local global'
yellowButtonMessages:
#(line circle arc polyLine rectangle clear delete front back plusOne minusOne copy local global')

Listing 3.1

access to a previously selected object is provided (instantiated by **nil**), leading to Listing 3.2.

Creating and Copying Graphics Objects

A typical user action to create a new part consists of the construction of a line. After the corresponding menu option was selected, the user presses the mouse button and tracks it to a second position. Interaction feedback is provided by a rubberband. When the button is released the line is completed and used as content of a newly created part of the hierarchy. Restoration of the display is automatically provided by GEO++.

The copy operation creates a new part with a slightly changed transformation, referring to the same content as the original part. Because the original part was picked, it can be inquired from the view; the message content offers its content, which is used for the new part. This is the way equivalent parts are created by the user (see Listing 3.3 and Figure 3.5).

Picking and Dragging

The inside view activity message will select an item or drag a selected one.

EditView	*Initialize*

class name	**EditView**
superclass	ViewDevice
instance variable names	root selected
class methods	

open

myView←(super new) init.	"create view device and associate input and echo devices"

myView locator: (MouseLocator new).
myView pick: (MousePick new).
myView rubberBand: (Rubberband new).
myView dragger: (Dragger new).

myController←ViewController new.	"create controller"
myView controller:myController.	"define VC pair"
myView label:'GEOEditor'.	"label view"

instance methods

init

root←Group new.	"create empty GEO++ group to store the graphics editor's part hierarchy"
selected←nil.	"initialize picked object"

root	"deliver root"
↑ root	

selected	"deliver selected object"
↑ selected	

deselect	"deselect object"

selected isNil ifFalse: [selected highlightingOff. selected ¨ nil.]

Listing 3.2

When the inside view message is sent to the controller, the mouse event has been performed and the location is accessible by the variable **eventPosition**. This is the right position for the pick device looking for the picked object. A normal pick asking for the current location of the mouse may deliver an incorrect result if the user, wishing to drag an item, changed the mouse position too much between the event and the time when the mouse position is inquired by the pick device. Therefore a new pick method was introduced,

class name   **EditController**
superclass   ViewController
instance methods

line   "Let the user generate a line"
myLocator←(self view) locator.   "Inquire locator from my view"
loc←myLocator waitButton.   "Wait until button pressed"
aLine←GEOLine new.   "Create new empty line"
endRubber←view rubberBand from:loc."Provide rubberband feedback"
aLine beginPoint:loc; endPoint:endRubber.
                                "Edit line by inserting
                                begin point end point"
shift←aLine boundingBox origin.
aLine←aLine moveBy:0@0–shift.   "Shift line to origin"
myRoot←(self view)root.   "Ask view for hierarchy."
aPart←LinePart for:myRoot content:aLine moveBy:shift.
                                "Create part:"
view selected:aPart.   "Highlight part"

copy   "Copy selected object"
(selected←view selected) isNil ifTrue: [↑ self].
                                "Inquire picked object:"
myRoot←(self view) root.   "Give root"
partClass←selected class.   "Inquire the part's class"
                                "Insert content of original in copy,
aPart←partClass for:myRoot   use original's transformation and
   makePart:(selected content)   change it by an amount of (4,4)"
   moveBy:((selected translation)+(4@4)).
view selected:aPart.   "Select and highlight copy"

Listing 3.3

as mentioned above, that offers the picked object not by inquiring the mouse but by using a location offered from the outside, that is, from the calling method

```
pickedObject ← pick location:aPoint.
```

Now the inside view activity will take the picked object, provide it with a drag echo, and decide whether the user has really dragged it to a different position. If real dragging was accomplished, the transformation of the

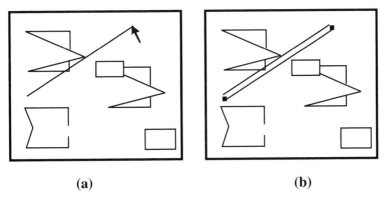

(a)   **(b)**

Figure 3.5: Creation (a) and duplication (b) of a line

picked part will be changed, resulting in a screen update as shown in Figure 3.6. During the dragging process the selected part remains unchanged. Only a dragging feedback is provided until the mouse button is released. Then the part hierarchy is updated using the GEO++ functionality. If the mouse button is released at the same position as the old one, this is interpreted as a kind of degenerate dragging and handled as a pure pick operation.

Extending the Editor to a Graph Editor

We extend the editor described above to reach the following goals:
- The user can create nodes and connect them by edges.
- Edges know about existing nodes. When a new edge is generated by a rubberband technique, the endpoints of an edge snap automatically into

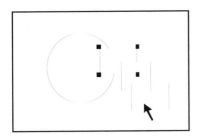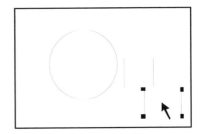

Figure 3.6: Dragging of a part

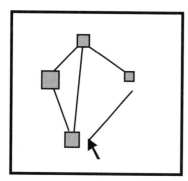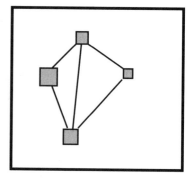

Figure 3.7: Adding an edge to a graph

the center of the two closest nodes when the mouse button is released (see Figure 3.7). In addition, the two adjacent nodes are informed about the new edge connecting them.
- Compared to the usual dragging operation, dragging of a node causes the adjacent edges to move smoothly with the node (see Figure 3.8). For doing this, the node informs all adjacent edges about its new center.
- When an edge is deleted, the adjacent nodes are informed to update their internal list about adjacent edges.
- When a node is deleted the adjacent edges are deleted as well.

The Classes GraphNode and Edge

To extend and change the behavior of the existing editor, we define two new

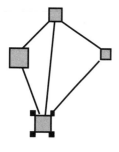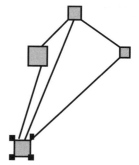

Figure 3.8: Moving a node

subclasses, **GraphNode** and **Edge**, of the predefined GEO++ classes **RectanglePart** and **LinePart**. In addition, the yellow button menu is redefined by adding the new menu labels and the corresponding menu messages, **edge** and **node**, in the same manner as shown in Listing 3.1. The relations between nodes and edges are modeled by an instance variable **nodes** of **Edge** and vice versa an instance variable **edges** of **GraphNode**. The variable **nodes** is defined as a key-value pair (an instance of the Smalltalk-80 class **Association**) for the two nodes connected by the edge; **edges** is defined as a set of key-value pairs where the key component holds the edge and the value component (with integer **value** 1 or 2) indicates whether the first or the second point of the edge is merging with the node in question.

Rather than listing all the code, which is quite simple, the message patterns (*protocol description*) for the methods of **GraphNode** and **Edge** together with a short comment is displayed in Listing 3.4.

GraphNode and Edge	*Protocol Descriptions*
class name	**GraphNode**
superclass	RectanglePart
instance variable names	edges
instance methods	
addEdge:edge mergePoint:i	"inform me that edge with its first or second endpoint is connected with my center"
removeEdge:anEdge	"remove edge from edges"
moveBy:aPoint	"move me, change merge points of edges"
delete	"delete me and my edges"
class name	**Edge**
superclass	LinePart
instance variable names	nodes
instance methods	
nodes:aPairOfNodes	"inform me about the pair of nodes to connect. Inform my nodes about me"
delete	"delete me and inform my pair of nodes about disconnection"

Listing 3.4

Advantage of Using Inheritance

What is the advantage of inheritance in our example? First, inheritance is an elegant principle to comprehend the new special parts as "normal" parts of the hierarchy. Second, there are technical advantages. Because edges and nodes are special parts, all methods besides the very special methods **moveBy:** and **delete** are inherited by **Part**. So all the numerous methods such as assigning attributes, picking an edge or a node, or posting the hierarchy can be applied to nodes and edges without writing a single line of code. Using object-oriented solutions, many trivial and boring pieces of code can be avoided.

Introducing a Graph Model

The extension in the previous section supports only basic construction and editing methods for a graph, derived by specializing a general purpose graphics editor. In the next step we ask whether the code developed so far could be *reused* to support the construction of interactive graph-oriented applications.

Suppose that the main object structure of an application is described as an abstract graph. There are many classes of applications (project planning, networking, route planning, or system analysis) where this is the case. By *abstract* we mean a representation of a graph without any layout information.

The whole application is defined as a class **GraphModel**. This class owns an instance variable named **nodes** whose elements are objects of a class named **Node** describing the nodes, and it owns a second instance variable named **relations** with elements of a class **Pair** describing the edges by referring to the adjacent nodes. In particular, the class **GraphModel** provides methods to edit the structure of the abstract graph as shown in Listing 3.5. We suppose that the functionality of the application is defined by a set of methods for **GraphModel**, **Node**, and **Pair** not listed here.

The methods in Listing 3.5 are particularly used by methods of **Node** and **Pair**. These classes have access to their graph model by an instance variable **myGraph**, which is initialized by the class method **new:**, as is common practice.

The basic editing methods for nodes and edges can then be defined very

GraphModel	*Partial Protocol Description*
class name	**GraphModel**
superclass	Object
instance variable names	nodes relations
instance methods	
addNode:node	"add a new node to the graph"
removeNode:node	"remove a node and all edges connected with it"
addPair:pairOfNodes	"add connection **pairOfNodes**"
addNodes:node1 and:node2	"connect nodes"
removePair:pairOfNodes	"disconnect **pairOfNodes**"

Listing 3.5

easily as shown in Listing 3.6a and 3.6b. **Pair** owns an instance variable of the predefined Smalltalk-80 class **Association** used to store the two components of the pair.

Node	*Partial Implementation Description*
class name	**Node**
superclass	Object
instance variable names	myGraph
class methods	
new: aGraph	"create a new node and inform it"
↑ (self new) graph:aGraph	"about its graph"
instance methods	
graph: aGraph	"initialize instance variable and"
myGraph ← aGraph.	"inform my graph"
self add	
graph	"deliver my graph to the outside"
↑ myGraph	
add	"add me to my graph"
(self graph) addNode:self	
remove	"remove me from my graph"
(self graph) removeNode:self	

Listing 3.6a

Pair	*Partial Implementation Description*
class name	**Pair**
superclass	Object
instance variable names	myGraph myAssociation
class methods	

new   "new empty pair"
↑ (super new) init

newFor: aGraph first: aNode1 second: aNode2
                                           "create a new pair with nodes"
↑ ((self new) graph:aGraph) first:node1 second:node2

instance methods

init   "initialize instance variable"
myAssociation ← Association new
graph: aGraph   "initialize instance variable"
myGraph ← aGraph
graph   "deliver myGraph to the outside"
↑ myGraph
first: node1 second: node2   "define pair and inform my graph"
myAssociation key:node1 value:node2.
self add
add   "add myself to my graph"
(self graph) addPair:self
remove   "remove me from my graph"
(self graph) removePair:self

Listing 3.6b

Defining a Model-View-Controller Triad

To constitute the links between the application and its graphics representation a full model-view-controller triad has to be defined. The triad is established with

```
myModel ← GraphModel new
myView model:myModel controller:myController.
```

From model to view

The next step is to add a graph layout algorithm **display:** that translates the abstract graph into a visual representation on the screen. The main part of such an algorithm, not described here, consists of the calculation of the positions for the nodes. The graphical representation can be performed by GEO++ using the classes **GraphNode** and **Edge** described above. This algorithm should be part of the view. We call this view **GraphView** and define it as subclass of **ViewDevice**. To define a one-to-one relation between abstract nodes and graphics nodes, we add a dictionary (instance of class **Dictionary**, defining a set of associations) named **nodeBridge**; a second dictionary, **edgeBridge**, is defined for the edges as illustrated in Figure 3.9.

Up to now we have not explained how the model will inform the view that it should start the layout algorithm. The usual way to do this would be a message from the model to the view. But doing this is against the philosophy behind the MVC triad. Informing the view is accomplished by an indirect addressing scheme (a so-called *dependency relation*) to avoid any information inside the model's methods about the graphics representation at the user interface. Therefore it is possible to modify the user interface or even to construct a completely different type of interface without any change of the model's code. This makes it easier to start with a first version of an interface

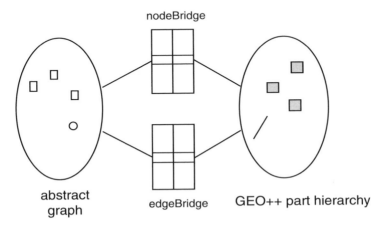

Figure 3.9: Coordination between model and representation through bridges

and to improve it stepwise without changing the application described by the model.

The model is able to address its view indirectly by sending a change message to *itself* (and not to the view):

```
self changed:#layout.
```

This message will trigger a predefined message **update:** as a reaction to the model's change message. The update message can then check whether the argument, in our case **#layout**, was used, and perform the display algorithm. The partial implementation in Listing 3.7 shows how the system works.

GraphView	*Partial Implementation Description*
class name	**GraphView**
superclass	ViewDevice
instance variable names	root selected nodeBridge edgeBr-
idge	
instance methods	

update: aParameter   "react to model's change
                                             messages"
aParameter = #layout ifTrue: [↑ self display: (self model)]
ifFalse: [. . . *possibly, evaluation of other values of aParameter due to
   additional change messages in model* . . .]
display: aGraphModel   "display model's graph "
calculate nodes' positions, then for each node **aNode** *with position*
   aNodePosition:
aGraphNode ← GraphNode for:root content:aSquare
moveBy:aNodePosition.
nodeBridge at:aGraphNode put:aNode.
calculate for each pair of nodes the line **aVector** *describing the
   difference from first to second node's position, then create edges*
anEdge ← Edge for:root content:aVector moveBy:positionFirst.
edgeBridge at:anEdge put:pair.
nodeBridge   "deliver **nodeBridge** to outside"
↑ nodeBridge
edgeBridge   "deliver **edgeBridge** to outside"
↑ edgeBridge

Listing 3.7

From view to model

The reverse direction, from view to model, is primarily supported by the existing functionality of the graphics editor. Only slight modifications are required in the sense that editing the graphics representation will update the model as well. To ensure this, the menu methods **edge**, **node**, and **delete** have to be supplemented by using the bridges constructed above. For the method **node**, for example, in addition to the existing method to create a new part

```
newGraphNode ← GraphNode for:root content:aSquare
    moveBy:mousePosition
```

the creation of a new graph node will be achieved by

```
newNode ← Node new,
```

the model will be informed by

```
self model addNode:newNode
```

and the bridge will be updated by

```
(view nodeBridge) at:aGraphNode put:newNode.
```

Improving the Integration by Using Inheritance

An analysis of the communication between model and view shows that there are still two separate worlds, the abstract graph on the one side and the graphical representation realized by GEO++ on the other side. These two separate worlds must be coordinated by the bridges introduced above, which may be troublesome in complex applications.

In the following we show how a stronger integration can be achieved without giving up the goal of a maximal reuse of existing code provided by the application classes (**GraphModel, Node, Pair**) and the graphics editor's classes (**GraphNode, Edge**, GEO++ classes). We use inheritance to melt the abstract graph objects together with the graphics objects into one entity providing and reflecting the behavior of both the application and the graphics presentation aspects. To achieve this goal, we first change the class hierarchy by defining the classes **GraphModel, Node**, and **Pair** as subclasses of **Group, GraphNode**, and **Edge**, respectively, as shown in Figure 3.10, where the old relations are shown by dotted lines and the new ones by bold lines.

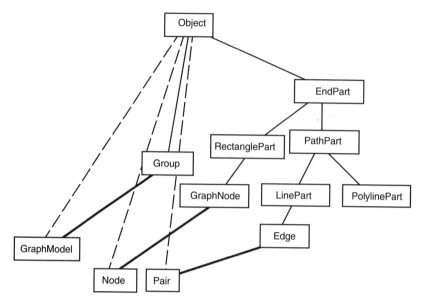

Figure 3.10: Melting model and representation by subclassing

The reorganization of the class hierarchy allows the application of the graphics editor's methods directly to the application objects. Thus, the **display:** method of **GraphView** (see Listing 3.7) can do without the bridge by replacing

```
aGraphNode ← GraphNode for:root content:aSquare
    moveBy:aNodePosition
nodeBridge at:aGraphNode put:aNode
```

and

```
anEdge ← Edge for:root content:aVector
    moveBy:positionFirst
edgeBridge at:anEdge put:pair
```

by the respective statements

```
aNode for:root content:aSquare moveBy:aNodePosition
```

and

```
pair for:root content:aVector moveBy:positionFirst.
```

To discuss the other direction, from view to model, we look first to the menu methods to add a new node. The four statements of the first solution

```
newGraphNode ← GraphNode for:root content:aSquare
    moveBy:mousePosition
```

```
newNode ← Node new
self model addNode:newNode
(view nodeBridge) at:aGraphNode put:newNode
```

are now replaced by the single statement:

```
newGraphNode ← Node for:root content:aSquare
    moveBy:mousePosition.
```

Compared to the original code for the graphics editor, only the name of the class was changed from **GraphNode** to **Node**. To add an edge, one has also to replace the class name **Edge** in the menu message **edge** of the old graphics editor by **Pair**.

In addition, the graph, which now coincides with the root of the hierarchy, has to be informed about a new edge or a deleted one. This can be done by overriding the **nodes:** and **delete** methods inherited from **Edge**. These overriding methods must be added (without changing any existing code of **Pair**) as shown in Listing 3.8.

Discussion

Subclassing provides a strong integration of both the application-oriented and the graphics aspects. Artificial bridges as displayed in Figure 3.9 can be avoided and the mental model of the application programmer—to see the graphical functionality of the graph as well as the application-specific behavior as methods of one entity—is directly supported by the software

Pair	*Overridden methods*
class name	**Pair**
superclass	Edge
instance variable names	myGraph myAssociation
instance methods	
nodes: aPairOfNodes	"override inherited method"
super nodes:aPairOfNodes.	
self graph: (self root)	
delete	"override delete"
super delete.	
self remove	

Listing 3.8

concept. All this can even be achieved without giving up the goal of optimal software reuse, as the example has shown.

There are, however, some points open for discussion. In our case, the application classes **GraphModel**, **Node**, and **Pair** are defined as subclasses of **Object**, the root of the Smalltalk-80 class hierarchy. Therefore, all methods inherited by these classes are also known to the new subclasses after having reorganized the hierarchy. In the general case where the application classes are part of a specific class hierarchy, reorganizing the application classes by defining them as subclasses of GEO++ classes is only possible by using multiple inheritance, not provided by the Smalltalk-80 environment, as shown in Figure 3.11a for **Node**. Some compromise can be reached by defining subclasses of the GEO++ classes in question and introducing an additional instance variable, sharing the respective instances of the application classes by reference (see Figure 3.11b). This solution can also do without establishing bridges, but in our example for **NewNode** it requires additional application methods that use the application methods of the instance variable internally.

Conclusion

What is the result of our experience? Before we realized the application, we believed the way to manipulate part hierarchies as described in Wisskirchen

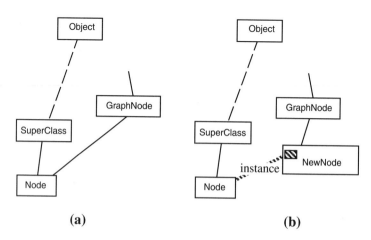

(a)   (b)

Figure 3.11: Integration by multiple inheritance (a) and by introducing an instance variable (b)

[1990] seemed well defined to us. The experiment has indeed shown that we did not need to modify the previous specification. The question of how to integrate GEO++ into the MVC concept could be answered by defining the right type of view and declaring it as an abstract device. The main differences in our earlier expectations (and in the specifications of PHIGS) appeared with the specification of input and echo devices. To come to a concise specification of the user interface, all the alternatives to handle the mouse for pointing, dragging, and selecting had to be supported by the application programmer's interface described by GEO++. Thus we came to the same conclusion as Myers [1990] that the GKS and PHIGS input model is unsatisfactory to support state-of-the-art input techniques.

The main advantages in using an object-oriented approach to interactive graphics lie in the fundamental model of this approach. Graphics objects as higher level structures with associated methods and organized as classes—objects in the sense of object-oriented programming—harmonize well with an intuitive feeling about graphics objects. The strong integration of data and methods often avoids complex bridges between application-dependent behavior and graphical representation. And last but not least, inheritance can be employed to customize a graphics kernel for specific needs, resulting in a high degree of software reuse.

References

Blake, Edwin and Peter Wisskirchen (eds.) [1990]. *Advances in Object-Oriented Graphics.* EUROGRAPHICS Sem. Series. Berlin, Heidelberg: Springer-Verlag.

Enderle, Guenther, K. Kansy, and G. Pfaff [1987]. *Computer Graphics Programming. GKS—The Graphics Standard,* 2nd edition. Berlin, Heidelberg: Springer-Verlag.

Goldberg, Adele and David Robson [1983]. *Smalltalk-80: The Language and Its Implementation.* Reading: Addison-Wesley.

Goldberg, Adele [1984]. *Smalltalk-80: The Interactive Programming Environment.* Reading: Addison-Wesley.

ISO [1985]. *Information Processing Systems: Computer Graphics—Graphical Kernel System GKS, Functional Description.* International Standard 7942.

ISO [1989]. *Programmer's Hierarchical Interactive Graphics System (PHIGS).* International Standard ISO/IEC 9592.

Kansy, Klaus and Peter Wisskirchen [1990]. "The new graphics standard—object-oriented," in Blake and Wisskirchen [1990].

Krasner, G. E., and S.T. Pope [1988]. "A cookbook for using the model-view-controller user interface paradigm in Smalltalk-80." *Journal of Object-Oriented Programming*, August, 1990, pp. 1, 3, 26-48.

Myers, Brad A. [1990]. "A New Model for Handling Input." *ACM Transactions on Information Systems,* 8(3), July, 1990.

Wisskirchen, P. [1989]. "GEO++ —A system for both modelling and display." *Proceedings Eurographics '89* (Hamburg, Sept. 1989). Amsterdam: Elsevier, pp. 403-414.

Wisskirchen, P. [1990]. *Object-Oriented Graphics.* Berlin, Heidelberg, New York: Springer-Verlag.

Chapter 4

GOII: An Object-Oriented Framework for Computer Graphics

Peter C. Bahrs
Wayne D. Dominick
Dennis R. Moreau

A primary objective of computer graphics applications is to model objects and activities, to allow manipulation of them, and to provide feedback. This is not a trivial task. Real objects reflect and refract light in ways that can be captured by a common camera (see Figure 4.1). The camera is first aligned to provide the desired view. A picture is taken, the film is processed, and a

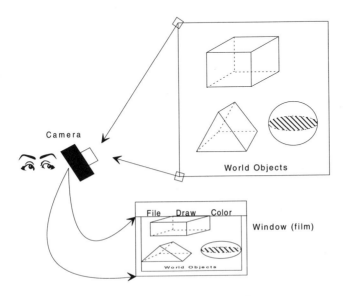

Figure 4.1: Camera metaphor

photograph is produced. In computer science we model the camera, the objects to be viewed, and the film, with mathematical approximations, algorithms, and data structures. These models are computationally intensive even for relatively simple scenes.

GO∥[1] is a specification for an object-oriented framework for concurrent graphics in heterogeneous environments designed to address this problem. GO∥ provides a hardware- and software-independent object-oriented graphics environment with additional functionality and flexibility not found in existing graphics systems. This chapter concentrates on the GO∥ graphical specifications rather than concurrency issues (see [Bahrs 1991]) and implementation details (see [Bahrs and Harnett 1991]). The graphical dimensions of GO∥ discussed in this chapter include the following.

- three-dimensional modeling
- two-dimensional picture manipulation
- graphical user interfaces
- image processing
- hierarchical and recursive modeling
- an object-based rendering pipeline
- user-defined graphics classes and protocols
- pick correlation
- configurations

GO∥ Class Hierarchy

Figures 4.2 and 4.3 show the three-dimensional, graphical user interface, image, and two-dimensional class hierarchy in GO∥.

Class **Shape3D** encapsulates graphical structure and behavior common to all derived class that can potentially "draw" themselves. The graphical user interface classes incorporate the similar specifications found in Actor with modifications primarily in the classes derived from **Shape**.

Class Specification and Syntax

The GO∥ specification contains an object-oriented programming language for graphical algorithm development. Language features include multiple inheritance, predefined graphical class hierarchies, encapsulation, polymor-

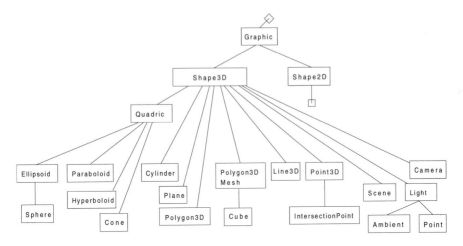

**Figure 4.2: GOll class hierarchy Part 1
(small boxes indicate additional class structure)**

phism, user-defined functions, user-defined classes, activities (program-matic threads of control), coercion, implicit reflective behaviors, aliasing, broadcast messaging, object migration, object mutation, and concurrent debugging.

An object is created by first defining a class containing the structure (local state) and behavior definitions (methods), followed by a request for

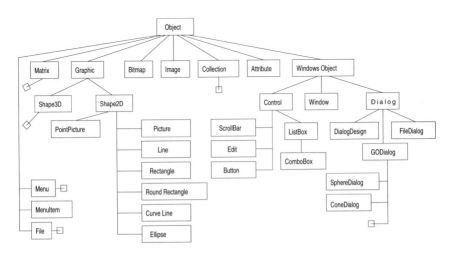

**Figure 4.3: GOll class hierarchy Part 2
(small boxes indicate additional class structure)**

instantiation. The instantiation syntax is

```
Class object_identifier
```

where *Class* is the name of a base or user-defined class and *identifier* is the object's name. An instantiated object is accessed by sending it a message denoting one of its behaviors along with appropriate parameters. We use a variant of the dot notation used in C++:

```
object_identifier.(behavior parameter1...parameterN).
```

We also employ the dot notation to discuss components of the GOII specification. For example,

```
Shape3D.attribute
```

refers to the attribute structure object in the **Shape3D** class definition. This syntax should not cause any ambiguity to the reader because we follow the rule that instances of a class are prefixed with an *a* or *an* (for example, **aSphere**, **aBuilding**). Therefore, object names begin with a lowercase letter and class names begin with an uppercase letter.

The graphical specifications in GOII are denoted using an abstraction of the UNITY syntax [Chandy and Misra 1989]. Listing 4.1 shows the base class **Shape3D** from which the majority of GOII classes are derived.

Objects are identified by
- a textual description stored in Shape3D.name,
- the static identifier given in the application source, and
- the implementation.

Associated with an object are a transformation matrix and an attribute. The transformation is applied to the structure of the object whenever the object is asked to draw itself. The attribute defines the surface characteristics of the object. The **Shape3D.drawObject** method defines what the object uses to draw itself. In the case of three-dimensional classes, such as **Sphere** and **Plane**, **drawObject** is *self*. The **Camera** and **Light** classes are examples where the **drawObject** will reference another object to be used for displaying. Setting this value to *nil* can temporarily hide an object. **Shape3D.baseClass** maintains a set of class names that are used to tailor the GOII architecture to a hardware platform.[2] The dialog is an interactive mechanism to display and edit the contents of instantiatable classes derived from **Shape3D**. The dialog refers to a windowing interface class object, composed of control windows.

Figure 4.4 illustrates the structure and behavior of a **Sphere**, derived from class **Shape3D**. Figure 4.4a is the dialog interface to the object and Figure 4.4b is the messaging interface. Figure 4.4c shows the derived structure inherited from **Shape3D**.

Class *Shape3D*
inherit: *Object*
class structure:
    classNames ≡ { *Sphere, Ellipsoid, Paraboloid, Cone, Cylinder,*
        Hyperboloid, Polygon3D, Line3D, Point3D }
    asClass ≡ { *asSphere, asEllipsoid, asParaboloid, asCone, asCylinder,*
        asHyperboloid, asPolygon3D, asLine3D, asPoint3D }
    baseClass ∈ classNames
structure:
    name ∈ *String*   transformation ∈ *Matrix*
    attribute ∈ *Attribute*   drawObject ∈ *Shape3D*
    dialog ∈ *Window*
always:
    name > ""
initially:
class behavior:
    new: *Shape3D* → init(new(*Object*)) ∧ *self*
    createWithDialog: *Shape3D* → init(new(*Object*)) ∧ dialog ∧ *self*
public behavior:
    name: *self* → name
    transformation: *self* → transformation
    attribute: *self* → attribute
    drawObject: *self* → drawObject
    dialog: *self* → dialog
    print: *self* → print(class(*self*)) ∧ print(name) ∧
        ∀ s ∈ *self*.classStructure: print(s) ∧ ∀ s ∈ *self*.structure: print(s) ∧
        print(transformation) ∧ print(attribute) ∧ print(name(drawObject)) ∧
        print(name(dialog))
    writeFile: *self* ↔ aFile → *self*   readFile: *self* ↔ aFile → *self*
    getDlg: *self* → dialog
    setName: *self* ↔ aString → name=aString
    setDlg: *self* ↔ aDialog → dialog=aDialog
    setTransformation: *self* ↔ aMatrix → transformation
    setAttribute: *self* ↔ anAttribute → attribute
    setDrawObject: *self* ↔ aShape3D → aShape3D
    setBaseClass: *self* ↔ aClass → aClass ∈ classNames ∧ baseClass=aClass
    asBaseObjects: *self* → asClass[index(classNames, baseClass)](*self*)
    asCube: *self* → nil   asEllipsoid: *self* → nil
    asSphere: *self* → nil   asCylinder: *self* → nil
    asCone: *self* → nil   asHyperboloid: *self* → nil
    asParaboloid: *self* → nil   asPolygon3D: *self* → nil
private behavior:

Listing 4.1

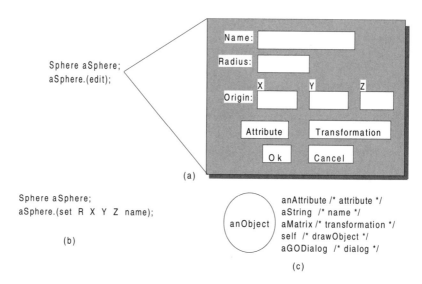

Sphere aSphere;
aSphere.(edit);

(a)

Sphere aSphere;
aSphere.(set R X Y Z name);

(b)

anObject

anAttribute /* attribute */
aString /* name */
aMatrix /* transformation */
self /* drawObject */
aGODialog /* dialog */

(c)

Figure 4.4: Object creation and editing through (a) dialog and (b) messaging; (c) class Shape3D derived structure

The **print** message is used to display internal structure in a textual form. Structure objects are accessed via **help** methods (for example, **anObject.(attribute)** returns the attribute associated with **anObject**). GOII objects also have the ability to read from and write to a file.

The *as* specifications (**asCube, asCone**) denote coercion mechanisms for interobject messaging. Coercion between three-dimensional objects attempts to create a volume with similar dimensions, transformation, attribute, and name as the coerced object. The specifications for the *as* messages are defined in each derived graphical class. The specifications for **asPolygons3D** and **doesIntersect** are explained individually and collectively in successive sections of this chapter, where their roles in object-based rendering algorithms are discussed.

drawObject

The element **Shape3D.drawObject** is used as a "mask" in the sense that an object may use another object as its three-dimensional representation. The **Camera** and **Light** classes define abstract entities, which normally are not rendered. GOII allows these objects to be rendered by setting their **drawObjects** to an instantiated drawable object.

Consider the following example.

```
Sphere aSphere;  Light aLight;
aSphere.(set "earth", aPoint, 100000);
aLight.(edit);
aLight.(setDrawObject aSphere);
```

This feature allows us to "draw" Lights and Cameras in a **Scene** similar to what happens in the real world. Lights and cameras are included with the Scene's objects during rendering in the GOII architecture. Drawing **aLight** is equivalent to drawing **aSphere**. To "hide" any object, we need only to set **drawObject** to *nil*.

baseClass and asPolygons3D

The GOII prototype implementation environment is composed of cooperating interpretation engines that take full advantage of their respective hosts' hardware and software capabilities. These capabilities may include the ability to perform graphical operations in hardware, such as rotation and shading, and to use optimized libraries.

Of particular interest in this section is the ability of a host environment to accept modeling primitives, including simple points, polygons, spheres, or even user-defined graphics. **Shape3D.baseClass** takes as values the names of classes that can be implemented by the host environment efficiently and effectively. Rendering algorithms can thus be tailored to render objects at an abstraction level conforming to device-specific capabilities. A coercion algorithm must then be defined to transform GOII primitives into the **baseClass**.

The GOII specifications include the transformation of all three-dimensional modeling primitives into **Polygon3D** objects. **Polygon3D** and **Polygon3DMesh** objects are prevalent in numerous graphics systems. The **asPolygons3D** message transforms three-dimensional objects into a collection of **Polygon3D** objects.

doesIntersect

The **asPolygons3D** message is used to provide modeling primitives that correlate well with rendering algorithms for a hardware environment. These algorithms include z buffer, painter's algorithm, and radiosity techniques.

Another class of algorithms, called ray tracing, is based on modeling light interaction with real objects. These algorithms map efficiently to host environments that support mathematical operations in hardware (matrix multiplications, ray intersections, and lighting calculations) and provide for concurrent execution of operations.

The **doesIntersect** message on an object is used by the object-based ray tracing algorithms defined later. The response to a **doesIntersect** message is a collection of **IntersectionPoint3D** objects. An **IntersectionPoint3D** is derived from **Point3D** with the addition of references to light sources, a source object, and an attribute. Figure 4.5 illustrates the interaction with a **Scene** via the **asPolygons3D** and doesIntersect messages.

User-Defined Class Protocols

User-defined graphics may inherit from (*is a*) and contain (*has a*) any component of GOll. They must adhere to message protocols defined thus far. These include the following.

- doesIntersect
- asPolygons3D
- new
- createWithDialog
- edit
- print
- readFile

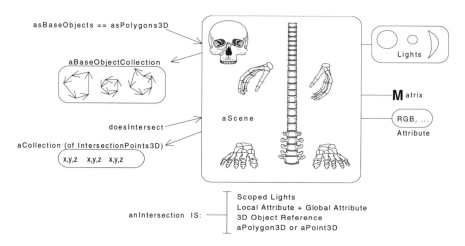

Figure 4.5: Scene pre-rendering messages

- writeFile

When adhered to, these protocols enable the creation of complex and hierarchical user-defined graphical elements that are treated as any of the base graphical components by the **Scene, Camera,** and object-based rendering algorithms. The identified user-defined class protocols are valid only for the existing rendering algorithms discussed in this chapter. The addition of a new rendering algorithm requires the following modifications to the GOII specification:

- definition of the new "draw" message for graphical classes
- definition of the rendering algorithm in the **Camera** class
- definition of a **Scene** traversal algorithm

Scene

The **Scene** class provides the ability to create sophisticated compositions of graphical objects, lights, and transformations. The structuring, editing, and traversal properties found in HOOPS™ [Ithaca 1988] and PHIGS [Foley et al. 1990], recursive modeling, and the benefits of object-oriented programming are achieved through the **Scene** class.

Scene maintains a collection of **Shape3D** objects, a collection of **Lights**, a transformation **Matrix**, an **Attribute**, and a depth value (see Figure 4.6).

Objects derived from class **Shape3D** and user-defined classes can be added to a Scene for rendering, including lights and cameras. A Scene can also contain other Scenes; cycles may exist in this composition. A scene will traverse itself as a result of a **doesIntersect** or **asBaseObjects** message.

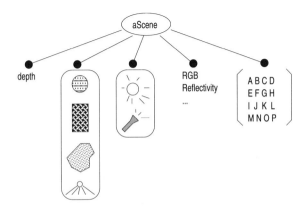

Figure 4.6: The scene object

Listing 4.2 shows the traversal algorithms for these two messages.

The **asBaseObjects** algorithm recursively converts an existing **Scene** to a **Scene** composed of **baseObject** objects. This includes light sources and cameras because they may be rendered via their **drawObject**.

The **doesIntersect** algorithm is invoked by a rendering message issued from a ray tracing algorithm. We are concerned with determining the intersection points of the **Scene** with respect to a given vector and transformation matrix. During traversal, graphical transformations are combined according to the global-local matrix composition defined in PHIGS. The **Scene** accepts an initial transformation and combines it with the Scene's local transformation. The new transformation is recursively applied to each

---

asBaseObjects: self → aCollection
```
Scene newScene;
setDepth(newScene, depth(self));
setTransformation(newScene, transformation(self));
setName(newScene, name(self));
∀ O ∈ objects
{   if O ≡ self ∧ decrement(depth) ≡ 0
    then /* skip it */
    else
    /* this GO‖ specification returns PolygonMesh objects */
        add(newScene, asBaseObject(O));
    endif
}
∀ O ∈ Lights: aCollection = asBaseObject(O);
setLights(newScene, aCollection);
restore(depth);
return newScene
```

doesIntersect: self ↔ aMatrix ↔ aVector → aCollection
```
newMatrix = aMatrix * matrix(self)
for all objects lights using O
if O ≡ self ∧ decrement(depth) ≡ O
    then /* skip it */
else intersectionPoints += doesIntersect(O, newMatrix, aVector);
endif
restore(depth);
∀ ι ∈ intersectionPoints: addLights(i, lights(self))
return intersectionPoints
```

Listing 4.2

object contained in the **Scene**. The **Scene** provides for changes in coordinates for objects in addition to the viewing coordinate system transformation, as is the case when an initial global transformation matrix specifies a Camera's UVN coordinate system.

Scene.depth is used to control the degree of self-referencing. As cycles may exist in the graphical composition, the traversal algorithms reach a fixed point when **Scene.depth** self-references have been reached. We show later that this is a powerful modeling feature not found in existing graphics systems.

Camera

The **Camera** class is used to specify views of a **Scene**. Multiple cameras can be defined and a **Scene** may have multiple views. The camera contains structure and behavior for the view plane normal (VPN), view reference point (VRP), viewing up vector (VUP), perspective reference point (PRP), view distance, projection type, window, clipping boundaries, quality (wire, hidden-line, hidden-surface, shading), and algorithm (z buffer, painter's algorithm, ray trace).

The **aCamera.(asMatrix)** message returns a transformation (**Matrix**) representation of the view maintained by **aCamera**. This transformation is typically used as an initial matrix in the rendering process.

Object-Based Rendering Algorithms

All object-oriented systems that deal with the rendering of objects must answer a fundamental question (from both a theoretical and practical viewpoint): *Should an object draw itself?* The response is: *It depends on what "draw" means!* In order to draw an object, that object must respond to a protocol message requesting its spatial location, spatial extents, or representation as a collection of base objects that *can* be drawn. The presence of such a set of base objects suggests that we can draw any user-defined object if that object can reply to a drawing protocol message with a collection of these base objects. The polygon is an example of a base object that numerous algorithms use for rendering. Accordingly, to implement a rendering algorithm, objects need only respond to drawing protocol messages for that algorithm. This strategy is employed in GOII. The base class specification is set as

```
scene.(setBaseClass aClass);
```

where **aClass** is the name of a base class (such as **Polygon3D**, **Line3D**, **Sphere**). The class variable **Shape3D.classStructure.baseClass** is changed by this message.

This research defines specifications for three general classes of object-based rendering algorithms: ray tracing, painter's algorithm, and z buffer. As this section proceeds, it should become evident that the incorporation of other rendering algorithms, such as radiosity, is straightforward. The benefits of object-oriented design, encapsulation, resource sharing, and object composition facilitate such modifications. The overall rendering architecture is shown in Figure 4.7.

The **Camera** class contains a method to take a "snapshot" of a **Scene** and produce a **Picture** object. The **Picture** is a two-dimensional structured representation of the three-dimensional **Scene**. Two-dimensional **Picture** editing operations include zooming, scrolling, and pick correlation.

The contents of the **Picture** object are simple two-dimensional drawing primitives such as circle, polygon, line, and point. To transform this structure into a flat **Image** object, we simply apply a scan line algorithm to each two-dimensional primitive into the **Image** object.

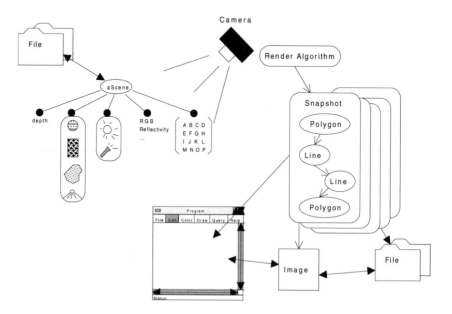

Figure 4.7: Object-based rendering architecture

Object-Based Ray Tracing Algorithm

This section presents an algorithm for ray tracing objects in an object-based rendering architecture, shown in Listing 4.3. The procedural-based ray tracing algorithm found in [Rogers 1985] is used as a guideline.

The algorithm operates as follows:
1. For each (x, y) on the world window (virtual screen):
2. Create a ray from the camera eyepoint through (x, y) and find an intersection point within the camera-orientation transformed scene.
3. Intersect each created ray with the scene. Returned from the scene is a

---

Class Camera:
rayTrace: *self* ↔ aScene → aPicture
    aPicture = new(Picture);
    ∀ i = self.(world).(left)...self.(world).(right) ∧
      j = self.(world).(bottom...self.(world).(top)
      initialRay = set(new (Ray), "initial", prp, point3D(i, j, 0));
      aStack.(push initialRay);
      loop while not aStack.(empty)
        currentRay = aStack.(pop);
        if currentRay.(intersected)
          setAttribute (currentRay, set (new(Attribute),
            intensity(currentRay)));
        else
          intPts = doesIntersect (aScene, asMatrix(self), currentRay);
          intPt = closest(intPts, currentRay);
          if not intPt
            setAttribute (currentRay, set(new(Attribute),
              background(currentRay)));
          else
            aStack.(push currentRay);
            if reflectedRay(intPt)
              aStack.(push reflectedRay(intPt));
            if refractedRay (intPt)
              aStack.(push refractedRay(intPt));
         endif
        endif
      endLoop
    add(aPicture, intensity(currentRay), i, j);

Listing 4.3

collection of intersection points. Each intersection point references the object it intersected; contains a **Point3D**, which is the intersection; and contains a collection of light sources "visible" to the path traversed in the scene.

4. Select the closest intersection point to the viewer.
5. Generate reflection and refraction rays for each intersection point. Repeat the above for each of these rays.
6. If a ray does not intersect the scene, set the intensity for this ray to the background color. If it does, calculate the intensity value. Propagate this value back to the previous ray.
7. Using a stack, hold current intersecting rays until their refracted and reflected rays have performed steps 1-6. Then combine intensities. A modification to the algorithm is needed after the **setAttribute** function in the **currentRay.(intersected)** test, if a limit is to be set on the depth to which to ray trace.

Object-Based Z Buffer Algorithm

This section presents an algorithm for rendering objects with a z buffer approach, shown in Listing 4.4. The procedural-based z buffer algorithm in [Foley et al. 1990] is used as a guideline.

The algorithm proceeds as follows:

1. Transform the scene into a **Polygon3D**-oriented scene, preserving structure, transformations, and lights.
2. We want to zbuffer paint each polygon into a 2D picture object. The camera's view plane transformation is the initial transformation for each object, and the scene's lights are the lights visible. Pass these to the paint algorithm and fill the buffer with **Points**.
3. If a **Polygon3D** is encountered, combine global and local transformations and transform the polygon. If the polygon is a front face, clip it. Then scan fill the polygon's 2D projection into the buffer. Recall that the 2D polygon has a reference to the source 3D object.
4. Scan fill calculates the intensity of the source object using the current lights and gives this value to each point.

These object-based rendering algorithms preserve references to the source object after source→2D and 2D→**Point** transformations.

Class Camera:

zBuffer: *self* ↔ aScene → aPicture
    aPicture = new(Picture);
    aScene.(setBaseClass Polygon3D);
    newScene.(= aScene.(asBaseObjects));
    /* now newScene is hierarchically similar to scene but is composed */
    /* of polygon3Dmesh, polygon3D, and Scene objects. Now fill the */
    /* zbuffer with Point objects. Each Point contains pointers to the*/
    /* original object. The initial transformation is a view plane */
    /* transformation. The initial object is a scene and the initial lights are */
    /* from the scene */
    self.(zPaint aPicture self.(asMatrix) aScene lights.(aScene));
    return aPicture;

Class Camera:

zPaint: *self* ↔ aPicture ↔ aMatrix ↔ aShape3D ↔ someLights → aBuffer
    if aShape3D.(class).(== Polygon3D)
        newMatrix.(= aShape3D.(matrix).(mult aMatrix));
        newShape.(= newMatrix.(multPoly aShape3D));
        if newShape.(isFontFace newShape)
            self.(Fill aPicture self.(project newShape) someLights)
    else
    if aShape3D.(class).(== Polygon3DMesh)
        ∀ p ∈ aShape3D: self.(zPaint aPicture aMatrix p someLights)
    else
    if aShape3D.(class).(== Scene)
        ∀ o ∈ aShape3D: self.(zPaint aPicture aMatrix *aShape3D.(matrix)
            someLights aShape3D.(lights))
    if aShape3D.(class).(== Collection)
        ∀ c ∈ aShape3D:
            self.(zPaint aPicture identity(new(Matrix)) someLights)

Class Camera:

Fill: *self* ↔ aPicture ↔ aShape ↔ someLights → self
    /* by point for zBuffer */
    ∀ pt ∈ aShape: if aPicture.(at pt.(x) pt.(y)).(z) < pt.(z)
            pt.(setAttribute calcIntensity(self pt.(source) someLights))
                ∧ aPicture.(add pt)
    /* by Shape2D for painters */
    aShape.(setAttribute calcIntensity(self pt.(source) someLights))
                ∧ aPicture.(add aShape)

Listing 4.4

Object-Based Painter's Algorithm

This section presents an algorithm, shown in Listing 4.5, for rendering objects using a painter's algorithm approach based on [Foley et al. 1990].
    This algorithm operates as follows:
1. Transform the scene into a **Polygon3D**-oriented scene, preserving structure, transformations, and lights.

Class Camera:
painters: *self* ↔ aScene → aPicture
    aPicture = new(Picture);
    aScene.(setBaseClass Polygon3D);
    newScene.(= aScene.(asBaseObjects));
    /* now newScene is hierarchically similar to scene but is composed of */
    /* polygon3Dmesh, polygon3D, and Scene objects. Now fill the zbuffer */
    /* with Point objects. Each Point contains pointers to the original object. */
    /* The initial transformation is a view plane transformation. The initial */
    /* object is a scene and the initial lights are from the scene */
    aCollection.(= self.(paintersAlg self.(asMatrix) aScene lights.(aScene)));
    self.(sort aCollection)
    self.(Fill aPicture self.(project newShape) someLights);
    return aPicture;

Class Camera:
paintersAlg: *self* ↔ aMatrix ↔ aShape3D ↔ someLights → aBuffer
    if aShape3D.(class).(== Polygon3D)
        newMatrix.(= aShape3D.(matrix).(mult aMatrix));
        newShape.(= newMatrix.(multPoly aShape3D));
        if newShape.(isFontFace newShape)
            return self.(project newShape)
    else
    if aShape3D.(class).(== Polygon3DMesh)
        ∀ p ∈ aShape3D:
            aCollection.(+=self.(paintersAlg aMatrix p someLights))
        return aCollection;
    else
    if aShape3D.(class).(== Scene)
        ∀ o ∈ aShape3D: aCollection.(+=self.(paintersAlg
            aMatrix *aShape3D.(matrix) someLights aShape3D.(lights))
        return aCollection;

Listing 4.5

2. The camera's view plane transformation is the initial transformation for each object; the scene's lights are the lights visible.
3. If a **Polygon3D** is encountered, combine global and local transformations and transform the polygon. If the polygon is a front face, clip it. Then return a collection of transformed polygons.
4. After the painter's message, sort the polygons. They have been transformed but retain their z value and source object reference. Then use **Fill** to fill the polygon's contents.

Two-Dimensional Structure

The output from a rendering algorithm is a structured class **Picture**. **Picture** is based on the two-dimensional structuring class of the same name in Actor [Whitewater 1990]. The functionality of **Picture** is similar to a display list used in GKS and CORE. The picture objects are a hierarchical structure containing polygons, curves, lines, circles, ellipses, squares, colors, brushes, and other pictures. The following is a list of operations common to a **Picture** structure.

- aPicture.(add aShape)
- aPicture.(remove aShape)
- aPicture.([] i aShape)
- aShape.(= aPicture.([] j))
- aPicture.(first)
- aPicture.(last)
- aPicture.(size)
- aPicture.(removeDeep aShape)
- aPicture.(writeFile)
- aPicture.(readFile)
- aPicture.(at i j)
- aPicture.(put aShape i j)

The **Picture** class is to two-dimensional shapes (**Shape**) as **Scene** is to three-dimensional shapes (**Shape3D**). The modification made for GOll to employ **Pictures** is to modify the **Graphic** class such that each graphic contains a reference to the source three-dimensional **Shape3D** from which it was generated. The picture is the entity that responds to draw messages sent to a window. The picture displays itself by recursively displaying its components.

The Camera's **Fill** message instructs the **Picture** to take a polygon, calculate its intensity, and add it to the 2D structure. The polygon can be decomposed into **Points**, **Squares**, or left as polygons and added to **Picture**. In any case, they retain their identity as 2D objects with references to source 3D objects.[3]

Pick Correlation

Pick correlation in GOII is facilitated by the object-oriented modeling primitives. Throughout the rendering pipeline, as objects are decomposed into base objects or intersection points, the reference to a source object is retained.[4] Therefore, we can perform simple two-dimensional pick correlation. The selected object[5] contains a reference to the source object from which editing may be performed (see Figure 4.8).

The typical pick correlation mechanism is to "click" through the objects and show bounding two-dimensional corners around the current object. Another method is to present a popup window containing names of objects that occupy this projected two-dimensional space.

Configuration

All GOII modeling primitives have messages **readFile** and **writeFile** defined so that their contents can be saved and retrieved for future editing. The configuration files are ASCII flat files and are opcode based. For example:

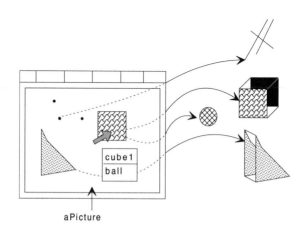

Figure 4.8: Two-dimensional objects retain 3D reference for pick correlation

```
Sphere:earth transformation:t1 attribute:earthColor
Matrix:transformation1 Rx:10 Ry:12
Attribute:earthColor Red:20 Green:120 Blue:189
```

is a partial listing of what is required to save the contents of a **Sphere** object.

Modeling Example

In this section, we present some modeling examples using the GOII architecture. Consider the following code fragments and Figure 4.9.

```
/* instantiate objects */
H2O waterMolecule;
Scene waterDemo;
Matrix transform1;
PointLight light1;
Attribute waterColor;
Camera view1;
/* build GO|| structure */
waterDemo.(add waterMolecule);
transform1.(translate 10 0 0);
setTransformation.(waterMolecule transform1);
```

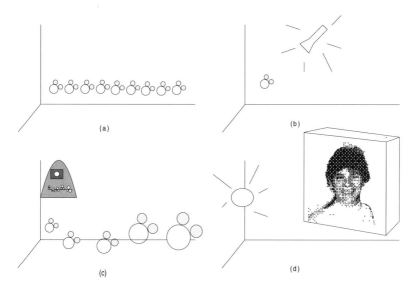

Figure 4.9: Example GOII modeling capabilities

```
waterColor.( /*set values for blue, clear water*/ )
waterDemo.(setDepth 10);
waterDemo.(add waterDemo);
view1.(setVRP 0 1 0);/*set remaining camera values*/
/* now render the picture and draw it in a window */
Window w;
w.(picture).(= view1.(rayTrace waterDemo))
```

What does this algorithm do? We have created one water molecule object and added it to a scene. We added an attribute and a transformation. The scene is self-referencing to ten levels. The rayTrace algorithm is invoked and the results are displayed in a window. One scene object, one user-defined primitive composed of three spheres, and several viewing and attribute objects and we have created a series of H_2O molecules as shown in Figure 4.9a.

Let's make some additions by appending code to the program shown above.

```
setDrawObject(light1, aFlashLight);
setDepth(waterDemo 1);
w.(picture).(= view1.(rayTrace waterDemo))
```

This addition displays one water molecule and a visible light source that appears as a flashlight (see Figure 4.9b).

```
Paraboloid p;   /* set values and a transformation */
Scene newScene;
newScene.(add waterDemo);
/* build a transformation consisting of scaling,
   translation, and rotation, then add it to
   waterDemo */
/* build transformation and set lighting models */
/* give the camera a drawObject that looks like a
   Camera */
w.(picture).(= view1.(rayTrace waterDemo))
```

This set of additions displays a series of water molecules spinning around the x axis,[6] again, by using only one scene and one object. The **waterDemo** scene is a component of **newScene**. The paraboloid contains reflections of the camera and the molecules (see Figure 4.9c).

```
/* build a new scene and add a cube and one light
   source - the light source looks like a ball */
Portrait aPortrait;
setDrawObject (camera, aPortrait);
```

This program fragment shows the complexity and expressiveness of the

**Color Plate 1: Angry George with a red face and a black eye
(Craighill and Fong)**

Color Plate 2: A landscape world object (Egbert and Kubitz)

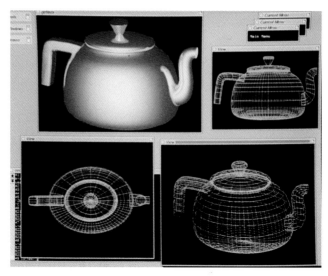

Color Plate 3: A rendered design from ALPHA_1 (Thomas)

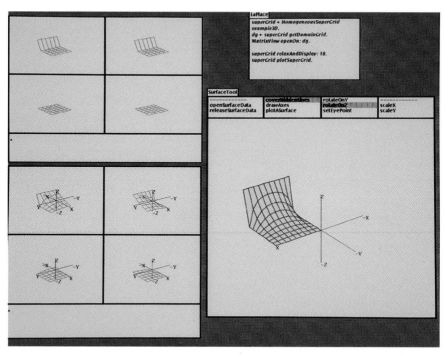

Color Plate 4: SurfaceTool spreadsheet on a domain decomposition object (Walther and Peskin). Each subview shows a "subdomain object," which computes its solution for a region of the problem's physical space

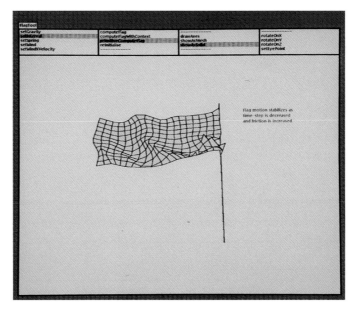

Color Plate 5: Visualization tool on flag simulation (Walther and Peskin). The user can vary the values of the forces

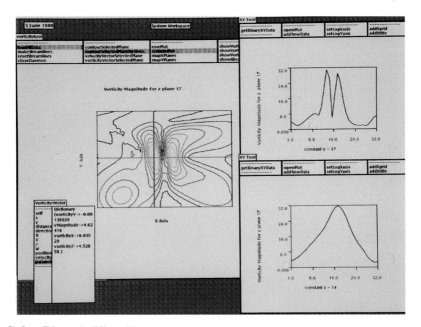

Color Plate 6: Visualization tool opened on a warehouse of vorticity objects (Walther and Peskin). The data represents velocities and vorticities in a 32 by 32 by 32 model of vorticity tube behavior

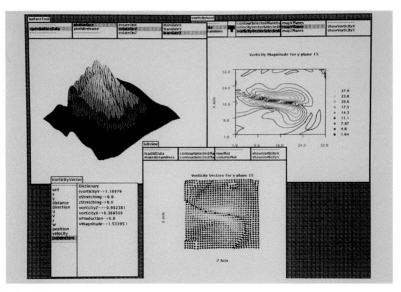

Color Plate 7: Visual queries to a warehouse (Walther and Peskin).
The tool shown in the previous plate has been asked to spawn several
visualizations of its data

Color Plate 8: The JACKS image (Melcher and Owen)

drawObject. In this case, a user-defined object creates a representation of a portrait through the use of textures in the attribute (see Figure 4.9d).

GOll Object-Based Rendering Pipeline

This section summarizes the individual stages of the object-based rendering pipeline proposed in GOll. Figure 4.10 illustrates this process.
1. Create primitive and user-defined graphical objects, images, and windows. Create attributes, lights, transformations, scenes, and cameras.
2. Create hierarchical scenes and user-defined objects. Set attributes, transformations, lights, names, draw objects, and base objects.
3. Choose view, scene, and rendering mode.
4. Render the scene in the specified mode and with the specified view. This process is the "black box" rendering pipeline that is prevalent in existing system. The various existing rendering pipelines are encapsulated into a dynamically configurable component of the overall object-based render-

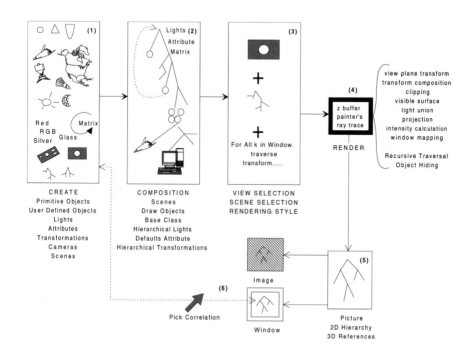

Figure 4.10: The GOll object-based rendering pipeline

ing pipeline. This step includes the decision processes to actualize recursive modeling resolution, object hiding determination, draw object resolution, and lighting unions. The general algorithm used for all of the rendering procedures is to first transform the scene into a set of base objects that are convenient to this algorithm and optimized to the supporting platform. The transformed scene is then traversed according to the particular "draw" message requirements. Traversal of the scene includes transformation composition, light union, and default attribute referencing.

5. Produce a two-dimensional hierarchical picture. The picture is a collection of objects that can "draw themselves" in a two-dimensional world. Each object maintains its source three-dimensional object identity.

6. Display the two-dimensional picture in a **Window** or create a "flat" **Image**. During display, the picture and window provide zooming, panning (scrolling), and pick correlation. The Image provides image-processing abilities on the attribute-oriented image.

In summary, the GOll object-based rendering pipeline not only encapsulates and provides existing modeling, transformational, rendering, and viewing capabilities, but adds significant features and techniques not easily modeled in existing systems.

Research Status

GOll is currently prototyped in two environments. The concurrent, reflective, heterogeneous, and graphical user interface specifications are implemented on a network of Sun-3™s, Sun-4™s, Encore™ Multimax™, and IBM™ RTs. This decision was motivated by two criteria: hardware availability and software tools. The aforementioned hardware environment is the authors' primary development environment. Secondly, the software tools (the X Window System, the C and C++ programming languages, the Berkeley UNIX™, SunOS™, and UMAX™ operating systems, and the Si communication libraries) are stable development environments. This prototype is 100 percent operational; distributed programs can be executed.

The second prototype environment implements the three-dimensional, graphical user interface, and image-processing specifications of GOll. This environment is implemented in Actor 3.0 under the Microsoft Windows 3.0 windowing system. The specifications are 100 percent complete and the prototype is 75 percent operational.

The significance and contributions of the GOll research and development effort include the following:

- a *complete and consistent multiple paradigm specification* for designing object-oriented graphical concurrent environments
- identification of class specifications, class hierarchies, interobject messaging constraints, protocols and algorithms for *object-oriented three-dimensional graphics systems*, which did not exist previously
- the specification for an *object-based rendering pipeline*, which did not exist previously
- the specification of a central storage structure (**Scene**) capable of modeling, with ease, existing graphical specifications, and supplementing this ability with *recursive modeling, hierarchical light sources, user-defined three-dimensional objects, direct pick correlation*, and *graphical encapsulation*, not found previously in existing systems

Current research and development activities for the GOll specification include the following:

- Supplementing the development environment with a Cogent XTM computer and a Silicon Graphics workstation
- Completion of a graphical user interface for the concurrent debugger, computing grid manager, and object-migration facilities
- Investigation into object-based radiosity, solid modeling, and animation algorithms

Notes

1. Pronounced "geaux" for concurrent graphical objects.
2. As with concurrency, device independence and heterogeneous computing are discussed in [Bahrs 1991].
3. [Bahrs 1991] contains the transformation from **Picture** to **Image**.
4. This specification increases the memory requirements substantially, however, a second **Scene** traversal is not needed (as performed in PHIGS and HOOPS™). Future testing and evaluation are needed to justify the merits of either technique.
5. There may be more than one selected object based on the rendering algorithm chosen. When ray tracing is used, the source ray intersects initally with zero or more objects for each pixel. These object references may be stored in the **Picture**. If z buffering is used, a similar approach is used. The granularity of the **drawObject** in the **Picture** is the **Point**. A painter's algorithm can produce complex polygons in the **Picture**.

Hence, we store only one object reference per whole polygon.

6. This recursive modeling capability of GO∥'s **Scene** is ideal for simulation and scientific modeling where large amounts of similar data are displayed in patterns that can be calculated, such as DNA modeling.

References

Bahrs, Peter C. [1991], *An Object-Oriented Framework for Concurrent Graphics in Heterogeneous Environments*. PhD. Dissertation. The Center for Advanced Computer Studies, University of Southwestern Louisiana. Lafayette, Louisiana, April 1991.

Bahrs, Peter C. and Sheila A. Harnett [1991], "An Object-Oriented Framework for Concurrent Graphics in Heterogeneous Environments: Implementation Source." *USL DBMS.NASA/PC R&D Working Paper Series*. DBMS.NASA/PC R&D-30. The Center for Advanced Computer Studies, University of Southwestern Louisiana. Lafayette, Louisiana, April 1991.

Bennett, John K. [1987], "The Design and Implementation of Distributed Smalltalk." *Object-Oriented Programming: Systems, Languages and Applications.* Conference Proceedings OOPSLA '87. Orlando, Florida, 1987, pp. 318-330.

Chandy, K. Mani and Jayadev Misra [1989], *Parallel Program Design: A Foundation.* Reading: Addison-Wesley, 1989.

Cox, Brad [1986], *Object Oriented Programming: An Evolutionary Approach.* Reading: Addison Wesley, 1986.

Foley, James D., Andries van Dam, Steven K. Feiner, and John F. Hughes [1990], *Computer Graphics Principles and Practice.* 2nd edition. Reading: Addison-Wesley, 1990.

Goldberg, A. and D. Robson [1983], *Smalltalk-80: The Language and Its Implementation.* Reading: Addison-Wesley, 1983.

Haines, Eric [1989], "Essential Ray Tracing Algorithms." In *An Introduction to Ray Tracing.* Andrew S. Glassner, editor. San Diego: Academic Press, 1989, pp. 33-77.

Hanrahan, Pat [1989], "A Survey of Ray-Surface Intersection Algorithms." In *An Introduction to Ray Tracing.* Andrew S. Glassner, editor. San Diego: Academic Press, 1989, pp. 79-119.

"Information Processing Systems—Computer Graphics—Graphical Kernel System (GKS) Functional Description." [ISO 1985a] ISO 7942. ISO Central Secretariat, August 1985.

"PHIGS: Programmer's Hierarchical Interactive Graphics System—Functional Description." [ISO 1985b] TC97/SC21/N819. ISO Central Secretariat, September 1985.

HOOPS Graphics Software. [Ithaca 1988] Ithaca Software. Alameda, California, 1988.

Mallgren, William [1982], *Formal Specification of Interactive Graphics Programming Languages.* ACM Distinguished Dissertation. Cambridge: MIT Press, 1982.

Meyer, B. [1988], *Object-Oriented Software Construction.* Hemel Hempstead: Prentice-Hall, 1988.

Meyer, B. [1987], "Reusability: The Case for Object-Oriented Design." *IEEE Software*, 4(2), March 1987, pp. 50-64.

Micallef, Josephine [1988], "Encapsulation, Reusability and Extensibility in Object-Oriented Programming Languages." *Journal of Object-Oriented Programming*, 1(1). May 1988, pp. 12-19.

Rogers, David F. [1985], *Procedural Elements for Computer Graphics.* New York: McGraw-Hill, 1985.

Shu, Nan C. [1988], *Visual Programming.* New York: Van Nostrand Reinhold, 1988.

Stroustrup, Bjarne [1986], *The C++ Programming Language.* Reading: Addison-Wesley, 1986.

Whitewater Group [1990], *Actor 3.0.* The Whitewater Group. Evanston, Illinois, 1990.

Chapter 5

The Graphical Application Support System

Parris K. Egbert
William J. Kubitz

Two main processes occur in producing a view of a graphical object on a computer screen: modeling and rendering. Traditional graphics systems have emphasized the requirements of the rendering portion of the system in order to minimize the time required to generate an image. A by-product of this emphasis is that users of the system have been forced to program at a level convenient to the renderer, not to the application. The Graphical Application Support System (GRASSY) attempts to reverse this thinking and bring graphics programming up to a level convenient to the programmer. This is done through the use of object-oriented design and implementation for the graphics system and for its interfaces to the renderer and the application.

GRASSY Overview

GRASSY is a 3D modeling system designed for ease of use by the application. Most graphics systems in use today have been built by determining which types of graphics primitives are most easily and efficiently rendered, and then using these graphics primitives as the only modeling objects. This forces the application to build its models using only these low-level graphics primitives, which are almost always inappropriate for the application. GRASSY uses the principles of abstraction, class hierarchy, encapsulation, and inheritance to provide a higher level of modeling and graphics support to the application. The main goals of GRASSY are the following:

1. to allow an application user to build complex models at a high level of abstraction using only application semantics
2. to allow an application programmer to easily add new application modeling objects that are not currently available in the system
3. to provide a broad set of application graphical objects (having application semantics) from which the application modeling objects can be built
4. to provide a graphics support level that is largely application-independent so that the application need have little knowledge of the underlying graphics system
5. to provide an interface between the modeling and rendering systems that allows easy extension of the rendering system, while allowing renderers to use built-in efficiencies

The remainder of this chapter describes the way in which GRASSY approaches these goals. Color Plate 2 is a sample scene that has been modeled using GRASSY and will serve as the central reference for the discussion of GRASSY that follows.

The Application Programming Interface

Color Plate 2 shows a view of a visualization of a landscape world object. Here the application is landscape, the visualization is a particular representation of the underlying world object, and the view is the image of that visualization generated from a particular viewpoint in three-dimensional space. The world object is the hierarchical object representation in world coordinates of all the objects that contribute to this image. A world object is created by executing the code:

```
WorldObject world_object = WorldObject();
```

This creates an instance of the class **WorldObject** and prepares it to be used by the application. A **WorldObject** is used to keep track of all the application objects that are to be visualized by the application. In the example of Color Plate 2, the world object is composed of eleven application objects that have been modeled using GRASSY. These are a ground object, a mountain object, a sky object, three tree objects, two chair objects, a table object, and two glass objects. The code to create and establish the locations of these application objects is given in Listing 5.1. Note that GRASSY is implemented in C++, where the syntax of messaging and instance variable access is similar to C function calls and field references.

```
/* Create the application objects */
Tree tree1 = Tree(100, 150, 10);
Tree tree2 = Tree(380, 160, 200);
Tree tree3 = Tree(540, 100, 300);
Table table = Table(210, 40, 350);
Chair chair1 = Chair(100, 40, 370);
Chair chair2 = Chair(380, 40, 370);
Glass glass1 = Glass(310, 107, 380);
Glass glass2 = Glass(230, 103, 380);
Mountain mountain = Mountain(0, 200, 100);
Sky sky = Sky();
Ground ground = Ground();
```

Listing 5.1: Creating the application objects for the landscape scene

The code in Listing 5.1 creates instances of the application classes **Tree**, **Table**, **Chair**, **Glass**, **Mountain**, **Sky**, and **Ground**. These classes must have been previously defined by the application. In the case of the first tree in this scene, the code

```
Tree tree1 = Tree(100, 150, 10);
```

creates an instance of the class **Tree**, names that instance **tree1**, and stores the world coordinate point (100, 150, 10) as the location of that tree. The other object instances are created similarly. Once an application object has been created, it must have a graphical object associated with it to facilitate the visualization of the object. Listing 5.2 shows the code required to create and associate the graphical objects with the application objects in this scene. The first line of code shown in Listing 5.2 performs two functions. First, the embedded code

```
new GO_MapleTree();
```

creates an instance of the class **GO_MapleTree**. **GO_MapleTree** is a graphical object class that is defined in GRASSY. Creating an instance of this class creates an object that can later be used to represent graphically the application object with which it is associated. The association between the graphical object and the application object is done by executing the code

```
tree1.setGraphicalObject(new GO_MapleTree());
```

The other graphical objects are created and associated with application objects in a similar fashion.

Graphical objects can be created using default attribute values, as provided by GRASSY, or by the application specifying the desired attributes.

```
/* Associate graphical objects with the application
      objects */
tree1.setGraphicalObject(new GO_MapleTree());
tree2.setGraphicalObject(new GO_MapleTree());
tree3.setGraphicalObject(new GO_MapleTree());
table.setGraphicalObject(new GO_Table());
chair1.setGraphicalObject(new GO_Chair());
chair2.setGraphicalObject(new GO_Chair());
glass1.setGraphicalObject(new GO_Goblet());
glass2.setGraphicalObject(new GO_Goblet());
mountain.setGraphicalObject(new GO_Mountain());
sky.setGraphicalObject(new GO_Sky());
ground.setGraphicalObject(new GO_Ground());
```

Listing 5.2: Code to associate graphical objects with the application objects

For example, rather than creating a default **GO_MapleTree**, the application may wish to specify various attributes about its particular maple tree, such as the height of the tree, the color of the bark, and so on. Attributes such as these can be incorporated into the graphical object by passing the appropriate data values from the application object to the graphical object.

The next step in creating a visualization of the application objects is to associate particular renderer objects with the application objects. When the system is requested to generate a view of the **WorldObject**, each application object contained in the **WorldObject** will use its associated renderer to generate its visualization. In this example, one renderer object is used to generate the visualizations of all of the application objects. This renderer is a simple display list renderer that performs its graphics rendering using the Graphics Library™ from Silicon Graphics [1988b]. To create the renderer, to initialize it, and to prepare it for use by the application, the following code is executed:

```
GL_renderer renderer = GL_renderer();
```

This line of code creates an instance of the class **GL_Renderer** and stores that instance in the variable named renderer. Once the renderer has been created, we can associate it with the application objects. Listing 5.3 shows this being done for the landscape scene.

With the graphical objects and renderer objects in place, the application object is now ready to be added into the world object. Listing 5.4 shows the code to perform this operation. Once this has been done, the world object is

```
tree1.setRenderer(renderer);
tree2.setRenderer(renderer);
tree3.setRenderer(renderer);
table.setRenderer(renderer);
chair1.setRenderer(renderer);
chair2.setRenderer(renderer);
glass1.setRenderer(renderer);
glass2.setRenderer(renderer);
mountain.setRenderer(renderer);
sky.setRenderer(renderer);
ground.setRenderer(renderer);
```

Listing 5.3: Associating renderers with application objects in the landscape scene

ready to be viewed. This is done by sending a view message to it. The following line of code shows the form of this method.

```
world_object.view();
```

Upon receipt of this message, the world object sends **view** messages to each of the application objects contained within it. These application objects then pass a **render** message to their graphical objects. When the graphical objects receive this message, they send the appropriate object attributes (including geometry, color, and so on) to the renderer object that is associated with them. The renderer then produces a visualization of the world object.

```
world_object.addObject(tree1);
world_object.addObject(tree2);
world_object.addObject(tree3);
world_object.addObject(table);
world_object.addObject(chair1);
world_object.addObject(chair2);
world_object.addObject(glass1);
world_object.addObject(glass2);
world_object.addObject(mountain);
world_object.addObject(sky);
world_object.addObject(ground);
```

Listing 5.4. Adding application objects to the world object

To clarify some of the terminology used in this chapter, a *view* is the manner in which a visualization of an object is to be seen by the viewer. The view is established by specifying the *location* of the viewer and the *direction* the viewer is looking. The same visualization of an object can be viewed from any position. *Changing* a view entails changing the position the world object is to be viewed from and/or changing the direction of the view.

A *visualization* of an object is the manner in which the object is represented on the screen. It is possible to generate many different visualizations of the same object. A visualization is a function of the object itself, the graphical object associated with the object, and the renderer used to render the object. Altering any of these parameters will produce a different visualization. For example, suppose the application had defined a class **Box**, and had created an instance of that class. To view this object on the screen requires that a graphical object be associated with this application object. In this case, a **GO_Box** graphical object might be used. In addition, a renderer object must also be associated with the **Box** object. Once this has been done, a visualization of the **Box** can now be generated. If we desire to use a different renderer (perhaps one that produces a more realistic image of the **Box**), we could associate this new renderer with the **Box** object and generate a different visualization of it. In this case, the underlying object hasn't changed, nor has the graphical object that is associated with it, but a different visualization is produced. Likewise, we could associate a different graphical object with the **Box**. In this case, the **GO_Cube** graphical object might be sufficient for the application. Using this new graphical object, a new visualization of the **Box** is generated.

The Design of GRASSY

Modeling Abstraction

The first goal of GRASSY, as mentioned in the previous section, is to allow an application user to model at a high level of abstraction. Since renderers typically work with low-level graphics primitives, a gap exists between the level at which humans wish to model and the level at which computers perform rendering. GRASSY bridges this gap by defining graphical objects in a layered fashion, as depicted in Figure 5.1. The objects at the lowest layer are designed for ease of use by the renderer. Objects at the highest layer are designed for ease of use by application programmers. Intermediate objects provide a smooth transition between the two outermost layers. The layers, from bottom to top, are as follows:

1. The Primitive Graphical Object (PGO) Level. This level includes the objects that all renderers are capable of rendering. This is the lowest level of the GRASS system. At this level the emphasis is on efficient rendering of the graphics primitives. Although applications are allowed to use objects at this level, they will rarely wish to do so, since these objects are very low level and well below the level at which humans typically think.

2. The Composite Graphical Object (CGO) Level. Objects at this level are modeled at a higher level than those of the PGO level. Many objects at this level are created by instancing combinations of objects from the

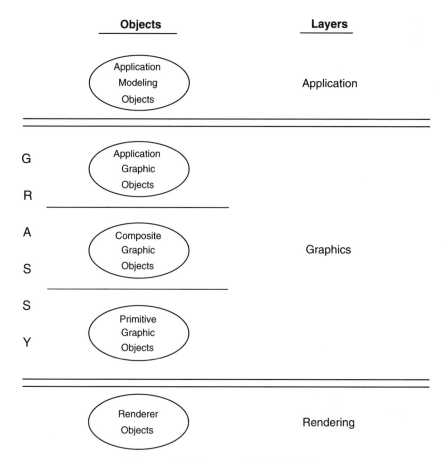

Figure 5.1: Layers in GRASSY

PGO level. Objects at this level are at a lower level of abstraction than most applications desire, and at a level higher than some renderers will be able to use. However, the CGOs are constructed so as to allow easy implementation of application graphic objects (AGOs), which are then used to build application modeling objects (AMOs).

3. The Application Graphical Object (AGO) Level. Objects at this level are designed to be easily used by the application. They are created by instancing combinations of objects from the CGO and PGO levels. Few, if any, renderers will be able to render objects at this level, but applications will be able to use these objects much more easily than objects at the lower levels. At this level objects have both graphics and application semantics associated with them.

The application exists above the top layer of GRASSY. Application modeling objects lie at this level. An object of this type will typically contain a large amount of application data. This data is used heavily by the application, but only a small portion of it is pertinent to producing a graphical representation of the application object. The graphical object(s) associated with the application object supplies the various visualization forms for the object and the application object supplies the location and other attributes for the object. The application also supplies the viewer information to the graphics layer. Thus the only issues addressed by GRASSY, as far as application objects go, are the ways in which an application initializes, associates with, alters, and views a graphical object. All other application data, which has no impact on generating a screen image, is irrelevant to GRASSY.

The system does not preclude either the application or the renderers from using objects at any layer. For example, when using constructive solid geometry (CSG), the PGO and/or CGO level objects may be directly usable by the application. Similarly, a renderer may be able to efficiently render objects at the CGO level. Thus, if desired, the application and/or the renderers can use objects at any level of the hierarchy. What the system does provide, however, is a mechanism for modeling at a high level, while allowing renderers to be optimized around a small, low-level subset of the modeling objects. It also allows all modeling objects to be visualized in multiple forms by associating different AGOs with the modeling objects.

By using this decoupled, layered approach, new AGOs can be added to the system very easily. The AGOs that an application wishes to add to the system can be built by using existing objects from the lower levels. In addition, renderers can be optimized without concern for which specific applications will be using them.

System Extensibility

The second goal of GRASSY is to provide easy extensibility. To meet this goal, the traditional application modeling and rendering layers have been decoupled so that extensions can be made in either domain without causing major revisions to the other. In order to decouple these two portions of the system and still allow them to work together, well-defined interfaces between the application modeling layer and GRASSY, and between GRASSY and the renderers, must exist. It is not feasible for every graphical object to know about each renderer, nor for each renderer to be able to render every graphical object. At the same time, however, we do not want to make the system so decoupled that renderers are precluded from using the efficiencies that are built into them. For example, if a particular renderer is designed to render spheres very efficiently, the system should send it spheres whenever possible, regardless of the level at which spheres are defined in GRASSY.

The extensibility criterion is met in the following manner. The PGO level is designed such that objects at that level can be rendered by all renderers. This forces the number of objects in this set to be very small. Currently there are three objects at this level. These objects are **GO_PointList**, **GO_LineList**, and **GO_PolygonList**. All renderers in the system must be built so that they can render all of the objects at the PGO level. Any new renderer that is to be added must be able to render all of the PGO objects.

Objects at the CGO level are built in one of two ways. The first way is to build a CGO by combining instances of PGOs in some fashion. The CGO being built is responsible for maintaining the relationships that exist between its PGO objects. To render a CGO that is constructed in this fashion, a render message is sent to the CGO object, along with the particular renderer that is to be used. The CGO object sends a render message to each of the PGOs that comprise it, passing the renderer as part of the message. The PGO level objects then pass their data to the renderer as though they were the sole PGO being rendered, that is, they have no knowledge of the other PGOs that are being rendered, nor do they need any. Figure 5.2 shows the message flow diagram for rendering a CGO object defined in this fashion.

As an example, we may wish to define a sphere as a CGO object. We could specify the sphere by calculating a polygonal approximation to the sphere and storing those polygons (which have previously been defined at the PGO level). Rendering a sphere defined in this manner would consist of sending all of these polygons to the renderer.

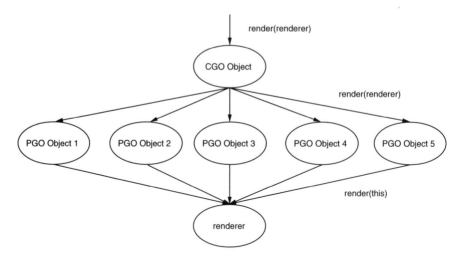

Figure 5.2: Rendering a CGO level object composed of multiple PGO objects

The second method of defining a CGO is to build it as a distinct graphical object and to provide a method for fracturing the object into one or more PGOs. When the object receives a render message, it makes a call to the fracturing method, passing the renderer as a parameter. To make the interface standard for all of these objects, this fracturing method is always given the name *transformInto*. This method fractures the CGO into one or more PGO level objects. It then sends render messages to the renderer, passing these PGO objects as parameters. The renderer then renders those objects. Figure 5.3 shows the message flow diagram for rendering a CGO level object constructed in this manner. Using this method, a sphere would be defined by a center point and a radius. We would also be required to supply the mechanism for transforming the sphere into one of the PGOs in the system. In this case a sphere polygonization routine would fulfill the requirement. When the **GO_Sphere** object was to be rendered, it would call its **transformInto** method. This routine would calculate the polygons that would approximate the sphere and send those polygons to the renderer. The renderer would then render them.

By using either of these two methods for creating CGOs, we are guaranteed that all of the CGOs in the system will be transformable to one or more PGOs. Since these PGOs are renderable by the renderers, we are guaranteed that the CGOs will be renderable.

Application graphical objects provide the highest level of abstraction in

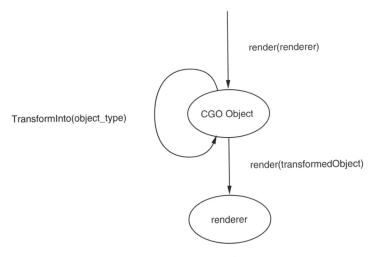

TransformInto(object_type)

render(renderer)

CGO Object

render(transformedObject)

renderer

Figure 5.3: Rendering a singularly defined CGO level object

GRASSY. An AGO is created by combining instances of lower-level CGOs and PGOs and associating application semantics with the resulting object. Since all PGOs and CGOs are renderable by the renderers, the AGOs are also renderable. For example, we may wish to define a barbell as an AGO level object. Assume that the objects **GO_Sphere** and **GO_Cylinder** have been defined at the CGO level. The **GO_Barbell** object would be built by instancing two **GO_Sphere** objects and one **GO_Cylinder** object and placing these objects in the correct locations. When the **GO_Barbell** is to be rendered, it simply passes the render message to the **GO_Spheres** and **GO_Cylinder** that comprise it, and these objects take care of the actual rendering. Figure 5.4 shows the message flow diagram for this process. Since the **GO_Sphere** and **GO_Cylinder** objects have been defined at the CGO level, we know that they can be rendered by the renderer. Thus the **GO_Barbell** is also renderable.

Application modeling objects are built by the application. To be able to produce a visualization of an application object, the application must have associated with it one or more graphical objects. The only graphical objects that can be used here are AGO level objects, but the system does not prohibit pseudo CGO or PGO level objects from being used, as long as they are redefined at the AGO level and application semantics are associated with them. When the application wishes to generate a visualization of an application object, it sends a message requesting this to the object. The object, in turn, sends a render message to the AGO object(s) associated with it.

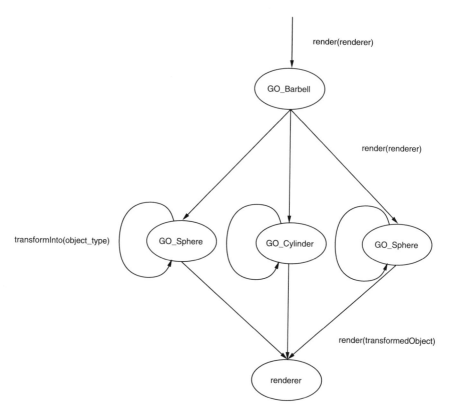

Figure 5.4: Rendering the GO_Barbell object

Because these objects are all expressible in terms of CGO or PGO objects, and because all objects at these levels are renderable, the visualization of the application object will also be renderable.

This scheme ensures that all modeling objects in the system can be rendered by all renderers. It also lends easy extensibility to the system. New application models can be created by instancing the appropriate AGOs in the system and associating the desired application semantics with those AGOs. If a particular AGO is desired that is not currently in the system, it can be created by using the existing CGOs and PGOs. Similarly, if a desired CGO is not currently in the system, it can be added by combining PGOs in an appropriate manner or by defining the new CGO and supplying a method for fracturing it into one or more PGOs.

Since PGOs are the basic interface between modeling and rendering, it is more difficult to extend this level. To add another object at this level requires that all renderers in the system be updated so that they are capable of rendering this new PGO. It is expected that one will never, or at least very rarely, need to expand this level of GRASSY.

By using this layered approach in which the interface between GRASSY and the renderers is defined to be a small set of easily renderable objects, we also provide for easy extensibility of the rendering portion of the system. Different applications will have different requirements as to the quality of rendering they desire and the amount of time they are willing to spend rendering an image. In many applications, users wish to have a scene rendered very quickly, initially, so that they can determine if objects in the scene are positioned correctly or the view of the scene is set up correctly. Once they have determined that object placement is correct in the scene, they desire to render the scene in a more realistic manner. Thus, not only will different applications desire to use different renderers, but it will often be the case that one particular application will want to use different renderers at different stages of development. This is handled in GRASSY by allowing different rendering styles and techniques to be present in the system simultaneously. Objects are rendered by sending them a render message with the particular renderer as a parameter of that message. Rendering an object with a different renderer is done by sending a different renderer as that parameter.

To extend the rendering portion of the system, new renderers may be added as necessary. The minimal requirements a renderer must adhere to are the following:

1. The renderer must respond to a message of the form **render(obj_type, obj)**, where **obj_type** is the type of object to render and **obj** is the actual GRASSY object to render.

2. The renderer must be able to render all of the objects at the PGO level.

Any renderer that meets the above requirements can be incorporated into the system. This allows renderers to be built without knowledge of all of the modeling objects in the system. The only objects a renderer must concern itself with are those at the lowest level of GRASSY. Thus, renderers can be optimized around this small set of objects without regard for the higher-level objects in the system. This can simplify the renderers considerably. If a renderer has the ability to render higher-level objects, it can do so. In fact, image generation time can often be reduced by rendering higher-level objects, but renderers are not required to have this ability. The ability to render higher-level objects can be built into the renderer at the time the renderer is created, or it can be added at a later time.

Application Graphic Objects

The third goal for GRASSY is to provide a broad set of generic application graphic objects for all applications while allowing the flexibility required for adding new application-specific AGOs as needed. Thus, although it is not possible to provide all objects that every application may require, we hope to provide a sufficiently broad range so that the effort involved in adding new application graphical objects to the system is minimized. The generic application graphic objects to be included in GRASSY have been determined using both a top-down and a bottom-up approach. To determine the generic objects most useful to applications, we have considered a few specific applications and assessed their requirements. In addition, we have chosen other objects that we feel will be useful for a broad range of applications. At the same time, we have looked at the lower graphics levels of GRASSY to see how they can be expanded and enhanced to better support the requirements of application modeling. By using this bidirectional approach, we have been able to determine a large number of graphical objects that can easily be used to build the application graphical objects in the system and retain characteristics that will allow for easy rendering. Using these objects as the building blocks for the application graphical objects, we have been able to determine a fairly broad suite of generic objects at the AGO level. The AGO objects in GRASSY are shown in Figures 5.7 through 5.14, in connection with the discussion of the GRASSY class hierarchies.

Renderer Efficiency

Most renderers will be able to render objects above the PGO level, but the objects that various renderers will be capable of rendering will differ. The system must allow renderers the option of rendering objects more complex than those at the PGO level, but must not force all renderers to be able to render objects above that level.

Rather than allowing only PGO level objects to be rendered, GRASSY allows higher-level objects to be provided to renderers that are capable of accepting them. This is managed by maintaining information on the active renderers in the system, as well as on the graphical objects each renderer is capable of accepting. This information is stored in a table called the renderer capability table. There is one row in the table for each renderer in the system. Each row in the table contains a tuple of the form (**r_type**, **obj_list**), where

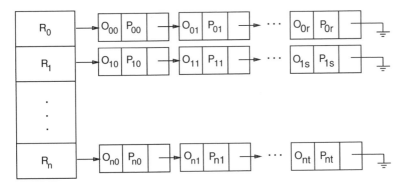

Figure 5.5: The renderer capability table

r_type specifies the type of renderer, and **obj_list** is a list of the graphical objects that type of renderer can accept, with a priority associated with each object type. The priority is determined by the efficiency with which the renderer can render that particular graphical object type.

Figure 5.5 shows a diagram of how this table is organized. In this diagram there are $n + 1$ renderers. Renderer R_0 is capable of rendering $r + 1$ different object types. It renders object O_{00} with an assigned priority of P_{00}, object O_{01} with a priority of P_{01}, and so on. Likewise, renderer R_1 is capable of rendering $s + 1$ objects. It renders object O_{10} with an assigned priority P_{10}, and so on. The renderer capability table is consulted when an object is to be rendered to determine the type of data that should be sent to the renderer.

In addition to the renderer capability table, there is another table in the system called the graphical object conversion table. This table contains a list of the graphical objects in the system along with the graphical object types into which they can convert themselves. The format of the table is similar to the renderer capability table. There is one row in the table for each graphical object in the system. Each row contains an (**obj_type, obj_list**) tuple, where **obj_type** specifies the graphical object type for this row, and **obj_list** is a list of the graphical objects into which this graphical object type can convert itself, along with a priority for each object type. The priority is based on the difficulty associated with transforming this graphical object type into the new graphical object type.

These tables are used together to determine the graphic object type to send to a renderer. When a graphical object is to be rendered, it is sent a render message. For example, the code that initiated the rendering of **tree1** in Color Plate 2 is

```
tree1.view(renderer);
```

This message was generated by the **WorldObject** when it received a render message itself. The **tree1** application object then passes the renderer to its associated graphical object so that the graphical object can be rendered. Since all application objects that are to be viewed will perform the same function when they receive a view message, this method is defined in their superclass. All application objects will inherit this method from their superclass and hence need not redefine it themselves. The definition of the view method for application objects is given in the following.

```
ApplicationObject :: render()
{
   if ((this->graphicalObject != NULL) &&
       (this->renderer != NULL))
   {
     (this->graphicalObject)->render(this->renderer);
   }
}
```

This code first determines whether or not a graphical object and a renderer have been associated with this application object. If so, a render message is sent to the graphical object. Otherwise, no action is taken.

The graphical object that was associated with the **tree1** object was an instance of the **GO_MapleTree** class. When this graphical object receives the render message, it determines the graphical object type to send to the renderer. It makes this determination by using the renderer capability table and the graphical object conversion table. Figure 5.6 shows the entries in these tables corresponding to the **GO_MapleTree** graphical object and the **GL_Renderer** rendering object. First, the entry in the graphical object conversion table corresponding to **GO_MapleTree** is considered. Using this entry, we extract the object list associated with **GO_MapleTree**. This list will contain graphical object types that class **GO_MapleTree** knows how to convert itself to. Initially, the first item on the list is considered. In this example, the first object type on the list is **GO_MapleTree**. At this point, the renderer capability table is consulted to determine whether or not this renderer can accept this graphical object type. The entry in the renderer capability table corresponding to this particular renderer is retrieved. The object list for this renderer is examined to see if the object type from the object conversion table is contained in it. If so, we know that **GO_MapleTree** is capable of converting to this type, and that the renderer is capable of accepting this graphical object type. In this example, the **GL_Renderer** does not know how to render objects of type **GO_MapleTree**, so the next item from the graphical object conversion table is considered. In the case of **GO_MapleTree**, the next object type on the list is **GO_PolygonList**. The

**Graphic Object
Conversion
Table**

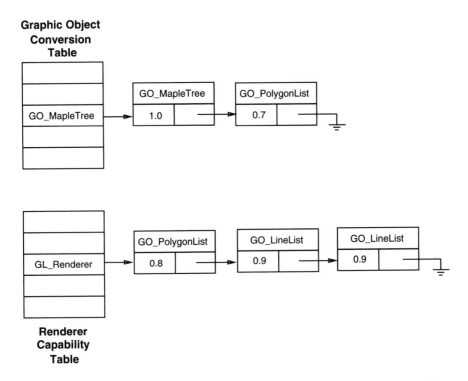

**Renderer
Capability
Table**

**Figure 5.6: Using the two tables to determine the object type to send to
the renderer**

renderer capability table is consulted to see if the renderer is capable of
rendering this type of object.

The **GL_Renderer** can indeed render type **GO_PolygonList**, so we
have found a potential object type for rendering. However, there may be a
different graphical object type that is more efficient to use. By combining
the priorities associated with this object type from the object conversion
table and the renderer capability table, we can determine an overall priority
associated with this object type. This overall priority is saved for future
comparisons. Then, the next object on the list from the object conversion
table is considered. If this object also appears on the list from the renderer
capability table, its overall priority is determined. This priority is then
compared against the overall priority of the first object type. If it has a higher
priority, the old object type is discarded and this one is retained. At the end
of this process, the best object type will have been determined. Best is
defined by the highest overall priority of the object types that appeared on
both the object conversion list and the renderer capability list. In this case

there are no more object types from the graphical object conversion table, so the object type that was found to be best is **GO_PolygonList**. If the best object type happens to be the type of the original object, the object need not perform any conversion—it can simply send its data to the renderer as is. If this is not the case, the object converts itself into the new object type and sends that data to the renderer. Since the best object type found in the case of the **GO_MapleTree** was **GO_PolygonList**, the **GO_MapleTree** must first convert itself to a **GO_PolygonList** object and send this object to the renderer.

The process an object goes through to be rendered is the same regardless of the object type. Thus, the definition of the render method is placed in the root node of all graphical objects. This means that graphical objects need not define the render method themselves—they simply inherit it from their superclass. If an object type requires a new render method, it can be changed but, in general, new objects will not require a change. The following code defines the render method that all graphical objects inherit.

```
GraphicalObject :: render(Renderer *aRenderer)
{
    int objectType = combinedTable.getObjectType
                    (this->getType(), aRenderer);
    if (objectType == this->getType()) {
        aRenderer->render(objectType, this);
    }
    else {
        Primitive *newPrimitive =
                    this->transformInto(objectType);
        aRenderer->render(objectType, newPrimitive);
    }
}
```

The **combinedTable** object maintains the renderer capability and graphical object conversion tables. In addition, it is responsible for determining, from those two tables, the best type of object for a given renderer and object type. The first line of code given here sends the particular object type and renderer to **combinedTable**, and **combinedTable** returns the object type into which it should transform itself. If the object type that the object should transform itself into is the type of the object itself, no transformation need be done. The object sends its data to the renderer and the renderer produces the image. If the object type returned from this message is different from the type of this object, a transformation must be done. This object is sent a **transformInto** message, with the object type it is to convert itself into. Once this object performs the conversion, the new object is then sent to the renderer.

When a new renderer is added to the system, a new entry is created in the renderer capability table. This is done by sending a message to the table with a renderer type and an object/priority list. The table then inserts the new renderer type into itself along with the associated list. If this is inadvertently forgotten, the transformations of the graphical objects simply default to one of the PGOs in the set, and thus are still renderable. Similarly, when a new graphical object is added to the system, a new entry must be made in the graphical object conversion table. This is done in the same manner as the renderer capability table. The graphical object conversion table is sent a message indicating the new object type and the object types currently in the system into which this new one can transform itself. The table then incorporates this information for future use by the objects. If this entry into the graphical object conversion table is omitted, the object will be unable to determine the most efficient object type to send to the renderer. In this case it simply transforms itself into one of the PGOs and sends that object to the renderer. This mechanism of sending higher-level objects to the renderers will allow renderers to capitalize on the efficiencies that are inherent in them, whether they be in software or hardware.

Class Hierarchies in GRASSY

There are two separate class hierarchies an application must be concerned with when using GRASSY, the application object hierarchy and the graphical object hierarchy. The application object hierarchy is determined by the application. Classes are placed in the hierarchy in a manner that is convenient to the application. Figure 5.7 shows an application object hierarchy that might be used in a landscape architecture application.

Subclasses in the hierarchy are specializations of their superclasses, and they inherit the attributes present in the superclasses. Thus, objects that share some common set of attributes are placed in the hierarchy so as to have a common superclass. The attributes that are used to determine the classing structure are dependent on the application. For example, in Figure 5.7 a **Maple** tree is defined to be a subclass of **Deciduous**. A **Maple** tree object inherits all of the attributes defined in the object **Deciduous**, and in turn defines new attributes that distinguish it as a Maple tree. The application determined that the characteristics that separate a deciduous tree from an evergreen tree were significant enough to divide trees into these two categories. A different application may consider a different property of trees to be

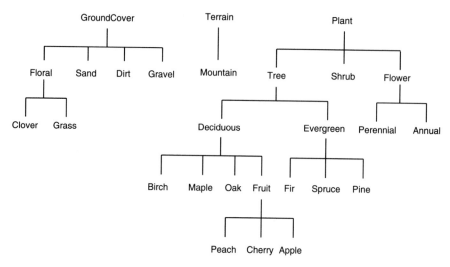

Figure 5.7: A landscape architecture application hierarchy

more important and thus structure the class hierarchy differently.

The other class hierarchy used is the graphical object class hierarchy. This is defined in GRASSY to be used by the application. It is defined much differently than the application class hierarchy. In this case, objects are classed according to the way in which their graphical representation is implemented. For example, a fire and a cloud can both be represented as a particle system that changes over time. Thus, these two objects are both subclasses of the class **GO_DynamicParticleSystem**. In an application, these objects would likely be unrelated and would be placed in two completely different class hierarchies. Because of the similarity in the way they would be stored in GRASSY, they are subclasses of the same superclass. This hierarchy was created by looking at the most plausible method of storing graphical data about an object, then putting objects with similar characteristics as subclasses of the same superclass. Figures 5.8 through 5.15 show the breakdown of the graphical class hierarchy in GRASSY. Figure 5.8 shows the root level and part of the next lower level. The object class **GraphicalObject** is defined at the root level. All objects that support visualizations in GRASSY are subclasses of this class. The three subclasses shown in this figure, **GO_PointList**, **GO_LineList**, and **GO_PolygonList**, are the objects in GRASSY defined at the PGO level.

Figure 5.9 shows all of the CGO level objects that are defined at the first level of the hierarchy. These include classes of objects that are still quite general, but that don't naturally fit as subclasses of **GO_PointList**,

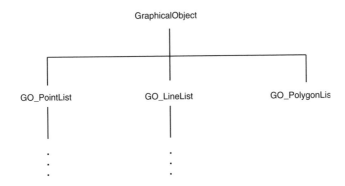

Figure 5.8: PGO objects in the graphical object class hierarchy

GO_LineList, or **GO_PolygonList**. The **GO_Dynamic** class contains objects types that have intrinsically dynamic characteristics. Objects of this type will be used for applications such as computational fluid dynamics and other types of scientific visualization. The class **GO_TextObject** will include object types necessary for producing text on the screen. This class is currently undefined, but will be defined in the future. The class **GO_Analytical** contains subclasses that represent analytically defined objects. These include the conic sections, spheres, and the like. The **GO_VolumetricData** class is used to view three-dimensional volumes of data. This data can be either scalar or vector. Applications such as medical imaging will use objects of this type to visualize their data. The **GO_Surface**

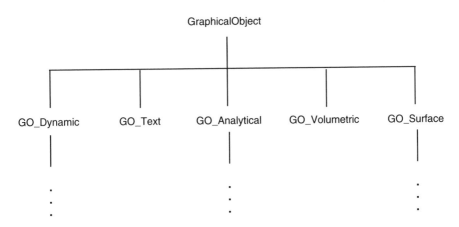

Figure 5.9: First-level CGO objects in the graphical object class hierarchy

class is used as a superclass of objects defined as surfaces. The actual definition and implementation of the subclasses will vary, but all will inherit the traits common to surfaces from this superclass.

Figures 5.10 through 5.15 show the CGO objects that are defined at the lower levels of the hierarchy, as well as the AGO level objects. In general, the AGO objects are the objects at the leaf nodes. These AGOs are the highest level of graphical object in GRASSY. They represent the highest level of graphical information that can be used by the application. AGOs become part of application objects when the application uses these AGOs as part of (that is, the graphical part of) application modeling objects. When used by an application modeling object, the AGO takes on the semantics of the application and can be indirectly manipulated through its associated application object.

Figure 5.10 shows the classes that are defined as subclasses of **GO_PointList**. These are the classes that are stored on the computer as a list of points. They include **GO_Polymarker**, **GO_ParticleSystem**, **GO_TriangleStrip**, and **GO_QuadMesh**. The **GO_Polymarker** class is used to represent objects known in PHIGS or GKS as polymarkers. These are a sequence of points that are represented on the screen by some symbol, such as a dot, circle, or asterisk. They are often used for plotting graphs and other such purposes.

The **GO_ParticleSystem** class is used for visualizing particle systems, as described by Reeves [1983]. Particle systems have been used to represent various types of objects such as fire, clouds, grass, and smoke. Because each

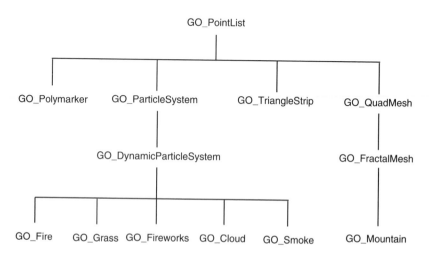

Figure 5.10: Subclasses of class GO_PointList

of these object types is a specialization of particle systems, there are corresponding graphical objects for them, which are subclasses of class **GO_ParticleSystem**.

A triangle strip is stored in the computer as a list of points that will be connected to form a chain of triangles. Thus, this class is included as a subclass of **GO_PointList**. At the present time, we have not determined any objects that fit nicely as subclasses of **GO_TriangleStrip**.

The last subclass of **GO_PointList** is **GO_QuadMesh**. This class includes objects that are described naturally by a quadrilateral mesh. One subclass of **GO_QuadMesh** is **GO_FractalMesh**. This class has as its underlying data a quad mesh. It then performs a midpoint displacement algorithm on that data to create a fractal mesh (see Pietgen and Saupe [1988] for a description of this algorithm). This mesh is then interpreted as desired by its subclasses to create various types of objects. Currently the only subclass of **GO_FractalMesh** is **GO_Mountain**. This is the graphical object that was used in Color Plate 2 to create the mountain in the background.

Another subclass of the root class is **GO_LineList**. Figure 5.11 shows the subclasses of this class. Included as subclasses of **GO_LineList** are those objects that can be easily represented on the computer as a list of lines.

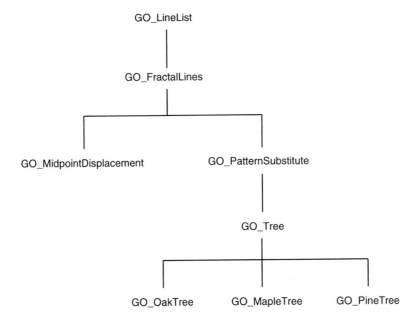

Figure 5.11: Subclasses of class GO_LineList

Currently the only subclass of **GO_LineList** is **GO_FractalLines**. This class takes an initial list of lines and performs a fractal substitution algorithm on them to generate a list of fractal lines. These fractal lines can then be used to represent various object types. The trees in Color Plate 2 were generated using this technique and are formed by creating instances of the class **GO_MapleTree**. **GO_MapleTree** is a subclass of **GO_Tree**, which is a subclass of **GO_PatternSubstitute**, which is in turn a subclass of **GO_FractalLines**.

Figure 5.12 shows the subclasses of **GO_Analytical**. These are object types that can be defined analytically, such as the conic sections, tori, and the like. Each of the subclasses of **GO_Analytical** are CGO level objects. They can be further subclassed and specialized to create AGO level objects. For example, **GO_Sphere** is one subclass of **GO_Analytical**. It is subclassed to create the class **GO_Ball**. This class is further subclassed to create the class **GO_Basketball**, which is an AGO level object. The class **GO_Basketball** inherits all of the attributes of **GO_Ball**, and in addition specifies other attributes that make it unique from other subclasses of **GO_Ball**. Thus, attributes specific to basketballs will be stored in the class **GO_Basketball**, and attributes that are common to all balls will be stored in the class **GO_Ball**.

Figure 5.13 shows the subclasses of **GO_Surface**. These subclasses are various techniques for specifying surfaces. Currently two techniques, **GO_FractalSurface** and **GO_NURBSSurface**, are specified. The class **GO_FractalSurface** is used for surfaces that are to be generated by fractal

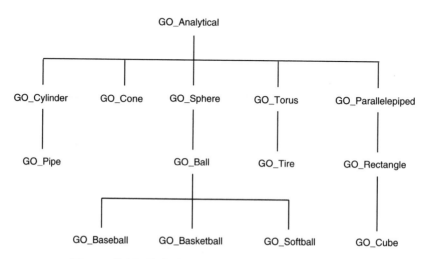

Figure 5.12: Subclasses of class GO_Analytical

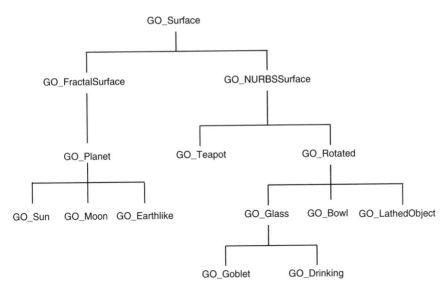

Figure 5.13: Subclasses of class GO_Surface

techniques. Planets are one example of objects of this type. Thus, **GO_Planet** is a subclass of **GO_FractalSurface**. A **GO_Planet** can be further refined to a specific type by specifying appropriate attributes of a **GO_Planet**. There are three subclasses of **GO_Planet** that do this specialization. These are **GO_Sun**, **GO_Moon**, and **GO_Earthlike**.

The other class of surface is **GO_NURBSSurface**. This class includes objects that can be easily representable by a NURBS surface. There are many objects that fall into this category, and more subclasses of **GO_NURBSSurface** can be added. There is a specialization of NURBS surfaces common to many objects. These objects can be represented as a NURBS curve that has been rotated about an axis. Thus, a subclass of **GO_NURBSSurface** has been created to accommodate these types of objects. This subclass is named **GO_Rotated**. The goblets in Color Plate 2 are subclasses of this object class. Classes for other objects that can be created and represented in a like manner are created as subclasses of **GO_Rotated**.

The class **GO_Dynamic** contains simple objects that will move over time. Figure 5.14 shows these objects. These objects will be used for scientific visualization or particle animation. Subclasses of **GO_Dynamic** are **GO_Ribbon**, which animates a ribbon through time, **GO_Tube**, which allows a cylindrical tube to move through time, and **GO_Path**, which simply traces the path a particle follows.

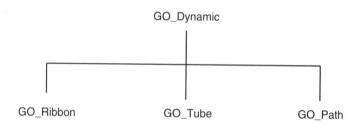

Figure 5.14: Subclasses of class GO_Dynamic

GO_Composite is the superclass for classes of objects that are created by combining other objects. Figure 5.15 shows this class along with its subclasses. There are two subclasses of **GO_Composite**. These are **GO_SimpleCompositeObject** and **GO_CSGObject**. The first of these, **GO_SimpleCompositeObject**, contains objects that are combined by a simple UNION operation: that is, the underlying objects are simply referred to without having to worry about them intersecting or colliding. **GO_CSGObjects** are more complicated objects. These objects can be created by performing UNION, INTERSECTION, and DIFFERENCE operations on various objects. This object type has not yet been implemented in GRASSY.

Implementation

Because of the easy separation of the components of GRASSY into distinct entities, and because of the desire for reusability and extensibility, GRASSY

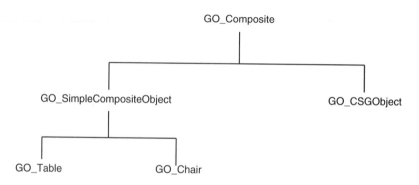

Figure 5.15: Subclasses of class GO_Composite

has been designed in an object-oriented fashion. The programming language we have used is C++. Other object-oriented graphics systems have attempted to implement existing graphics systems using an object-oriented approach. Wisskirchen [1989], [1990] are examples of this. One of the ways our system differs from these is the way in which modeling is approached.

At the present time we have defined the PGO level, a good portion of the CGO level, and some objects at the AGO level. We are currently looking at several different applications to determine the proper set of objects to include at the AGO level. We hope to find a set of common AGO objects that can be used by a variety of applications. Some application specific AGOs must be added by the application programmer. We have used three different renderers in this project to date. The first was a simple X line drawing renderer (see Gettys, Scheifler, and Newman [1989]). We wanted to create a prototype system in GRASSY and show that it worked, without spending a lot of time on the rendering portion. Once we determined that the prototype system worked, we used a more sophisticated renderer to get higher quality pictures. The second renderer we incorporated into the system was UIPEX©—The University of Illinois implementation of PEX, as described by Egbert [1990], Sung [1990] and Rost, Friedberg, and Nishimoto [1989]. UIPEX provided more capabilities that improved the images greatly. After successfully using UIPEX as a renderer in the system, we then implemented another renderer using the Graphics Library from Silicon Graphics [1988a], [1988b]. This provided a wider variety of colors available for the images.

Because of the well-defined interface between the graphical objects and the renderers, incorporating different renderers into the system has been very simple and required only a minimal amount of time and effort. In the future we plan on incorporating different style renderers, including a ray trace renderer and a radiosity renderer. We expect to see a quick and easy integration of these rendering styles into the system.

Conclusions

The GRASSY system approach has proved to be an effective way to implement modeling in a graphics system. In particular, GRASSY allows modeling to be done at a higher level of complexity than is done in current graphics systems. GRASSY provides a wide range of graphical objects in an attempt to make application programming simpler. Included in these object types are fractals, particle systems, volumetric data, NURBS surfaces, and traditional object types such as spheres and cylinders. GRASSY provides a simple mechanism for combining lower-level objects to form higher-level ones and to otherwise take advantage of objects already existing in the system. It also provides a clean separation between portions of the system so that new capabilities and techniques can be added in a simple fashion, with a minimum of side effects on other portions of the system. Thus, extending the modeling or rendering system is very easy. In addition, the interface between the modeling and rendering portions of the system is designed so that the modeling portion will not restrict the manner in which renderers may be optimized.

References

Egbert, Parris K. [1990], "UIPEX: Design of the Application Programmer Interface." Master's Thesis, Department of Computer Science, University of Illinois at Urbana-Champaign, 1990.

Gettys, James, Robert Scheifler, and Ron Newman [1989], *Xlib—C Language X Interface, X Version 11, Release 4*. MIT X Consortium Standard, 1989.

Pietgen, Heinz-Otto and Dietmar Saupe [1988], *The Science of Fractal Images*. Heidelberg, Berlin: Springer-Verlag, 1988.

Reeves, William T. [1983], "Particle Systems—A Technique for Modeling a Class of Fuzzy Objects." *Computer Graphics* 17(3), July 1983, pp. 359-376.

Rost, Randi J., Jeffrey D. Friedberg, and Peter L. Nishimoto [1989], "PEX: A Network-Transparent 3D Graphics System." *IEEE Computer Graphics and Applications* 9(4), July 1989, pp. 14-26.

Silicon Graphics, Inc. [1988a], *Graphics Library Reference Manual*, C Edition. Document number 007-1203-020, 1988.

Silicon Graphics, Inc. [1988b], *GT Graphics Library User's Guide*. Document number 007-1202-010, 1988.

Sung, Kelvin H. C. [1990], "UIPEX: A 3D Graphics Extension to the X Window System." Master's Thesis, Department of Computer Science, University of Illinois at Urbana-Champaign, 1990.

Wisskirchen, Peter [1989], "GEO++ —a System for Both Modelling and Display." *Eurographics '89 Conference Proceedings*, Amsterdam: Elsevier, 1989, pp. 403-414.

Wisskirchen, Peter [1990], *Object-Oriented Graphics*. Heidelberg, Berlin: Springer-Verlag, 1990.

Chapter 6

Object-Oriented Programming in Computer Graphics: ALPHA_1—A Case Study

Spencer Thomas

The Alpha_1 system is an experimental mechanical computer-aided design system developed at the University of Utah. It comprises a collection of programs and modules written in C and LISP. An example of a rendered design with ALPHA_1 is shown in Color Plate 3. An object-oriented programming (OOP) paradigm has been used since the project began in 1980. Use of this paradigm has tremendously simplified programming tasks and has expedited system development. It is difficult to conceive of implementing a system of this magnitude (approximately 250,000 lines of code) without using similar technology.

Although the system was recently converted to C++, the C implementation is described here, illustrating that it is eminently possible to use OOP techniques in a conventional programming language. The relatively minor differences between the C and C++ versions are briefly described.

Motivation

There were originally several motivations for using an object-oriented programming approach. Primary among them were (1) a desire to automate common operations such as storage management and I/O and (2) a need for polymorphism—that is, to be able to apply an operation to a data object regardless of its "true" type. Other benefits we expected to gain were easy extensibility—new object types and operations could be added as needed; simplification of programming tasks; and efficient and simple interprogram communication. In addition, there was a need to deal with *complex* objects, composed of a number of C "structs" linked together with pointers.

Certain operations must be performed on all objects, regardless of type. For example, all objects must be dynamically allocated, initialized, perhaps copied, and eventually disposed of. In our system, the code for these *storage management* operations is automatically generated from the object description. Not only does this save programmer time and tedium, but the code is guaranteed to be correct and will be automatically updated whenever the object description is changed.

Objects are self-identifying; that is, each carries a *tag* that uniquely identifies its type. *Generic functions* use the tag to appropriately apply the type-specific function for a given operation. This *object polymorphism* allows the programmer to treat objects identically and generically, except in those rare cases when a particular object type must be specially handled. For example, objects may be placed on a linked list without regard to their types, and then all objects on the list may be processed by a generic function such as *draw*.

Extensibility is important in a developing, experimental system. New types of objects and new functions will be added to the system as it grows. Object polymorphism and generic functions guarantee that as new object types are added, existing programs will be able to handle them (up to program-specific operations) without modification. This means that a program will at least not crash when it encounters a new type of object in an input stream, although it may not be able to "do anything" with it. For example, if a new type of graphical object, say a fractal, were added to the system, a rendering program would be able to read files containing fractals, but it would not be able to render them until some fractal-specific rendering code had been written.

In order to communicate between programs, even using just files or pipes, objects must be written to and read from the files or pipes. This is not difficult for simple objects comprising a single "struct," but becomes more difficult for complex objects. The system automatically generates correct binary I/O from the object description, so that a complex object may be transmitted between programs as a single unit. The application programmer just "dumps" the object from one program and "loads" it into the other. The I/O functions will automatically compensate for differences in byte order or number format between different computer systems, making such communication truly portable.

Finally, the task of the application programmer is simplified. The tedium of correctly implementing storage management and other operations is taken over by the system. The use of polymorphic objects simplifies code that must process many object types similarly. The programmer is freed to concentrate on the algorithm at hand, and to deal only with the special cases, since the ordinary case is already covered.

By encapsulating data and operations into objects, OOP techniques provide an additional level of abstraction that, in essence, brings the programming language closer to the language of the original problem domain. The programmer does not need to expend as much time and effort translating from the problem domain into the language-restricted implementation.

Architecture

An object is a single C struct or a C struct containing pointers to other objects or (possibly circular) linked lists of objects. Aside from the list pointers, there may be no cycles in the rooted directed acyclic graph induced by this structure. In fact, the graph must be treelike. This constraint is not strictly enforced, but the I/O routines will not correctly relink nontree structures, except for linked lists. An object containing subobjects will be treated as a single unit for the purposes of operations such as copy and dispose. Each object contains a *tag* field that uniquely identifies its type.

Objects are described with a notation similar to that used to declare structs in C. The major enhancements are:

- Three types of pointers are used. These are pointers to subobjects, pointers to lists of subobjects, and reference pointers to other objects. Reference pointers will not be correctly restored after an I/O operation, nor will the object referred to by such a pointer be automatically copied, freed, and so on.
- Initial values may be provided for fields of the object; whenever an instance is created, its fields will be initialized to the given values.
- An object may contain a single dynamically sized array, with the size specified by a field in the object. The size of the array must be given when the instance is created.

A program called *structgen* reads the object description and produces a C header file and code for all the automatically implemented operations.

The architecture supports a limited set of classes and subclasses. There are three system-defined classes; all object classes are immediate subclasses of one of the system classes. The predefined classes are **object**; **list-object**, for objects that can be placed in a linked list; and **attr-object**, for objects that have an attribute list. **Attr-object** is a subclass of **list-object**, which is a

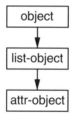

Figure 6.1: Object class hierarchy

subclass of **object** (Figure 6.1).

In place of the traditional class hierarchy is a lattice, in which classes are grouped according to the kinds of operations that can be performed on them (Figure 6.2). Related operations are grouped into *protocols*, and each class *subscribes* to a set of protocols. For example, all classes subscribe to the *storage management* protocol, which contains the operations **new**, **copy**, **dispose**, **make** (creates a new instance and fills it with given values), and a few others. Most objects subscribe to the *binary I/O* protocol, whereas only a few subscribe to *raster display*. List operations can be applied only to objects that are subclasses of **list-object** and attribute list operations only to those objects that are subclasses of **attr-object**. It is possible to ask whether a particular operation can be applied to a given instance. Most operations can be applied generically (such as **new** or **copy**), but some cannot (for example, the **make** operation has a class-specific argument list).

A useful protocol, to which all objects automatically subscribe, is the *debug* protocol. It contains a single operation, **debug**, which prints all the information contained in an object, including its subobjects, in a human-readable form. At any point, a call to the generic **debug-object** function will print its argument on the standard error output. The operation may also be invoked from a debugger and usually provides a significantly more useful output than the debugger's built-in print operation. A list of objects may be

	Color	Surface	Time Curve	Polygon
Storage Management	●	●	●	●
Attribute		●	●	●
Binary I/O	●	●	●	●
Raster display		●		●
Spline evaluation		●	●	

Figure 6.2: Sample object–protocol lattice

debugged by calling the **debug-object-list** function with a pointer to the first element of the list.

I/O Operations

The object tag field is actually a pointer to an object descriptor record (see Runtime Environment in the next section, on implementation) that completely describes the format of the object. This record is used by polymorphic I/O functions to read and write the object. (The first time an object appears in an input file, it is preceded by its descriptor record.) This scheme has several benefits over providing separate input and output functions for each object type. It significantly reduces the amount of code in the program, because there is only one input procedure and one output procedure, instead of one each per object type. This is most important for the input procedure, which may be required to convert byte-ordering and floating-point format for files generated on a different type of computer. In addition, it is possible for the program to read and write objects of which it has no compiled-in knowledge. Before the polymorphic I/O functions were written, a common, frustrating error message was "No input function for object type xxx." Now, a program can ignore unrecognized input objects or copy them to its output, on the assumption that another program "down the line" will use them.

A problem with storing permanent data in a binary file format is that if the format changes, it outdates all existing data files. The use of self-describing objects means that a program can convert objects stored in the old format to the new format as they are read in. Specifically, each input field is placed in the object field of the same name, if it exists, and new object fields are left with their default initial value. This scheme handles most changes to objects, as they usually involve the addition or deletion of one or more fields (instance variables). If an incompatible change is made, a special conversion program can easily be written that will read old objects and write new ones.

Efficiency does not suffer with this scheme for several reasons. First, many objects are read or written in a single "chunk." Extra I/O operations are necessary only for subobjects connected with pointers. The input procedure needs to do extra data manipulation in only three cases—if the input byte-ordering or floating-point format is different from that used by the CPU, if an old version of an object is read, or if an "unknown" object is read. These conditions can be detected when the object descriptor is read, by comparing it to the in-core descriptor. Finally, the time needed to rearrange an input object is usually small compared to the physical I/O time.

To summarize, the use of polymorphic I/O operations with self-describing objects provides machine independence, upward compatibility of binary data files when objects change, and the ability to read and write objects that are otherwise "unknown" to the program.

Architecture Summary

Objects are complex structures linked with pointers, built on a limited class hierarchy. Object classes are grouped more by the operations that apply to them than by a class hierarchy. Similar operations are grouped into protocols, to which objects subscribe. Generic functions provide object polymorphism, and polymorphic functions can manipulate objects on the basis of a descriptor record, even if no knowledge of that object type is compiled into the program. Polymorphic functions form the basis for machine-independent, transparent binary I/O.

Implementation

The implementation can be broken down into two parts: generation of C data structures and functions from object descriptions, and the runtime environment. Each of these will be described through the use of examples.

Object Structure Declaration

The **poly_obj** class describes a polygon with multiple contours and per-vertex rendering information (normal, color, and the like). The structure description for **poly_obj** is given in Listing 6.1. Line 3 names the object. This is the type name that will be used in the C programs.

The LINKS statement on line 5 specifies that this object can be part of a doubly linked list (and thus is a subclass of **list-obj**). On line 6, the ATTR_LIST statement further specifies that the object will have an attribute list and is therefore a subclass of **attr-obj** (an object with ATTR_LIST is automatically given LINKS).

Lines 7 and 8 declare the fields of the struct. The field *closed_poly* is a

```
1  TYPE( int boolean_type )
2
3  OBJECT( poly_obj )
4  {
5     LINKS;
6     ATTR_LIST;
7     boolean_type  closed_poly;
8     poly_cntr_obj @p_cntr;
9  }
10
11 OBJECT( poly_cntr_obj )
12 {
13    LINKS;
14    pt_vector_obj *vert;
15    pt_vector_obj *norm;
16    pt_vector_obj *uv;
17    pt_vector_obj *color;
18    pt_vector_obj *shd;
19 }
```

Listing 6.1

Boolean value that will be true if the object describes a polygon (if it is false, the object describes a polyline). The type *boolean_type* is a C type equivalent to the primitive integer type, and is declared in the TYPE statement on line 1. Finally, the *p_cntr* field is a pointer to a list of **poly_cntr_obj** objects (the @ sign indicates a pointer to a list of objects).

All the C primitive data types are recognized, as well as a few special types such as *string* (a pointer to char) and *point_type* (a structure containing three real numbers). Strings, in particular, are handled specially; the storage management functions allocate storage for string values when initializing or copying an object and will free the storage when an object containing a string is disposed of. Any unrecognized type name is assumed to be an object class.

The structure definition for **poly_cntr_obj** is also shown in Listing 6.1. The **poly_cntr_obj** class is a subclass of **list-obj** but not of **attr-obj**. It consists of pointers to (up to) five **pt_vector_obj** objects that contain the actual data. The character ' * ' indicates a pointer to a subobject. (The third type of pointer, referring to something which is not part of the object, is indicated by the character ' > '). Any or all of the pointers on lines 15–18 may be NULL if data of that type is not present.

To complete the example, Listing 6.2 shows the structure declaration for a **pt_vector_obj**. **Pt_vector_obj** is actually a special case of **matrix_obj**, as is declared on line 25. **Matrix_obj** is a class that implements a matrix of real numbers with one to three dimensions (the size and number of dimensions are fixed when the matrix is created). A two- or three-dimensional matrix can be considered as a one- or two-dimensional array of points, respectively. In this case, the *pt_tag* element on line 13 specifies the type of point. It may take on values (defined elsewhere) such as E3 for a three-dimensional Euclidean point, or P3 for a three-dimensional homogeneous point.

Note the variably sized array structure element on line 18. The value for *total* must be specified when an instance is created, so that the right amount of storage to hold it can be allocated. Normally, this is done by a high-level

```
1    TYPE( int point_tag_type )
2    TYPE( double mat_element_type )
3
4    /*************************************************
5     * TAGS( matrix_obj )
6     *
7     * Matrix data type.  Matrix subtypes include
8     * control polygons, knot vectors, and surface
9     * meshes. */
10   OBJECT(matrix_obj) /*Struct of matrix instance.*/
11   {
12     LINKS;
13     point_tag_type pt_tag;/*Type of matrix elts.*/
14     int   size[3];     /* Size in each dimension. */
15                        /* (1 for unused dims.) */
16     int   stride[3];   /* Increment for subscript. */
17     int   total;       /* Product of the size[i]. */
18     mat_element_type value[total];
19   }                    /* Value data vector. */
20   TYPE( matrix_obj mat_1d_obj )
21   TYPE( matrix_obj mat_2d_obj )
22   TYPE( matrix_obj mat_3d_obj )
23   TYPE( mat_1d_obj vector_obj )
24   TYPE( mat_2d_obj array_obj )
25   TYPE( mat_2d_obj pt_vector_obj )
26   TYPE( mat_3d_obj pt_array_obj )
```

Listing 6.2

matrix allocation function. Lines 20 through 26 define type aliases for the different uses of **matrix_obj**.

As a final example, consider the type **color_obj**, which might appear on the attribute list of a **poly_obj** to specify the color of the entire polygon (if it does not have per-vertex colors).

```
OBJECT( color_obj )
{
   LINKS;
   int r, g, b;
}
```

This is a subclass of **list-obj**, as it can be placed on an attribute list; however, it cannot have attributes of its own.

Automatically Generated C Code

Two types of code are generated automatically, by a program *structgen*, from the object structure definitions above. A ".h" file is created that defines the C data structures and declares the functions that implement the object methods. For each protocol, a ".c" file is created that contains definitions of the automatically generated functions. These will be illustrated in Listing 6.3 by excerpts from *Poly.h* and *S_poly.c* (by convention, file names beginning with a capital letter are machine generated).

The types **poly_cntr_obj** and **poly_obj** are declared in a file *Objects.h*,

```
typedef struct poly_obj poly_obj;
typedef struct poly_cntr_obj poly_cntr_obj;
```

along with all the other main object types. This allows pointers to these objects to be used without needing the full object declaration. Opaque declarations of this sort are the only form of information hiding available in the C language.

The tag values T_POLY_CNTR_OBJ and T_POLY_OBJ are similarly globally declared. Tag values are distributed from a "registry," so that they are permanent, unique, and consistent between programs. (It is the tag value in an input file that determines the identity of an object.)

The *structgen* program has inserted field declarations for the tag field (a pointer to the object descriptor record), the list links, and the pointer to the attribute list, if needed. Less obviously, it has also rearranged the remaining fields in the object. All fields of a given type are grouped together, and the types are ordered in (roughly) descending order by size. Padding is inserted if necessary to maintain structure element alignment. The idea is to minimize the adjustments that must be made when reading a structure from a file that may have been generated on a different machine.

```
1    /*************************************************
2     * TAG( poly_cntr_obj 16789511 0x01003007 )
3     */
4    struct poly_cntr_obj
5    {
6       obj_info_type *t_tag;
7       poly_cntr_obj *next, *prev;
8       pt_vector_obj *vert;
9       pt_vector_obj *norm;
10      pt_vector_obj *uv;
11      pt_vector_obj *color;
12      pt_vector_obj *shd;
13   };
14   extern poly_cntr_obj *new_poly_cntr_obj();
15   extern poly_cntr_obj *cp_poly_cntr_obj();
16   extern void fr_poly_cntr_obj();
17   #define is_poly_cntr_obj(ob) \
18      ((ob) && ((object *)(ob))->t_tag->tag \
        == T_POLY_CNTR_OBJ)
19   /*************************************************
20    * TAG( poly_obj 50343944 0x03003008 )
21    */
22   struct poly_obj
23   {
24      obj_info_type  *t_tag;
25      poly_obj       *next, *prev;
26      object         *attr_list;
27      poly_cntr_obj  *p_cntr;
28      boolean_type   closed_poly;
29   };
30   extern poly_obj *new_poly_obj();
31   extern poly_obj *cp_poly_obj();
32   extern void fr_poly_obj();
33   #define is_poly_obj(ob) \
34      ((ob) && ((object *)(ob)) -> t_tag -> tag \
        == T_POLY_OBJ)
```

Listing 6.3

Structgen has also inserted declarations of the functions that implement the automatically generated protocol operations (the list has been abbreviated for this example). Finally, a macro is created for each object class, making it easy to recognize instances of that class.

The automatically generated C code will be illustrated by looking at the **copy** methods for the types **poly_obj** and **poly_cntr_obj**. A **copy** method creates a copy of an object, including any subobjects it contains.

```
poly_obj *cp_poly_obj(poly_obj *_obj)
{
    poly_obj *this = new_poly_obj();
    if (_obj->attr_list)
        this->attr_list = cp_obj_list(_obj->attr_list);
    if (_obj->p_cntr)
        this->p_cntr = cp_obj_list(_obj->p_cntr);
    this->closed_poly = _obj->closed_poly;
    return this;
}
```

The **new_poly_obj** function allocates memory to hold a **poly_obj** structure and initializes the fields. In this case, that means setting all the pointer fields to NULL and filling in the tag field with a pointer to the **poly_obj** descriptor record. Then the fields of the original object are copied: If it had an attribute list, a copy is made. If the *p_cntr* field is not NULL, a copy of the list of contour objects is made (in the process, repeatedly invoking the copy method for **poly_cntr_obj**). Finally, the scalar field *closed_poly* is copied. The linked list pointers are not copied.

The copy method for the **poly_cntr_obj** is similar. Since all its fields are pointers, the object each points to is copied, if the field is not NULL. The copies are made via the macro *cp_obj*, which invokes the object-specific copy method through a function table (described in the next section).

```
poly_cntr_obj *cp_poly_cntr_obj(poly_cntr_obj *_obj)
{
    poly_cntr_obj *this = new_poly_cntr_obj();
    if (_obj->vert) this->vert=cp_obj(_obj->vert);
    if (_obj->norm) this->norm=cp_obj(_obj->norm);
    if (_obj->uv) this->uv=cp_obj(_obj->uv);
    if (_obj->color) this->color=cp_obj(_obj->color);
    if (_obj->shd) this->shd=cp_obj(_obj->shd);
    return this;
}
```

Runtime Environment

Object instances are self-identifying through their tag fields. The tag is a pointer to an object description block, which contains information about the object and its structure. This scheme is illustrated in Figure 6.3. (The "op table" and descriptor record are described later in this section.)

The descriptor records are created by the *structgen* program from the object description file. The descriptor record for a **poly_obj**, reformatted and commented for readability, is given in Listing 6.4.

On line 1, an array of field type descriptors is initialized. Each descriptor contains bit fields describing the field type (from a short list of "intrinsic" types); the pointer type, if the field is a pointer; the number of array dimensions, if the field is an array; and the number of fields of this type. This works because *structgen* has reordered the structure so that all fields of a given type are adjacent.

Starting on line 5, the object descriptor is filled in. The substructure on lines 6 to 17 is the object header that would appear in a binary file and completely describes the format of the object structure. The list of names on line 9 is used for text input and output and for matching fields in old binary input files, as described above. This object has no embedded C structures; if it did, line 11 would contain a pointer to an array of structure descriptors. Following the object header is some data that is computed and used at runtime. The bit-vector on line 21 is used to record whether or not the header for this object type has been written to an output file (because the object header must be written before the first instance of an object type, but it is

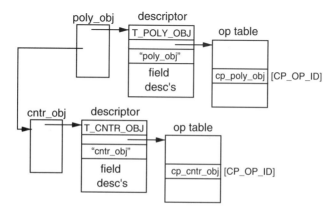

Figure 6.3: Tag and descriptor records

```
1 static unsigned i_poly_obj[] = {
        /* "Intrinsic" field types. */
2    0xa4000001, /* One subobject pointer. */
3    0x40000001, /* One integer. */
4 };
5 obj_info_type _OH_poly_obj_ =
6   {   {
7        T_POLY_OBJ, /* Polygon tag value. */
8        /* List of object and field names. */
9        "poly_obj\0p_cntr\0closed_poly\0",
10       i_poly_obj, /*Intrinsic field types, counts.*/
11       NULL, /*Embedded structure counts. */
12       NULL, /*Var. sized field descriptor. */
13       0,    /*Size of object (filled at run time).*/
14       2,    /*Number of fields. */
15       29,   /*Size of names array. */
16       2,    /*Number of intrinsic types. */
17       0 },  /*Number of structure fields. */
18    NULL,    /*Array of structure element
19             offsets. Filled at run time. */
20    0        /*Number of above. */
21    0        /*Bit-vector for output. */
22             /*Sample initialized object. */
23    (object_type *)&_in_poly_obj,
24    _poly_op_table /* Method vector for poly_obj.
```

Listing 6.4

inefficient to write it more than once). It is indexed by the file number. Finally, line 23 refers to the method dispatch vector.

In C, generic functions are implemented with a combination of macros and a function dispatch table. For example, the copy method is invoked by the macro *cp_obj*:

```
#define cp_obj(ob) \
((*((object *)(ob))->t_tag->op_table[CP_OP_ID])(ob))
```

Since some operations are not applicable to all object types, it is possible to query whether a generic operation can be applied to a given instance:

```
#define can_cp_obj(ob) \
    (((object *)(ob))->t_tag->op_table[CP_OP_ID])
```

Examination of these macros reveals an apparent defect in the scheme: The table subscript, CP_OP_ID, must be constant over all the separate pieces of code that are linked together into a program, including functions loaded from a library. Thus, the method IDs are constants that must be global to the entire system. This is a consequence of the object-oriented programming view that methods are part of the object. C programmers are not surprised when a program must be recompiled if a data structure is changed. Similarly, object-oriented programs must be recompiled if a method is added or deleted.

The *op_table* dispatch vectors are created by another utility program, *mk_op_table*, which uses the global list of operations and the structure definition files to create a method table for each object type. A default set of dispatch vectors is available in the system library. A program that defines its own *local* protocols also requires local dispatch vectors that include the new methods defined in the local protocols. The local methods are added to the end of the dispatch vector, so as not to disturb the placement of the global methods.

In the C++ version, method dispatching is done by the compiler using virtual functions. It is still the case that all methods must be globally declared, and the whole system must be recompiled whenever a global method is added, because each method is part of the major classes. C++ normally compiles a "virtual function table" for each source file. In a large system comprising hundreds of source files, this would generate many copies, and would use excessive amounts of memory. Therefore, the virtual function tables for all objects are separately generated and compiled and are loaded into each program. However, this means that all methods for all objects are loaded into each program.[1]

Applications

Two applications will be described: a scanline rendering program and a generic display package. The rendering program uses object polymorphism to simplify the main loop and individual scan-conversion functions. The display package provides a generic application programmer interface that converts subroutine calls into remote procedure calls (RPC) on a separate display driver program. The RPC stubs and message formats are automatically generated from the object structure description and subroutine calling sequences.

Rendering

To illustrate the code simplification that OOP makes possible, some code from the rendering program is presented below. The object abstraction hides implementation and housekeeping details, thus the resulting C code is not very far removed from a pseudocode description of the algorithm.

The raster display program uses several specialized protocols (some of which are also used by other programs). These include *raster display* and *bounding box*. The raster display protocol has three methods: **start**, which adds an object to the "start list" or "active list" of a standard scanline algorithm (depending on whether its bounding box overlaps the current scanline); **rdisp**, which renders an object that intersects the current scanline; and **p_rem**, which returns TRUE if the object should be removed from the active list. **rdisp** may return a list of objects, each of which will be **start**ed. **p_rem** will usually test the current *y* coordinate against the object bounding box, and return TRUE when *y* exceeds the object **Ymax**. However, for objects that are converted to other objects by **rdisp**, **p_rem** always returns TRUE. The bounding box protocol has one operation, **bbox**, which computes the bounding box of an object in a specified coordinate system (modeling, world, or screen). **Bbox** caches its result on the attribute list for efficiency.[2]

```
int curr_y;       /* A global variable. */
object *start[]; /* Global. One list per scanline.*/
object *active;  /* Global. */
object *o, *t;
while (o = read_obj() )
   if ( can_start_obj(o) )
      start_obj(o);
for ( curr_y = 0; curr_y <= ymax; curr_y++ ) {
   active = append( start[curr_y], active );
   /* Render all active objects. */
   for ( o in active )
      if ( t = rdisp_obj(o) )
         start_obj_list(t);
   /* Remove inactive objects. */
   for ( o in active )
      if ( p_rem(o) )
         remove(o, active);
}
```

Recall that the **rdisp** method may decompose the object into simpler objects instead of directly displaying it. For example, the **rdisp** method for a spline surface either converts the surface to two triangles, if it is flat, or subdivides the surface, if it is not. In either case, the triangles or subdivided surface pieces will be added to the start list (and the original surface removed). Simplified examples of the **start** and **rdisp** methods for a surface are shown in Listing 6.5.

An object-oriented approach with polymorphic objects and generic functions significantly simplifies the implementation of the scanline rendering program. The main program can be written in a style very close to the original pseudocode, because the generic functions provide the appropriate

```
start_surf( surface *s )
{
   surface *s1;
   bbox *bb;
   s1 = xform_obj(s, SCREEN_SPACE);
                           /* Transform to screen space.*/
   bb = bbox_obj(s1, SCREEN_SPACE);
   /* Add to appropriate start list, or to active
      list. Really should clip bbox against screen
      bounds first. */
   if ( bb->ymin <= curr_y ) {
     if ( bb->ymax > curr_y )
       append( active, s1 ); /* Add to active list.*/
   }
   else
     add( s1, start[bb->ymin] );
}

rdisp_surf( surface *s )
{
   object *res;
   if ( is_flat(s) )
     res=(object *)srf_to_polys(s); /* 2 triangles.*/
   else
     res=(object *)subdivide(s);    /* 2 surfaces.*/
   return res;
}
```

Listing 6.5

level of abstraction. The program modularity is enhanced and the main program does not have to be modified in order to add a new object type.

Generic Display Package

The display package was written to provide a generic interface to a wide variety of graphics displays, ranging from high-performance 3-D workstations, such as the Silicon Graphics Iris®, to the X Window System, to Tektronix™ terminal emulators running over a modem. Additionally, we wanted to be able to drive displays running on a remote host. This latter feature was initially motivated by the fact that, for a long time, the geometric editor component of the system, written in Lisp, did not run on the SGI computers. The combination of device independence with remote execution strongly suggested that an RPC protocol be used. Since we already had a machine-independent binary data format, we built the RPC protocol on top of it. The display architecture is shown in Figure 6.4.

Most of the display operations are implemented by generic functions (such as display object and add object to window), and assume a multiwindow display list model. For those displays without hardware display lists, we wrote a software display list package. It includes a traversal operation, which calls device-dependent draw functions (draw polygon, draw curve, and the like). The two-program model simplified this task, as each display driver program has to drive only a single display type. Thus, two-way dispatching (by object type and device) is not required in either the application or the driver. The display list implementation will not be described in

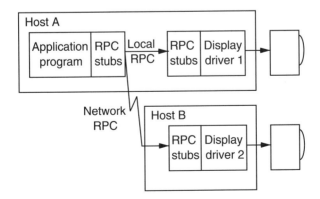

Figure 6.4: Display architecture

detail here, as it is fairly standard.

Figure 6.5 shows the basic process used to implement the RPC. C declarations of the display functions are translated into RPC message object declarations. Each object contains the arguments to the corresponding display function. If the function has a return value, a return value object is also built. Each declaration is also processed into a pair of "stub" functions. The one called by the application creates and sends the RPC request. The other receives the RPC request, unpacks it, and calls the actual display function. The RPC message object declarations are processed by *structgen* into binary I/O functions that are used by the stubs.

As an example, consider the function **disp_obj**, which adds an object to the display memory in the driver. It takes a single object as its argument and returns an identifier that can be used to refer to the display version of the object in later calls. The function declaration is shown on line 0 of Listing 6.6, and is processed by *RPCgen* into the object declarations (lines 1-7) and stub functions (lines 8-26). The display driver program has a main loop that looks, in part, like lines 27-36 (input event processing has been left out).

The display driver will send input events to the application. The function *await_reply*, called on line 15, intercepts and queues events and returns when a reply message of the specified type is received. The function *dp_obj*, called on lines 14 and 31, writes the message onto the RPC connection. (A pair of global variables determine the file descriptors used by *dp_obj* and *read_obj*.) The generic function *recv_obj*, called on line 29, invokes the appropriate receive stub, based on the object type of the message.

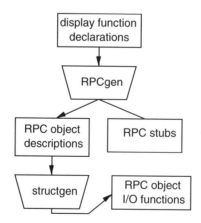

Figure 6.5: RPC code generation

```
0 display_id disp_obj( object *ob );

1 TYPE( long display_id )
2 OBJECT( disp_obj_msg ) {
3    object *ob;
4 }
5 OBJECT( disp_obj_repl ) {
6    display_id retval;
7 }
8 /* disp_obj send stub. */
9 display_id disp_obj( object *ob )
10 {
11    disp_obj_msg *msg = make_disp_obj_msg( ob );
12    disp_obj_repl *r_msg;
13    display_id rv;
14    dp_obj( msg ); fr_obj( msg );
15    r_msg = (disp_obj_repl *)await_reply \
                        ( T_DISP_OBJ_REPL );
16    rv = r_msg->retval;
17    fr_obj( r_msg );
18    return rv;
19 }
20 /* Receive stub. */
21 object *recv_disp_obj_msg( disp_obj_msg *msg )
22 {
23    disp_obj_repl *r_msg = new_disp_obj_repl();
24    r_msg->retval = disp_obj( msg->ob );
                        /* Call the real one. */
25    return r_msg;
26 }

27    while ( ob = read_obj() ) {
28       if ( can_recv_obj( ob ) ) {
29          retval = recv_obj( ob );
30          if ( retval ) {
31             dp_obj( retval );   /* Send reply. */
32             fr_obj( retval );
33          }
34       }
35       fr_obj( ob );
36    }
```

Listing 6.6

The existing object-oriented programming base, together with the automatic function generation facilities, made it easy to implement a simple machine-independent RPC mechanism. The RPC stubs and message descriptions were automatically generated from the function declarations. Device-independent, distributed, interactive, 3-D display was built on top of the RPC facility.

C++

The Alpha_1 system is still developing and growing. Recently, all the C code was converted to C++. The programmer-visible changes are mainly syntactic. For example, the generic function call *cp_obj(ob)* becomes *ob->cp_obj()*, and storage allocation and disposal are syntactically cleaner. We still use the *structgen* program to generate C++ class declarations and methods for storage management, I/O, and the like. Writing such functions by hand would still be tedious (although not as tedious as in C) and error prone. Use of C++ automates the object implementation details, most notably method dispatching, and thus simplifies system maintenance. Nothing got worse in the transition, and a number of "rough edges" in the original implementation improved.

Summary

We believe we gained several benefits from following the object-oriented approach. *Object polymorphism* means that special cases can be hidden in object-dependent methods, where they belong, instead of being made visible in supposedly generic code. The resulting "main-line" code ends up much closer to the original pseudocode abstraction and is easier to read, understand, and maintain. Programs are more easily *extensible* to handle new object types. Frequently, no changes are needed in the main body of the code, all that is needed is to write the appropriate methods for the new object types.

Polymorphic functions for I/O and storage management mean that programs can read and write "unknown" objects (objects whose descriptions are not compiled into the program). Because object descriptors are written into output files, programs can read data stored in outdated formats and can convert that data into the current format. This provides a form of *backward compatibility* for binary data files. The byte order, integer sizes, and floating point format with which it was created are specified in a file. The input routine can convert the data from the file format into the native machine format. Thus I/O is *transparent* and *machine independent*.

Programs are easier to *maintain* because most knowledge is localized at one point. The overall algorithm can be found in the "main-line" code, whereas object-specific functionality is confined to the methods for each object type. Program *modularity* is enhanced over traditional programming methods.

The code that implements methods for storage management and I/O is *automatically generated* from data structure descriptions. This ensures correctness of the code and alleviates programmer tedium. Complex objects built from pointer-connected structures are correctly created, copied, and freed. When an object description changes, the appropriate methods are automatically regenerated.

The only significant negative aspect to the object-oriented programming approach that we have seen is that new project members must overcome a learning curve before they can contribute to the system. Some aspects of the learning curve are common to object-oriented programming in general, and others are specific to our project. The very concept of object-oriented programming is new to many programmers. Once it has been absorbed, then they must learn about the existing collection of objects and methods.

The "language" that we use is really an extended version of C or C++, because we consider certain types (such as linked lists) and operations to be part of the language. Thus, even those who are familiar with OOP and C++ must learn the local dialect. Finally, the *structgen* machinery adds another layer of "magic" on top of an already complex system. However, complete understanding is not necessary, and most project members quickly become proficient.

In summary, I think that the use of object-oriented programming techniques for a project of this magnitude has been extremely successful. It is hard to quantify the impact of our methodology: we did not implement the system "both ways." However, I would not want to implement a system of this magnitude without some similar technology, because the mass of details would quickly become overwhelming.

Notes

1. This is an example of a corollary to Murphy's law: Things never get better.
2. OOP makes it easy to add such optimizations. The generic bounding box computation includes the caching action, which is then inherited by the class-specific bounding box methods.

Chapter 7

An Object-Oriented Approach to Animation Control

M. Pauline Baker

Contemporary animation systems use a variety of strategies for controlling activity. Some systems are based on keyframing; others use special-purpose scripting languages. Several research groups are investigating the use of higher-level specifications, including rules and constraints. The work described here is an experiment in unifying these different control strategies. Our goal is to incorporate a variety of control strategies in a system that extends easily to include new control techniques. This would provide a flexible environment in which the animator can mix and match control strategies according to personal preference or the nature of a particular task.

The object-oriented approach is a natural choice for structuring the system. Classes and inheritance provide support for abstraction, generalization, and specialization. Characteristics common to all control techniques can be abstracted and defined in a superclass. Class-specific features of various control mechanisms are encoded in subclasses. New control techniques can be added by defining new subclasses.

This chapter describes an object-oriented graphics environment and animation system. SWAMP (the reverse acronym of Proposed Model for Animating With Streams) includes a variety of animation techniques. To put this work in context, we first review contemporary computer animation control techniques.

Computer Animation

The use of the computer in animation has a relatively short history. Initially, tools were designed that mimicked the process of traditional manual animation. Subsequent animation systems have extended these techniques in new directions.

In doing animation by hand, an animator draws a number of *keyframes*, indicating how things should look at various key points in the animation. An assistant animator constructs the *in-betweens*—frames that must appear between the keyframes to give the illusion of smooth motion. If the animation sequence is to be recorded on film, 24 frames are needed for every second. The drawings are colored in, arranged in proper sequence, and recorded.

In the computerized version of this process, animators use interactive sketch editors to draw the keyframes of a motion and painting systems to color in the shape outlines. In-betweening is done by programs that interpolate between the successive keyframe positions of the animated figures. Computer-assisted animation is currently used for two-dimensional or "cartoon" animation.

A more sophisticated approach uses the computer to model the entire animation. The characters and objects of the motion sequence and their environment (all of which may be three-dimensional) are defined in numerical databases. Transformations are applied to the objects to achieve a change in position or orientation. Specifying how the model is transformed over time defines the animation sequence. As in computer-assisted animation, the concepts of interpolation and in-betweening apply. Any attribute of the model may be chosen for interpolation, however, from position of the objects to rotation angles, to color, to degree of transparency, and so on.

Modeled animation systems can be characterized by how the animator interacts with the system to specify motion. In *interactive keyframe* systems, the animator works directly with a screen image of an object, manipulating its parameters to achieve the desired position and orientation for each particular keyframe. Alternatively, in *scripted systems*, an animator uses an animation language and writes a script detailing each movement. The script is then executed to generate the animation frames.

As expected, each type of system has its advantages and disadvantages. A keyframe system provides an interactive environment with immediate visual feedback. However, the animation description is at a low level of detail and the animator must define values for a multitude of parameters.

Further, reuse of the motion specification is limited. Scripted systems offer the advantage of reusable motion specifications. Once a set of parameter changes have been encoded, they can be named and called again and again. The system is extensible and can grow with continued use. Scripting, however, is a form of programming—the problem must be translated into the set of constructs provided by the language.

Animation studios often use both types of systems, depending on the nature of the problem. Those motion sequences that are best expressed algorithmically or that would be particularly hard or tedious to keyframe (for example, an explosion with pieces flying in various directions) would be handled using the animation language of the scripting system. Keyframing is used to choreograph more straightforward motion sequences.

A major thrust in contemporary animation research is directed at generating motion automatically, or from task-level specifications. For example, one early system uses a hierarchical arrangement to control a skeleton ambulating over uneven terrain. High-level task descriptions are given to a task manager. The task manager decomposes the task into component skills and calls the appropriate low-level programs to move the skeleton.

In more recent work, an object's behavior is integrated into the definition of the object. Inherently object-oriented in design, these systems are usually object-oriented in implementation. Physically based primitives incorporate the laws of dynamics into geometric elements. For example, we might treat each vertex of a polygon as an element that has mass. Polygons are made up of vertices joined by springs, and polygons themselves are joined by hinges. Animation is created when forces are applied to particular vertices—the rest of the system reacts in accord with the laws of dynamics. Similar in spirit, behavioral modeling is aimed at coordinating the behavior of a collection of individual entities, such as a flock of birds. An individual bird is defined with built-in rules for flocking behavior (collision avoidance and velocity matching, for example). Flocking is achieved by making multiple copies of the bird and letting them interact.

Constraints play an important role in these new animation systems. Constraints express a relationship that must always hold between two entities. In the realm of three-dimensional animation, constraints serve as a mechanism for world modeling—that is, to build in rules about how objects behave in relation to one another. For example, the spring connecting two vertices represents a constraint relating the positions of the two elements. Moving element **A** exerts a force on **B**, pulling **B** so that it is again aligned with **A**'s position. The motion of the constrained object is generated automatically from the behavior of the constraining object.

Streams-Based Animation

As we have seen, animation can be controlled in a number of ways. Taken together, the set of control strategies offers considerable variety—the mechanisms differ in their expressive power, level of detail, and manner of use. However, the typical animation system supports only one or two of these strategies. The animator is limited to the control techniques provided.

Our goal is to design and build a system that offers all of these control mechanisms, and that extends easily to incorporate new techniques. Abstraction is the key to this endeavor. We need to identify the most general notion of an animation control strategy. Particular control mechanisms are concrete expressions of this abstraction. Working with the abstraction, we deal with control techniques in a uniform way and avoid getting lost in control-specific details. The object-oriented paradigm is especially useful in this regard, because it offers strong support for abstraction. Control techniques are defined as classes. An abstract superclass, representing the most general notion of an animation control strategy, is constructed to provide a common parent for the control techniques.

We need, then, to identify this common parent, based on the shared characteristics of all control techniques. Although they differ considerably in their operation, ultimately, all control mechanisms produce new values to use in updating objects. This suggests that *streams* can serve as an abstraction for control strategies. The notion of a stream is certainly not new; it is found in a number of areas within computer technology. Streams are sequences of values. In file systems terminology, streams provide an abstraction for entities that can be read from or written to, such as files and sockets. In Scheme and some other LISP dialects, streams are sequences of data objects, most often produced by delayed evaluation of generator functions. That is, a stream is defined to be a value, and a function that can produce the next value.

We use the notion of stream as an abstraction for animation control strategies. In object-oriented terms, **Stream** is an abstract superclass. It is capable of producing a series of values, and it offers this service to the remainder of the animation system. **Stream**'s subclasses are particular control techniques, each with their own class-specific way of producing values.

Streams-based animation is organized as shown in Figure 7.1. The Stream Production subsystem is a collection of Streams, possibly of different types. The Modeling & Display subsystem maintains and displays the

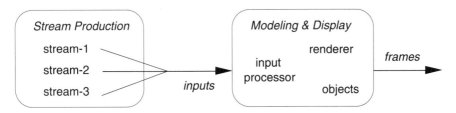

Figure 7.1: Streams-based animation separates Stream Production from Modeling & Display

animated objects. It operates like a finite-state machine, in which modeled objects are updated to new states as input values are received. An animation sequence is the succession of display frames produced by the series of states.

Related Work

In a limited sense, the streams model is related to the traditional input model found in graphics subroutine libraries such as GKS and PHIGS. These systems accept inputs from logical devices, including locators, valuators, and choice devices. A particular logical class might be implemented by one or more physical devices, but the physical implementation is hidden from the application. In streams-based animation, the source of a stream of values is hidden from the modeling and display subsystem.

A couple of other animation systems share the idea of feeding sequences of values to an object datastore to produce animation. In one system, "tracks" are used to record "events," such as a change in position. Tracks interpolate between events to generate new values. And the Advanced Visualizer™ from Wavefront Technologies reads "channel" information from a file to update and animate objects.

A number of systems use object-oriented, or closely related, paradigms. An early system called DIRECTOR (written by Kenneth Kahn and described in Magnenat-Thalmann [1985]), is based on "actors"—computational objects and related pieces of code that can send and receive messages. A second actor-based system, ASAS (by Reynolds [1982]), offers far more power and has influenced the design of many subsequent animation languages. Both of these systems are written in interactive languages (DIRECTOR in LOGO and ASAS in LISP) and allow for dynamic definition of new actors and their behaviors.

ASAS is primarily a scripting system, but also includes the notion of "animated numbers" called *newtons*, which can be used in any place where a number is appropriate. They update themselves to a new value after each use. Newtons are streams in the sense of LISP and Scheme. ASAS has a set of predefined newtons, representing different forms of interpolation. Animated numbers are also found in the CINEMIRA language, a Pascal preprocessor relying on data abstraction and providing built-in actor types, camera types, and scripts (see Magnenat-Thalmann [1985]).

Another system, OSCAR (described in Rumbaugh [1987]) provides for interactive instantiation of predefined object classes, including lights, cameras, and a variety of geometric primitives. Animation control is through keyframes or a form of procedural scripts. OSCAR provides "liasons" to "analysts," or external simulation programs. The control techniques are not unified but handled in control-specific ways.

SWAMP

SWAMP is an object-oriented graphics environment and streams-based animation system. It provides hierarchical object definition, windows, multiple views of objects, and the possibility of multiple renderers. Both textual and mouse-and-menu-style interfaces are provided and can be used together.

Three animation control strategies were included in the initial version of SWAMP. The user can animate through keyframes, or by making connections to a process written in C or FORTRAN, or by defining rules that specify relationships among a set of object attributes. These particular types of control strategy were chosen because they represent animation control at three distinct levels of abstraction. Keyframes provide a mechanism for explicit user control. Connecting to an external process written in a high-level language provides a means of procedurally specifying the animation. Rules provide a form of declarative control. The three control strategies can be used in any combination to produce a particular animation. The animator can approach each aspect of the animation with the control technique offering the most appropriate level of abstraction.

Implementation Notes

The SWAMP implementation uses a variety of languages. Most of the system is written in Common LISP, using the object-oriented extensions of

CLOS (Common LISP Object System). Those classes involved in modeling and display of objects include methods that call foreign code written in C, with PHIGS+ used for rendering and display. The mouse-and-menu interface is written in Sun Microsystems' NeWS™ windowing system.

The Common LISP Object System is an object-oriented extension to Common LISP. Its fundamental aspects include classes, instances, generic functions, and methods. A Class encapsulates the structure and behavior of some type of object. Instances of a class are structured and behave as defined for their class. A generic function is a function whose behavior depends on the classes of the arguments supplied to it. A method defines class-specific behavior within a generic function.

LISP was chosen as SWAMP's implementation language because of its ability to support exploratory work and rapid prototyping. Since CLOS represents the standard for object-oriented programming in LISP, it was chosen over Flavors. This section provides a brief overview of CLOS. The CLOS system is considerably more detailed and abundantly richer than what is described. Additionally, it is a system in evolution; what is described is not the most current implementation. For a complete description, see Keene [1989].

Classes are defined in CLOS using the *defclass* function, which takes as arguments a class name, a list of superclasses, and a list of instance variables, called *slots*. Instances are created with the *make-instance* function. For example, the code in Listing 7.1 defines a class named **Graphic-Primitive** with the slot *gray-value*. Two subclasses, **Point** and **Line**, are defined. **Point** and **Line** inherit the slot *gray-value* from **Graphic-Primitive**, and also define class-specific slots. Of the two points created with **make-instance**, *this-point* is given the default slot values for the coordinate location (0, 0), whereas for *that-point*, the location (100, 55) has been explicitly specified by the user. The **a-line** object is made up of *this-point*, *that-point*, and a grayscale specification.

Slot values can be accessed through the access functions defined for the slot. The expression

```
(gray-value a-line)
```

returns the current value of the slot *gray-value* in the object **a-line**. This value is updated through the call

```
(setf (gray-value a-line) 0.75)
```

Slot access can be limited by using *:reader* and *:writer* options within a slot definition, instead of *:accessor*.

Class-specific behavior is defined using *defmethod*, which takes as arguments a name, a list of one or more *specialized parameters*, and a body.

```
(defclass Graphic-Primitive ()
  ((gray-value :type (float 0.0 1.0)
    :accessor gray-value:initform 1.0)))
(defclass Point (Graphic-Primitive)
  ((x :type integer :accessor x :initform 0)
   (y :type integer :accessor y :initform 0)))
(defclass Line (Graphic-Primitive)
  ((p0 :type Point :accessor p0)
   (p1 :type Point :accessor p1)))
(setf this-point (make-instance 'Point))
(setf that-point (make-instance 'Point :x 100 :y 55))
(setf a-line (make-instance 'Line :p0 this-point
    :p1 that-point :gray-value 0.5))
```

Listing 7.1: CLOS code to define the classes Graphic-Primitive, Point, and Line, and to create instances

The method definitions

```
(defmethod draw ((pt Point))
  (class-specific code to display a point at
      (x pt), (y pt)))
(defmethod draw ((ln Line))
  (class-specific code to display a line from
      (p0 ln) to (p1 ln)))
```

define a generic function named **draw**. These method definitions specify that **draw** receives one parameter. The parameter is "specialized," consisting of both a parameter name and a class specifier (**Point** or **Line**). Specialized parameters determine what method within draw is executed. A call to **draw** might take the form

```
(draw a-line)
```

Since **a-line** is of class **Line**, it is the second method defined above that is executed.

Parameter lists for generic functions can contain multiple specialized parameters. For example, our system might include the classes **Raytracer** and **Hardware** to represent two different renderers. We might have a variety of **Graphic-Primitive** subclasses, including **Sphere** and **Cube**. The generic function **draw** would include the methods

```
(defmethod draw ((rend Raytracer) (obj Sphere))
    ...body...)
```

```
(defmethod draw ((rend Hardware) (obj Sphere))
   ...body...)
(defmethod draw ((rend Raytracer) (obj Cube))
   ...body...)
(defmethod draw ((rend Hardware) (obj Cube))
   ...body...)
```

In the early implementation of CLOS, use of multiple specialized parameters made an unfortunate impact on performance. Because performance and interactivity are important in SWAMP, we chose to forgo the benefits of multiple specializers and design SWAMP to use just one specializer in a method. For clarity, this is always the first parameter in a parameter list. Subsequent description of the SWAMP implementation frequently lists the methods defined for a class. A method entry takes the form

```
method-name receiver-object arguments
```

In SWAMP, then, calling a generic function is similar in appearance to sending a message to an object.

SWAMP's hardware environment consists of a Sun 4/260, equipped with a GX4000™ graphics board set from Raster Technologies, Inc. The GX4000 provided a hardware implementation of the PHIGS+ standard graphics subroutine library operating within the NeWS windowing system.

System Overview

The SWAMP implementation consists of three subsystems: Modeling & Display, Animation, and the User Interface. Figure 7.2 shows the most important classes within each subsystem. The Modeling & Display subsystem,

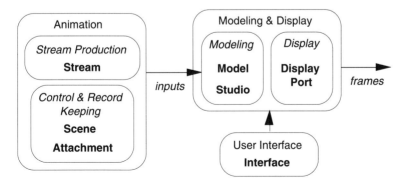

Figure 7.2: SWAMP consists of three functional subsystems

made up of **Model**, **Studio**, and **Display Port** subclasses, is an object-oriented graphics environment. Interface subclasses provide mouse-and-menu-style, as well as textual, interfaces. Within the Animation subsystem, control and record-keeping functions are handled by the **Scene** and **Attachment** classes; and the various **Stream** subclasses generate values for successive frames of the animation.

Together, the Modeling & Display subsystem and the Stream Production subdivision implement the heart of the streams-based animation model. The Scene object plays the role of intermediary between streams and animated objects, recording information about which streams are attached to which object attributes. It reads from the streams to obtain new values, which are then used to update the object attributes. As shown in Figure 7.3, the **Scene** synchronizes the operation of the system. From each stream, the Scene acquires a new parameter value by issuing a **get-next-value** message. It forwards the returned value to the object as an argument in an **edit** message. Streams are processed in a round-robin fashion, once each frame.

All of SWAMP's classes are descended from a root class, **Object**. Instances of **Object** respond to the following messages:

```
make prototype-object name
show object
edit object slot-name slot-value
```

The **make** message is sent to a prototype-object of some class. A prototype is an instance of a class created by SWAMP when a new class is defined, primarily as a receiver of **make** messages. A listing of the slot names and slot values of an instance is displayed in response to the **show** message. **Edit** is the primary interface to an object, since it allows the user to change slot values. Some subclasses specialize the **edit** method to notify other objects that a change has occurred. For example, when a camera object

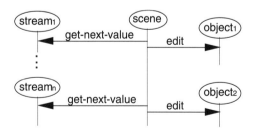

Figure 7.3: For each frame of animation, the scene requests a value from a stream and sends it in an *edit* message to the appropriate object

is edited, perhaps moving to a new position, it informs the visual display that an update is needed.

The following sections look at Object's subclasses, organized by their role within SWAMP. We take a short look at the user interface and then examine the modeling and display classes. SWAMP's animation capabilities are described in the subsequent section.

User Interface

The SWAMP implementation includes two interfaces: a textual interface and a mouse-and-menu interface. The classes **Textual Interface** and **NeWS Interface** are subclasses of the abstract class **Interface**. Either interface is adequate for interacting with the system. The interfaces can be used together within a session, allowing the user to switch back and forth between interface styles. The **switch-face** method allows the animator to switch from one interface to the other. Since CLOS does not provide class variables, a global variable *the-interface* is used to record which interface is currently active.

In the textual interface, input is simply the message protocols of the various classes. Messages are typed in parenthesized format and processed by the LISP interpreter. The user familiar with LISP can make use of the full capabilities of the LISP language, treating the SWAMP class protocols as a set of built-in functions.

The NeWS Interface

Increased ease-of-use and greater interactivity are provided through a mouse-and-menu-style interface, written in NeWS. NeWS is a networked windowing system using an extended PostScript language protocol and offering an extensible server, multiple execution threads, and lightweight processes. User interaction items, such as buttons and sliders, are arranged in an object-oriented hierarchy. New items can be added by new top-level classes or through subclassing.

The SWAMP interface is designed around a main control panel and a collection of *cards* of various types. The control panel and an example card (the Create card) are shown in Figure 7.4. The physical components of the main panel are (from right to left):

• A card area for displaying various cards. Each class in the system has a

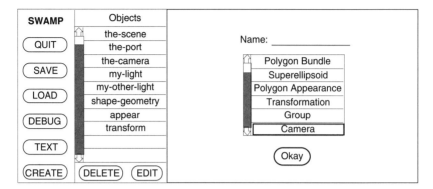

Figure 7.4: Main control panel for the NeWS interface

corresponding card. Additional cards are used for soliciting extra information about an operation from the user and for certain aspects of system management.

- A scrollable list with the heading "Objects." An entry is made for each object as it is created. The Delete button at the bottom of this list is used to destroy an object. The interface responds to the Edit button by displaying the selected object's card in the card area where it can be edited by the animator.

- Buttons used in object creation and in system management. The Create button causes the Create Card to be displayed. A return to the textual interface is accomplished by clicking on the Text button; Debug toggles the output of debugging information; the Load and Save buttons save and restore state; and the Quit button does just that.

Most of the user interaction with the system is carried out through the various cards. The Create Card is used to create named instances of the various classes. The user selects an object type from the scrollable list, supplies a name, and activates the Okay button.

The animator edits an object by interacting with the object's card. For example, adjusting the slider labeled "Red" on the card in Figure 7.5 to the value 0.75 changes the color of the light emitted by **my-light**. In response to the animator's action, the call

```
(edit my-light 'red 0.75)
```

is generated by the **NeWS Interface**, sent to the LISP interpreter, and dispatched to the correct object (**my-light**). The screen display is immediately updated.

SWAMP	Objects	Name: my-light		Class: Light

```
┌──────────┬──────────────┬────────────────────────────────────────────────┐
│  SWAMP   │   Objects    │ Name: my-light              Class: Light         │
│          ├──────────────┼──────────────────────────────────────────────────┤
│ ( QUIT ) │  the-scene   │ Type: ambient          Direction                │
│          │  the-port    │ Red  ─────────┤¹        X  ───────┬⁰             │
│ ( SAVE ) │  the-camera  │ Green ────────┤¹        Y  ───────┬⁰             │
│          │  my-light    │ Blue ─────────┤¹        Z  ──────────────┤¹      │
│ ( LOAD ) │ my-other-light│                                                 │
│          │shape-geometry│ Position               Attenuation              │
│ (DEBUG)  │   appear     │   X 0   Y 0   Z 1.5     X ⁰┼────────            │
│          │  transform   │                         Y ⁰┼────────            │
│ ( TEXT ) │              │ Concentration ²┼──────  Z ⁰┼────────            │
│          │              │ Spread ¹┼───────────                            │
│(CREATE)  │(DELETE)(EDIT)│                                                  │
└──────────┴──────────────┴──────────────────────────────────────────────────┘
```

Figure 7.5: An object is edited by manipulating the items on its card

Modeling and Display Environment

The classes providing the basic graphics environment of SWAMP are shown in Figure 7.6. The classes **Model**, **Studio**, **Display Port**, **Display Control**, and **Datastore** are all abstract superclasses. The **Model** class represents the actual items to be displayed, made up of geometric and attribute specifications such as color, size, and position. A subclass of **Model**, the class **Group**, is used to construct composite objects made up of **Model** objects. **Studio** subclasses each control some aspect of how items are to be viewed, including the camera position, lighting characteristics, and the range of available colors. Instances of the class **Display Port** are responsible for rendering **Group** objects and drawing in some area of the screen. In some

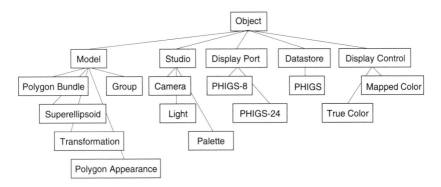

Figure 7.6: Classes in the Modeling & Display subsystem

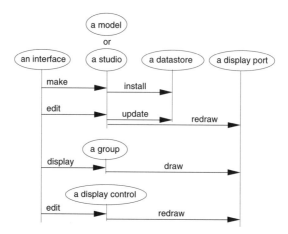

Figure 7.7: Relationships among the Model and Display classes

cases, a **Datastore** object may be employed to store information about **Model** and **Studio** objects in a renderer-specific way. A **Display Control** object groups particular cameras, lights, and palettes, and can be affiliated with one or more **Display Ports**.

Figure 7.7 gives an overall picture of how the classes interact. The **Model** and **Studio** classes engage the rest of the system when objects are created or changed. When a new instance is made of either of these classes, the class directs any existing Datastores to install the new object. If a **Model** or **Studio** instance is edited, the Datastores are directed to do an update, and any Display Ports are informed of the need to redraw. When a **Group** object is displayed, a request for drawing is issued to the **Display Port**. A redraw request is sent to the **Display Port** by a **Display Control** object when it is edited (such as when the user changes from one camera to another).

Modeling

Objects are modeled by making instances of primitives (the classes **Polygon Bundle**, **Superellipsoid**, **Transformation**, and **Polygon Appearance**) and combining them into an instance of the class **Group**.

Primitive Classes

Two types of geometric objects are included among the primitive classes.

The class **Polygon Bundle** is used to import a geometry stored in a file. The **Superellipsoid** class is an implementation of the elliptical form of super-quadrics. The appearance of geometric objects—**Polygon Bundles** or **Superellipsoids**—is influenced by instances of the other two modeling primitives. The **Polygon Appearance** class defines appearance attributes of an object, including color and degree of transparency. Size, orientation, and position of the geometric objects are determined by **Transformation** objects. Instances of this class include slots for the translation, scaling, and rotation transformations, as well as for specifying the order in which these operations are done.

Composite Objects

Group objects provide for construction of composite objects. Including objects in a group is done with the messages:

```
add-ref group object [place]
add-copy group object [place]
add-n-copy group object howmany [place]
remove-element group place
```

The **add-xxx** operations insert some object into a group. The **add-ref** function specifies that a reference to the object is to be included in this group. When a reference to object **A** is added to the group **B**, an entry for **A** is made to **B**'s *elements* slot. Additionally, **B** is added to **A**'s *references* list. An object can be referenced from any number of groups, and any subsequent changes to the object will be reflected in all the referencing groups. The **add-copy** operation allows a user to indicate that a copy of an object is to be created and included in this group. When a copy of **A** is added to **B**, a copy of **A** is generated, named, and included in **B**'s *elements* slot. Group objects can be built up in a nonsequential order through the use of the optional *place* parameter.

Objects that can be added to a group include instances of the classes **Polygon Bundle**, **Superellipsoid**, **Transformation**, and **Polygon Appearance**. Groups can be added to other groups to form hierarchical object descriptions. Objects that establish position information or appearance information (**Transformation** and **Polygon Appearance** objects) affect objects encountered later in their group or in descendant groups.

The modeling classes in SWAMP reflect a traditional separation between the geometry of an object and its attributes. It can be argued that in an object-oriented approach to modeling, a graphical object should include its appearance properties, such as color and transparency, along with its geometry. This is indeed the approach taken in some object-oriented systems. However, although this makes for well-defined primitives, it is an inefficient use of space and can make the system difficult to use. For a collection of objects that have the same geometry but different appearance attributes, the geometry must be repeated for every object. Further, changing color for a group of objects that should all look the same (for example, the four tires on a car), requires that color specifications be changed in each individual object. These problems are eliminated by separating the geometries from the appearance control objects. Multiple groups can share a single geometry or appearance control object by referencing it as a subpart.

Display of Modeled Objects

Modeled objects are displayed by a **Display Port** under the control of a **Display Control** object. Only instances of the class **Group** can be displayed, and only one group can be displayed in a **Display Port** at a time.

Display Port objects are responsible for the graphical display of objects within some particular area of the screen. Different **Display Port** classes use different rendering methods. For example, on a platform supporting hardware rendering of objects, a system could be implemented that includes both a **Hardware Display Port** (providing rapid drawing) and a software **Raytracer Display Port** (providing a more realistic picture). The user could display objects in the **Hardware Display Port** until their composition and placement were satisfactory and then switch to the **Raytracer Display Port** for a nicely rendered version of the scene. Although a **Display Port** class is in some sense the embodiment of a renderer, the two are not exactly equivalent in that multiple ports might be driven by a single renderer. **Display Port** instances respond to the messages **open**, **draw**, **redraw**, **erase**, and **close**.

Studio objects are primitive objects that represent some aspect of how a scene is to be viewed and rendered. There are three subclasses—**Camera**, **Light**, and **Palette**. The protocol for each of these classes is simply the protocol inherited from **Object**. Instances for the class **Camera** define a view, including specifications for eye position, viewing direction, field of view, and so on. **Light** objects have a type, position, color, and direction. **Palette** instances have a set of entries, with each entry consisting of a red, green, and blue color specification.

Instances of these classes are combined into **Display Control** objects. A **Display Control** object controls how an object is displayed in a particular port. The type of **Display Port** determines what kind of **Display Control** is needed. For example, a **Phigs-24 Display Port** needs specifications for a camera, lighting controls, hidden surface method, and whether it should display in wireframe or solid form. A **Phigs-8 Display Port** also needs information about a color table.

Summary

In summary, SWAMP's Modeling & Display environment includes the classes **Model**, **Studio**, **Display Port**, and **Display Control**. Modeling primitives are combined into instances of the class **Group**. Studio primitives, such as **Cameras** and **Lights**, are used in instances of the **Display Control** classes. The modeling and studio primitives record information about the objects from which they are referenced. When modeling or studio objects are edited, they inform their referencing objects; changes propagate up through the part-whole hierarchy.

Display Ports are areas of the screen, possibly driven by different rendering engines. If appropriate for the rendering engine, a **Datastore** object may be used in conjunction with the **Display Ports**. This object manages the object definitions in the renderer's private storage area. To maintain consistency across the various parts of the system, information about all **make** and **edit** operations involving modeling and studio objects must be relayed to the **Datastore**. Groups are displayed in **Display Ports**, with **Display Control** objects determining view and lighting characteristics of the display.

Scenes, Streams, and Animation

The classes **Scene**, **Target**, and **Attachment**, along with the **Stream** subclasses, are the primary classes involved in producing animation. An instance of the class **Scene** records the main objects in an animation—streams, targets, and the attachment of streams to targets—and controls the run of an animation. **Stream** objects generate values to be used by the scene in updating objects. **Targets** record the objects that undergo change during the animation. A **Target** can be a single object or a collection of similar objects. **Attachment** objects associate **Streams** with **Targets**.

The Scene

An instance of the class **Scene** serves as the director of animation, managing information about the players and their actions. A **Scene** instance maintains the display configuration (recording which groups are displayed in which display ports), keeps track of which Streams are attached to which objects, and controls the animation run. (See Figure 7.8.)

SWAMP has one scene object, **the-scene**. As part of its protocol, it responds to messages that change the configuration of groups and display ports. **the-scene** is also responsible for keeping track of the associations between streams and objects. It relies on a group of **Stream Managers** as assistants in this task. The **Stream Managers** serve to shield **the-scene** from the peculiarities of particular types of streams. (In object-oriented environments that support class methods, such as Smalltalk, the job of the **Stream Managers** could be handled by defining class methods for each of the **Stream** subclasses.) **Stream Managers** record the animator's specifications for which streams to use in updating which objects and respond to the messages:

```
add-entry manager arguments
remove-entry manager place
```

Add-entry takes a list of arguments that includes a stream, the object(s) to which it should be attached, and any additional information needed for the particular type of stream. **Remove-entry** removes a generator from participating in the scene. In the initial version of SWAMP, **the-scene** is assisted by **the-keyframe-manager**, **the-process-manager**, and **the-rule-manager**.

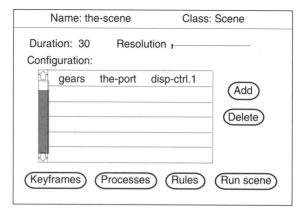

Figure 7.8: The card for a scene

New **Stream** types can be added by including the stream definition and its manager and informing **the-scene** of the presence of a new assistant.

From Control Strategies to Streams

The initial version of SWAMP includes the **Stream** subclasses **Spline**, **External Process**, and **Rule**. These objects respond to the messages **initialize**, **get-next-value**, and **shutdown**. **Initialize** starts the stream. The scene's duration and resolution are passed as an indication of how many values are expected from the stream. The stream object returns one such value on each receipt of the message **get-next-value**. The **shutdown** message is issued on completion of the scene, allowing the stream to do any necessary clean-up activities. The following sections briefly describe how different control techniques are each reduced to stream-like behavior and managed by their **Stream Managers**.

Keyframes and Splines

Keyframes provide a low-level form of control over the animation. To define a keyframe, the animator edits **Model** and **Studio** objects until they appear as they should for a particular frame of the sequence and then requests that this state be saved. **the-keyframe-manager** saves the current state in a snapshot. SWAMP records the current values of the slots of all the displayed objects. Any of the objects' slots can be manipulated through keyframing, and any number of keyframes can be defined.

The keyframes are used to create instances of the **Spline** class when the scene is run. A **Spline** is an object that interpolates across a set of control points to produce a stream of some requested number of values. **the-keyframe-manager** searches the scene's keyframes for slots whose values change over the set of frames. For each such slot, a spline is instantiated. The control points are pairs made up of the keyframe number and the value of the slot at this keyframe.

External Process Objects

An **External Process** object provides a mechanism for directing the animation from an independent process, allowing for a form of algorithmic control over the animation. The object manages communication between the process and the rest of the system. There are, of course, numerous ways to provide for procedural control. A specialized scripting language could be developed, or internal LISP functions could be used. The choice of including External Processes in the initial SWAMP system was influenced by our interest in eventually using the system to visualize scientific simulation codes, as described in a later section.

An **External Process** object can produce multiple streams, each identified by an integer tag. An auxiliary file, named *run-name.tag*, must be present to supply information about the process's capabilities for output. Editing the *run-name* slot of an **External Process** object causes SWAMP to locate and read the *.tag* file.

The animator specifies that a process stream play a part in the animation by sending the **add-entry** message to **the-process-manager**. Parameters for the attachment include the process name, a tag, and target information. A stream can be attached to multiple objects.

When a scene is run, the **initialize** method forks the process and establishes a communication channel. On subsequent calls to **get-next-value**, the **External Process** object reads from this channel. A small subroutine library is provided to allow the **External Process** object to communicate with **the-scene**.

Rules

Rules, as implemented in SWAMP, provide a simple form of declarative control over the animation. They enable the animator to constrain targets to maintain some relationship. For example, we might specify that a spotlight always point at the position of a particular object. Move the light and the object follows; move the object and the light tracks it. Establishing this relationship allows the animator to concentrate on how the object should move, without concern for the light. The **Rule** class in SWAMP is an attempt to provide this simple form of control.

Incorporating rules into SWAMP involves the two classes **Rule Template** and **Rule**. **Rule Templates** are used to define a relationship among a collection of participants. A rule is added to **the-scene** by identifying specific targets to participate in the rule. This creates an instance of the class **Rule**. At run time, **the-rule-manager** determines which rules can be satisfied, given the other attachments that exist for the scene, and makes an **Attachment** instance for each such rule.

An instance of the class **Rule Template** responds to the messages

```
add-method rule-template method place
remove-method rule-template place
fire-p rule-template participants known-targets
```

Add-method and **remove-method** are used to manipulate the set of solution methods making up the **Rule Template**, as discussed later in the example animation. The **fire-p** method returns true or false, depending on whether a particular set of Attachments are sufficient for triggering this rule.

In creating a rule, the animator must specify the *rule expression*. The rule expression is in general terms; it does not involve specific targets. A small language is provided for specifying the rule that includes the unary operators ~ (negation), *abs*, *round*, *sqrt*, *log*, *exp*, *sin*, and *cos*, and the binary operators =, *, /, +, and −. Operands can be constants or variables. An example rule expression is shown in the card in Figure 7.9.

Editing the rule-expression slot causes the **Rule Template** object to parse the expression, looking for a list of the variables involved. For each variable, the animator must specify how that variable is derived from the others, such that the rule relationship will be maintained. That is, for each variable v in V, the animator must write the expression that could be used to calculate v using the values of the variables $V - v$. The expression is v's *method*. As methods are added, the **Rule Template** object generates corresponding functional expressions, suitable for execution by the LISP interpreter. Each function is of a form that takes $V - v$ as input parameters, and returns v.

As with keyframes and external process controls, the animator specifies that some aspect of the animation is to be governed by a rule by sending the **add-entry** message to **the-rule-manager**. Arguments must include the **Rule Template** to be used and a list of the entities that are to participate in the rule. Participants are usually instances of the **Target** classes, but a constant may also serve as a rule participant. Adding a rule generates an

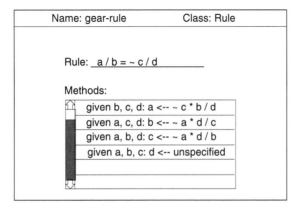

Figure 7.9: The card for a Rule Template object

instance of the **Rule** class. **Rule** is a subclass of **Stream** and is responsible for actually producing a stream and responding to the **get-next-value** message.

An individual rule establishes some relationship among a collection of targets. Adding a number of rules to the scene builds a rule network. During the run of a scene, changes to any target object in the network must be matched by changes in the other target objects, such that the rules are always satisfied. There will be no animation, of course, unless some of the targets involved in the rule network are also attached to other streams.

Resolving the rule network is the job of **the-rule-manager**. It is performed in response to the **generate-attachments** message issued by **the-scene**. This call should be made after the other stream managers have processed their information into attachments, because **the-rule-manager** must know what targets in the network are attached to other streams. Starting with this information, **the-rule-manager** searches the rule network for a set of data-flow dependencies, such that changes to already attached targets propagate through the rule network. The last step of the **generate-attachments** method is to create an attachment for each **Rule** that can be satisfied.

An Example Animation

Suppose **the-scene** is configured to display a **Group** named **gears** in its windows. **Gears** is made up of 4 subgroups, **gear.1** through **gear.4**. The gears are of various sizes with different numbers (10, 15, and 20) of teeth. They each include their own **Transformation** and **Polygon Appearance** instances.

To animate the gears, let's keyframe the **Camera** to change from a head-on view to something more oblique. Suppose we also attach an **External Process** object named **counter** to the *rotation-z* slot of **gear.3**'s **Transformation** object. **Counter** simply interpolates between starting and ending values supplied as parameters, producing a value for each frame.

For the collection of gears to turn properly, the relationship

$$\text{teeth}_0 / \text{teeth}_1 = \text{rotational speed}_0 / \text{rotational speed}_1$$

must always be true. We use a **Rule Template** object named **gear-rule**, shown in Figure 7.9, to express this relationship. We specify that **gear-rule** should be used, along with the appropriate constants for the number of teeth in the gears, to constrain the *rotation-z* slots of the **Transformation** objects in **gear.1** through **gear.4**, as shown in Figure 7.10.

gear-rule

```
A: Gear1, transform1, rz
B: 10
C: Gear2, transform2, rz
D: 20
```

gear-rule

```
A: Gear2, transform2, rz
B: 15
C: Gear3, transform3, rz
D: 10
```

gear-rule

```
A: Gear3, transform3, rz
B: 20
C: Gear4, transform4, rz
D: 15
```

Figure 7.10: The Rule Template object *gear-rule* is used three times, to link the rotations of pairs of gears

When the scene is run, the **Stream Managers** generate attachments. **the-keyframe-manager** attaches the Splines needed to smoothly change the view, while **the-process-manager** makes the simple attachment between **counter** and **gear.3**'s *rotation-z* slot. **the-rule-manager** works with these attachments and determines the chain of dependencies that can be used to satisfy the rule network. The set of attachments returned by the managers is given in Listing 7.2. **the-scene** processes these attachments once per frame, producing the animation suggested by Figure 7.11.

Discussion

As demonstrated by SWAMP, taking an object-oriented approach to control strategies provides a particularly flexible animation environment. The object-oriented paradigm supports abstraction, enabling us to define an abstract class representing the most general notion of animation control. We design the rest of the system to interface with this abstraction. Particular control strategies are defined as subclasses and provide the same services as

```
>(run the-scene)
    attachments are:
    Source          Target Obj        Slot
    SPLINE.1        THE-CAMERA        VPNX
    COUNTER         GEAR3-TRANS       RZ
    GEAR-RULE       GEAR4-TRANS       RZ
    GEAR-RULE       GEAR2-TRANS       RZ
    GEAR-RULE       GEAR1-TRANS       RZ
```

Listing 7.2: The attachments produced by the stream managers

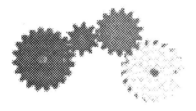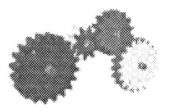

Figure 7.11: Scenes from the animated gears example

our Stream abstraction. Control-specific behaviors are hidden in the subclass definitions, so the system is shielded from the peculiarities of individual control techniques.

Use of the object-oriented paradigm also allows the animation system to be extended easily. The initial version of SWAMP has been extended to include a new primitive and two new control strategies, outlined in the following.

A color-mapped height field is a commonly used technique in the display of two-dimensional arrays of scientific data. A data array is used to provide height values for every (x, y) position in a two-dimensional grid. A second data array can be used as color indices for the vertex at each position (x, y, *height*). The class **Color-Mapped Height Field** was added to SWAMP as a subclass of **Model**. An instance has the slots *rows* and *columns*, indicating the size of the field. Other slots are present for height and color information. Each of these slots is a one-dimensional array of size *rows*columns*, to be attached to an external process that produces an array of values at each time step.

Figure 7.12 shows a height field, attached to a process simulating the life cycle of some population of insects and the predator insects that feed on them. The simulation accounts for the birth, maturation, movement, and death of the two insect groups throughout a field and outputs population

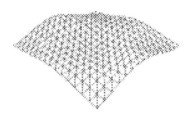

Figure 7.12: Height at each grid point shows population of immature prey

vectors for immature prey, mature prey, immature predators, and mature predators. In Figure 7.12, the mature predators substream has been attached to **height**.

The class **Interactor** was added, as a subclass of **Stream**, to allow the animator to interact with objects during the run of a scene. Interactors are mouse-sensitive items that can be attached to object slots. Like all Streams, instances of Interactor respond to the **initialize, shutdown**, and **get-next-value** messages.

Interactor has two subclasses: **Locator2** and **Vector Sketch** (see Figure 7.13). **Locator2** is a two-dimensional valuator that produces a substream for each dimension. A **Vector Sketch** is a user-interactive item that outputs a collection of values. It includes a box area in which the user can sketch out a set of values. The user can specify the number of entries, which are assumed to be evenly spaced across the horizontal dimension of the sketch area. The numeric range for the values to be generated (the vertical dimension of the sketch area) is set by the user.

Extending SWAMP in these directions required very few changes to the original code. The **Color-Mapped Height Field** introduced slots whose values are vectors, rather than single values, and this necessitated some adjustment. Other than these small changes, the system was unaffected by the addition of either the new primitive or the new control strategies. It is expected that additional controls and modeling primitives could be added just as easily.

A key tenet of the object-oriented paradigm is that object structure and behavior are encapsulated. This idea is played out in several research systems. Animated skeletons incorporate the "knowledge" of how to walk; snakes "know" how to slither. Physically based primitives include mass and

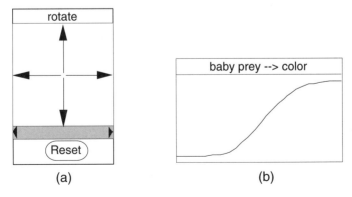

(a)   (b)

Figure 7.13: (a) a Locator2 and (b) a Vector Sketch

material attributes (such as elasticity or rigidity) and the ability to position and/or deform themselves in response to forces. In this approach to object-oriented animation, modeled objects incorporate behavioral capabilities in their definition.

However, for general-purpose animation, greater flexibility is achieved through lower-level building blocks. Even in the physically based arena, recent work by Pentland [1989] reports significant advantages from decoupling the object geometry and dynamics. Rather than relying on a point-wise representation for both, Thingworld chooses separate representations for geometry and dynamics, each suited to its piece of the problem. The results are more efficient calculation of dynamic interactions and the ability to map the dynamics to a variety of geometries, including B-spline surfaces and superquadrics.

In a similar manner, the streams model decouples animation specifications from the definitions of modeled objects. Graphical entities are defined in terms of their shape, appearance attributes, and position information. Behavioral information is not included. Behaviors, in the form of streams, are themselves defined as objects. This approach provides for greater flexibility and reusability in that behaviors can be mapped to geometry, appearance, or position of the modeling entities.

References

Keene, Sonya E. [1989]. *Object-Oriented Programming in Common LISP.* Reading, MA: Addison-Wesley.

Magnenat-Thalmann, Nadia, and Daniel Thalmann [1985]. *Computer Animation.* Tokyo: Springer-Verlag.

Pentland, Alan [1989]. "Good Vibrations: Using Modal Analysis in Modeling," *Computer Graphics*, 23(4), 1989, pp. 215-222.

Reynolds, Craig W. [1982]. "Computer Animation with Scripts and Actors," *Computer Graphics*, 16(3), 1982, pp. 289-296.

Rumbaugh, James, Michael Blaha, William Premerlani, Frederick Eddy, and William Lorenson [1991]. *Object-Oriented Modeling and Design.* Englewood Cliffs, NJ: Prentice-Hall.

Chapter 8

Object-Oriented Graphics for Interactive Visualization of Distributed Scientific Computations

Sandra S. Walther
Richard L. Peskin

In a true object-oriented system, objects are endowed with behavioral characteristics through internally referenced procedures that are dynamically bound at runtime. The objects respond to messages with a behavior that returns another object. Thus, a physical system can be represented by an object, and a stimulus to that system can be represented by a message. The result of sending a message is the return of an object that contains the data associated with the physical system's behavior. In this discussion, we are concerned with endowing these data objects with their own behavior so they can represent themselves graphically in response to user requests. We present these concepts using the framework of a scientific simulation system called SCENE.

SCENE (Scientific Computing Environment for Numerical Experimentation) is a scientific/engineering user interface designed for computational prototyping that utilizes object-oriented paradigms over a distributed system of facilities. SCENE features a graphical control environment executing in Smalltalk through which users can design and manipulate a computation running remotely on a variety of parallel and serial resources.

This research was supported in part by the National Science Foundation under NSF grant ECS-8814937 and by the Parallel Laboratory of the Center for Computer Aids for Industrial Productivity (CAIP). CAIP is supported by the New Jersey Commission on Science and Technology, Rutgers-The State University of New Jersey, and the CAIP Industrial Members.

SCENE is fully object-oriented in design and implementation and is itself a distributed application; the graphical interface and control elements are implemented in Smalltalk and the numerically intensive work, both for graphical manipulation (such as three-dimensional representation) and for computation of the numerical model, are implemented in C as the following: (1) *local primitives* (subroutines written in C and linked into the Smalltalk virtual machine) and/or (2) *remote primitives* (system calls to remote processes running outside the Smalltalk image and virtual machine on the local graphics workstation or via networking on a resource facility, such as a Sun SPARC™ server, an NCUBE™ hypercube, or a BBN Butterfly™). These remote processes are programs written in C that incorporate the object-oriented structure of the Smalltalk process that invoked their services. Figure 8.1 shows a schematic of the system. The graphical control environment has been implemented with ParcPlace 2.5 and 4.0 Smalltalk-80 on Sun-3™, Sun-4™, Ardent™ Titan™, and Macintosh™ workstations, in Tektronix Smalltalk version TB2.3a on the Tektronix 4317/4319 color workstations, and in Digitalk Smalltalk/V™ on the Macintosh.

SCENE is designed to provide scientific users with a "programless" access to a numerical laboratory. The basic system, described in Peskin et al.

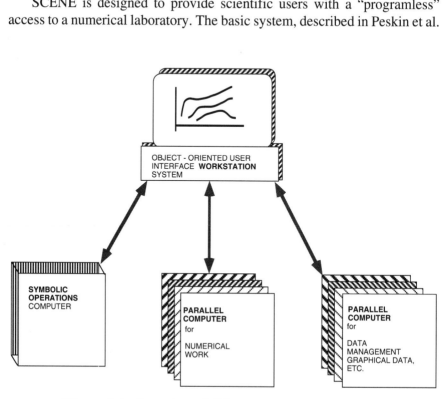

Figure 8.1: Overview of SCENE system components

[1989], includes numerous tools such as symbolic algebra systems and numerical subsystems to allow users to prototype physical problems in an interactive manner. The user enters equations in mathematical form, and the system provides a solution in a graphical form. The user can alter the model (by altering the equations) *in situ* and can see the new results immediately. These results are available in a variety of graphical output structures (for example, line plots, surface plots, contour plots, vector field plots, stream-lines) at the user's option. These graphical output structures (tools) and the computational entities they represent are themselves *objects*.

The central paradigm of SCENE is that of an object-oriented model-view-controller (MVC), which promotes intimate integration of the data set (model), the graphical presentation (view), and user interaction devices such as a mouse (controller). Under this paradigm, changes in the behavior of the phenomenon serving as the model can be reflected immediately in the graphic display, and user requests to cause changes in or to query the model can be indicated through graphic events. In SCENE, the user interacts with the computational model by manipulating a visualization tool (an MVC object) running in Smalltalk on a graphics workstation. The visualization tool provides graphical representations and control of the computational model according to the methods of its visualization classes. The types of MVC objects that we have developed (xytool, contourtool, surfacetool, vectortool, streamtool, meshtool) indicate clearly our orientation to object-oriented graphics; *a visualization object is a locus of representation and management for a type of information. Visualization objects are not merely graphic effects; they are expressions of the behavior of information.*

Scientific Visualization Objects

The visualization tools presently in use in SCENE have evolved over the past several years from our development of libraries of device-independent 2D and 3D graphics functions linked with device-dependent libraries to support interactive graphics on graphics terminals (Tektronix 4010/4014 standards) and later, on bitmapped workstations running SunView™ and the X Window System. Although not yet object-oriented in design, these versions of *xytool*, *contourtool*, and *surfacetool* were organized behavior-ally: The 2D library contained subroutines that presented xy data according to the Graphical Kernel System standard; the 3D library contained subrou-tines that presented and manipulated xyz data as three-dimensional shapes using standard transformation and perspective techniques. These graphic representational behaviors (the device-independent data transformation routines) were decoupled from the drawing and device-dependent display functions, as well as from the event management of the interface (SunView or X). This functional distinction between the graphic object (the data), its manifestation as a display behavior on a particular device, and the user control mechanisms of the interface environment mapped easily to the model-view-controller paradigm of Smalltalk. The evolution of SCENE's MVC object classification scheme has been described in a series of articles by Walther [1987], [1989], [1991]. Some recapitulation is provided here in conjunction with presenting the current state of the system.

The visualization tools are organized functionally around data, display, and control behaviors. Figure 8.2 shows the current classification. **Data-Model** is the class that comprises the basic two-dimensional graphing methods (GKS-compatible). It provides methods for managing, scaling, and transforming xy data. **DataView** includes the display methods supporting the *presentation* of xy plots, providing methods for placing tic marks, labels, titles, and notes, as well as methods for drawing lines and/or dots of different sizes and colors. **DataModel3D** is the class that comprises basic three-dimensional graphing methods, inheriting from **DataModel** whatever data-managing methods are common to them both (such as normalizing), and itself supports two implementation classes: **XYZData**, which concentrates on methods for representing and tracking three-dimensional trajectories,

VISUALIZATION CLASSES (Model-View-Controller Paradigm)

VisualizationObjects (Models)	DisplayBehaviors (Views)	Managers (Controllers)
Object	View	MouseMenuController
DataModel	DataView	DataViewController
DataModel3D	ContourView	ContourViewController
DataSurface	MeshView	VectorViewController
DataContour	VectorView	MeshViewController
PrimitiveContour	*XYVectorWarehouseView*	XYZViewController
MeshData	*XYWarehouseView*	DataSurfaceViewController
PrimitiveSurface	XYZView	FlagViewController
Flag	DataSurfaceView	StreamViewController
XYZData	FlagView	*VorticityViewController*
StreamData	*PrimitiveSurfaceView*	
XYZWarehouse	StreamView	
VorticityWarehouse	*XYZWarehouseView*	
DataVector	*VorticityWarehouseView*	
XYVectorWarehouse		
XYData		
LogisticEquation		
XYWarehouse		

Figure 8.2: Visualization interface classes for scientific modeling

and **DataSurface**, which provides methods specific to the representation of three-dimensional data as "see through" wireframes or as triangulated solid objects. **DataContour** comprises methods for extracting two-dimensional "cross cuts" from xyz data. **MeshData** includes methods for constructing two-dimensional adaptive meshes from a set of points specifying an enclosed region. **StreamData**, a subclass of **XYZData**, adds methods for representing data associated with points in three-dimensional space. **DataVector**, a subclass of **DataModel**, adds methods for representing distances and directions in a plane to the basic two-dimensional capabilities of its parent class. **VectorView**, a subclass of **DataView**, adds methods to draw arrows.

Those classes that focus on the methodologies needed to transform certain kinds of numeric information into specific visualization objects are treated as graphical *Models*. The display presentation methods (for example, how lines are drawn or areas colored) are incorporated into subclasses of the Smalltalk system class **View** (or **Pane** in Smalltalk/V), according to their special display behaviors. In a sense, they are analogous to device-specific "driver" libraries, because any platform-specific user primitives (such as hardware z buffering) would be added as methods of the **View** subclass that displays the type of data requiring that service. For example, **PrimitiveSurfaceView** is a class that draws surfaces with hidden lines removed using "native mode" graphics primitives. Not every graphics model class needs its own view class. For example, **XYData**, a subclass of **Data Model** that implements some model methods as *user primitives,* uses **DataView** for its displaying. By contrast, **XYWarehouse**, a subclass of **XYData**, implements some model methods as *remote processes* and speeds up its display performance by using **XYWarehouseView**, a subclass of **DataView** whose display methods themselves incorporate remote processes. This class structure is depicted in Figure 8.2. Subclassing is represented through indentation of class names. Class names shown in italics indicate classes that include methods linked to user primitives. Underlined class names shown in italics indicate classes that include methods calling remote processes.

Each view has a controller to manage requests for view and/or model behavior. Each controller has certain behaviors associated with specific mouse buttons (or mouse button equivalents). Functionally, Smalltalk supports three mouse activities, traditionally referred to as *red button, yellow button,* and *blue button.* The red button (the left button on a multi-buttoned mouse) is used for selecting and pointing; SCENE's controllers, subclassed off Smalltalk system class **MouseMenuController** (**Dispatcher** in Smalltalk/V), use the red button for their specialized selecting and pointing needs. For example, all the tools allow the user to indicate a place in the graphic area with a mouse click. In **DataViewController** and **VectorViewController**, the default red button activity (when no overriding options have been set) presents the user with a "zoom" cursor that allows selection of a rectangular area of any size within the view. The controller collects the display coordinates of the selected rectangle and, with the help of its view (which knows how to transform between data space and display space), delivers them as data values to its model; the model uses these data values to rescale its data set and opens another view on this portion of its data.

Controllers that have options to override the zoom feature as the default behavior (**DataViewController**, **VectorViewController**, and **Vorticity-WarehouseController**) deliver the selected display coordinate to the view to decode the value into data space. The model then uses that data space value to locate an actual data value in the data set. For **DataVector**, this requires using methods that identify the closest mesh point to the selected value and that then fetch the **vector** object associated with that mesh point. For **VorticityWarehouse**, similar methods are invoked, but they are executed as remote primitives. In either case, the user selection results in the inspection of the computational object (of the object type managed by the tool) at the requested location in data space. Figure 8.3 illustrates several visualization effects based on red button selection activity. The small view at the left is a zoomed view on a mouse-selected data region. The inspection box shows the instance variable values of a selected object. Path lines are interpolated at user-designated startpoints. (Data is from a two-dimensional flow with backward recirculation computed on a 32 processor BBN GP1000.)

MouseMenuController supports pop-up menu behavior as the activity associated with the *yellow button* (middle button on a three button mouse). This allows each tool to have a set of user demands accommodated through a menu that pops up only when the yellow button is invoked in the active tool area. The methods called by such a menu are methods of the local controller, but because the MVC paradigm in Smalltalk registers both the model and the view with the controller, those methods can in turn invoke methods in (by sending messages to) the model and/or the view. Most SCENE controller pop-up menus service user requests to change data style and color representation, to make hard copies, to inspect the model, and to perform other functions that are frequently used and convenient to control with menu selection.

The *blue button* (right button) supports the control of the tool as a "well-behaved" window. Its pop-up menu features the commands *move, resize, refresh, under, collapse,* and *close,* sending messages to the tool object whose view is "encased" in a window object that is itself a subclass of the Smalltalk system class **StandardSystemView**. It is worth noting that in

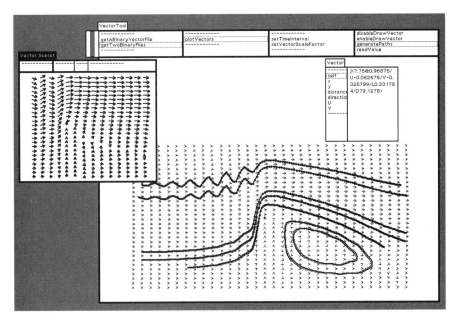

Figure 8.3: Vector visualization tool. Features shown illustrate visualization of vector flow, zoom, path interpolation, and retrieval of data values.

ParcPlace release 4.0 of Smalltalk-80, the encasing window is actually implemented directly as a graphic entity in the host workstation interface environment, namely the X Window System on most platforms and Macintosh windows on the Macintosh. (Smalltalk/V also uses Macintosh windows on the Macintosh.) This means that Smalltalk as an interface environment no longer has a characteristic Smalltalk look but rather takes on the appearance of the host environment's "window dressing." However, the tool classes are well encapsulated so that porting to Smalltalk/V and to ParcPlace version 4.0 required only some minor adjustments to methods accessing system features that had changed.

Currently, we are using a composite view design for our basic tool format featuring four scrolling menu sections or control panels across the top of the tool and a large graphics area in the remaining rectangle. These control panels are **SelectionInList** objects, based on Smalltalk system classes, and they provide added capability for user intervention into tool behavior beyond the transient pop-up menus described above. The list of menu labels and the selection handlers are *named* in the method that sets up the view, but the methods that are *invoked* are methods of the model. For example, we always use the left-most panel as the place where the user makes input requests. The specific requests made in that panel vary from model to model. In the method that sets up a tool view on a model, a layout method specifies the name *inputList* as its argument to the method registering the command list for the first panel. When that method is activated, it construes *inputList* as the name of a method in the object (model) that has invoked it. Thus, several models can invoke the same method to set up the same kind of view and yet can tailor the command panel to their own needs. This illustrates the usefulness of polymorphism in exploiting a "mix-and-match" approach to the design of graphics tool features.

Each of the **View** classes includes a class method to open a standalone tool that can access and display precomputed data from files. Tools can invoke other tools. For example, the user can open a contourtool on an xyz data set, display the data as a contour plot, and, from that tool control panel, spawn a surfacetool on the same data. One can also spawn a contourtool from a surfacetool. Each tool is fully autonomous; the user can make use of all features. Since both **contourtool** and **surfacetool** objects triangulate their data, the collection of triangles is an intermediate object that can deploy either contour or surface transformation methods. Of course, any object that wants some numbers graphed can declare an instance of **DataModel**, **DataContour**, or any other visualization class and directly invoke that class's graphing methods while it is computing. In effect, computation objects can deploy visualization objects just as any object in Smalltalk can deploy other objects. This is one of the most powerful features of object-oriented environments: *The total repertoire of objects is accessible and is ready to perform in response to a proper request.*

Graphic model objects can spawn subviews of selected regions of their own data, as mentioned above. Zoomed regions can be zoomed themselves until the resolution of their data is exhausted. Figure 8.4 shows **xyztool**, a tool object based on **XYZData** that visualizes data representing a particle over 10,000 time steps (ABC flow mixing model computed on 128 node NCUBE/ten). The view on the right shows the entire data set with a user-designated region (the small cube) specifying the parameters for a zoomed view. The user selects the zoomed region by indicating (via mouse clicks) the points on the three axes that bound the area of interest. In this case, the user has selected a region of dense particle concentration for further inspection. The view on the left is the result of the selection process. As a visualization tool, the zoomed view is independent of its parent view and is capable of all functionalities, including selecting and spawning a zoomed view of its part of the model.

Tools can also be constructed to track multiple objects acting concur-

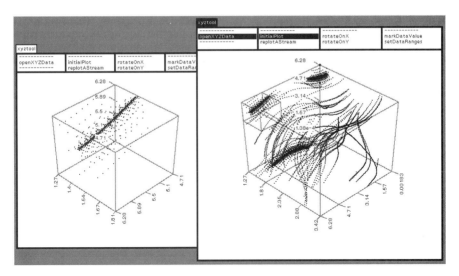

Figure 8.4: Three-dimensional visualization tool with zoom

rently. Color Plate 4 shows a tool organized as a composite view on a domain decomposition solver using object-oriented techniques. Each subview visualizes the behavior of a computational object that is computing a specific region of the problem. As each subdomain object completes a time step for its region, it notifies *its* view to update the graphic presentation. Upon completion of the computation, the subdomain objects can be asked to pool their solutions so that the unified result can be represented and studied in its own tool. Initial conditions are shown at the top left of the graph. The final computation of each subdomain is shown at the bottom left. The domain decomposition object itself, the solution as reconstituted for the entire region, can be viewed and manipulated in the tool shown at the right.

An alternative approach to the deployment paradigm for visualizing computational objects is to subclass a computational model directly off one of the primary visualization classes so that the graphic data behavior can be inherited and/or modified. As indicated in Figure 8.2, **LogisticEquation**, a class that defines numerical methods in order to explore the behavior of this equation, handles its data management, visualization, and interaction needs by subclassing its model off **XYData** (a faster version of **DataModel** which does its data transformations through user primitives) and its controller off **DataViewController** in order to add some menu items of its own. This approach creates a new MVC tool that is fully operational from the start but can be specialized in the process of prototyping the behavior of the computational model. Users new to SCENE (and to Smalltalk) have found this approach to be a very convenient and expeditious route to devising their own tool environments. In particular, meshtool, an automatic mesh-generating tool, was developed by a student researcher as a subclass of **DataContour**. A tool to model the behavior of a two-dimensional meshed surface (a flag) driven by physical forces was developed very quickly by subclassing the computational class **Flag** off the visualization class **PrimitiveSurface** (Color Plate 5). The **Flag** object behaves *graphically* as a surface represented in three dimensions. Its simulated *physical* behavior is driven by its own methods incorporating computations of physical forces acting on a surface specified as a field of points. This is one advantage of basing the visualization class behavior on the data behavior rather than on the graphic representation technique. To the extent that certain types of phenomena are modeled by certain types of computations (for example, iterations through a spatial mesh), they generate types of data models. *It is these data models that we have identified as our generic graphic objects.*

User Primitives

The strategies presently employed in SCENE evolved out of the desire to combine the prototyping features of the Smalltalk interface with the enhanced computation capabilities provided through distributed resources, including massively parallel systems. Computational steering, the interactive alteration of objects and/or procedures while a model is computing, requires an interpretive treatment of computation objects; object behavior must be interruptible so that objects and their methods can be altered without destroying the context of their behavior. This type of behavior is well supported in Smalltalk, and, with respect to the class of workstations on which we have implemented SCENE, Smalltalk performance has been acceptable for problems up to a certain size and computational intensity. For example, computing 100 steps of the formula for the logistic equation

```
z = r * z * (1 - z)
```

takes 15 milliseconds (in Smalltalk-80, ParcPlace version 2.5 on a Sun-4); computing 10,000 points takes 1000 milliseconds. Preparing that data for display (two-dimensional scaling and transforming) requires 500 milliseconds for 100 data points and 33,000 milliseconds for 10,000 data points. Computing three-dimensional graphic transformations for a surface based on a 20 by 20 mesh of xyz points takes 1700 milliseconds; computing those transformations for a surface based on a 32 by 32 mesh takes 4700 milliseconds. Sorting transformed polygons (to display surfaces with hidden lines removed) added 2600 milliseconds more to the graphic processing of a 20 by 20 surface and 4700 milliseconds to that of a 32 by 32 surface. Because we intended to use SCENE for bonafide scientific problems requiring the management of large numerical models (for example, a flow field based on a computational mesh of 100 by 100 by 100 complex numerical objects over a number of time steps), we devised and implemented a variety of strategies to enhance the performance of the MVC tools (the Smalltalk objects) without sacrificing the characteristics of the prototyping environment.

The first efforts were directed toward offloading computationally intensive methods as *user primitives*. Under that strategy, computational entities operating as instances of Smalltalk objects send information (stripped of "object" representation) as data-typed arguments to subroutines written in C and linked in as runable code in the Smalltalk virtual machine. The first candidate for conversion to a user primitive was the method in **DataSurface** whereby a matrix (an instance of class **Matrix**) unpacked itself into columns of triplets (instances of class **Triplet**—an 'xyz' point) and multiplied each value of a triplet object (instances of class **Float**) by a 4 by 4 matrix of triplets. The Smalltalk code for this method (actually, a method employing several other methods) is presented below.

```
transformASurface
"compute 3d transformation of each xyzpoint in a
   surface"
| aTriple newTriple |
aTriple := Triplet new.
1 to: (self surfaceMatrix columns) do:[:x |
   aTriple setX: (self normalXgrid) at: x).
   1 to: (self surfaceMatrix rows) do:[:y |
      aTriple setY: (self normalYgrid) at: y.
      aTriple setZ:(surface atRow: y column: x)
      newTriple := self transformPt: aTriple.
      aPoint := self makePerspectivePoint: newTriple.
      dataPoints atRow: y column: x put: aPoint]].
```

Profiling this functionality indicated that the single largest time expense (25.5 percent) was spent in the method **transformPt**, which multiplied the 4 by 4 matrix of triplets by each triplet. Thus, it appeared at first glance that the matrix multiply method itself should be reworked as a user primitive. However, this still left almost 75 percent of the total transformation processing time consumed by the storing and retrieving of objects. To achieve credible graphic throughput of surface data from meshes of a sufficient size to be informative to a scientific user (upwards of 20 by 20), we had to accelerate the entire process from the time the user requests a surface plot (with or without hidden lines removed) to the time the image shows up on the display. In fact, we added a user primitive to do multiplication of matrices for a different situation (to speed up the concatenation of a series of matrices required for three-dimensional representation). However, we also added a user primitive that takes the final transformation matrix and the data as its arguments and returns the equivalent display coordinates ready to be drawn. A 20 by 20 surface transformed by **DataSurface**, using only Smalltalk methods, required 1750 milliseconds (ParcPlace 2.5 on a Sun-4). The equivalent function done as a user primitive by **PrimitiveSurface** (the "high-speed" subclass of **DataSurface**) took only 550 milliseconds on the same system.

We have converted the hidden line removal methods to a primitive as well. In that case, the surface data is triangulated and then transformed. The distance of each triangle from the eyepoint is computed as the average of the distances from its three vertices. The triangles are then sorted according to distance. On systems without hardware z buffering, we use the painter's algorithm and send the triangles to the display to be drawn and filled in order of farthest to nearest. This allows the closest triangles to overdraw the farther ones and produces the correct effect, but at the cost of drawing *all* the triangles. On systems with z buffering (such as the Ardent Titan), we added a user primitive to tap that graphics capability. A subclass of **DataSurfaceView**, **PrimitiveSurfaceView**, answered the message **doASurface** by sending the sorted triangles in front to back order to its user primitive, which (by employing the C function in the system graphics library that accesses the z buffer) selected and drew only the visible (uncovered) vertices. That procedure took only 5400 milliseconds to display the completed 20 by 20 surface. By way of comparison, using Smalltalk without these primitives (using **DataSurfaceView**) and drawing *all* the triangles took 62,000 milliseconds to complete.

More details on constructing user primitives can be found in Walther [1989]. Essentially, we have adopted a two-pass approach to the development of graphic capabilities in SCENE, namely *exploratory* and *production* passes. The exploratory stage is Smalltalk's strength. Objects can be designed, tested, and discarded if they fail to pan out or retained as tentative commitments in a larger exploration. Performance speed is rarely an issue in this phase, because preliminary models, or at least their components, can be scaled down. However, a point occurs at which a set of primary objects has proven to be a reasonable conceptual design, but the dynamics of their behaviors must be drawn out with physically meaningful parameters and for an extensive duration. (This is true both for the prototyping of visualization behaviors, for example, the automatic triangulation of arbitrary shapes in meshtool and for the prototyping of physical behaviors, as in the simulation of air flow around an airplane wing.) Increasing the scale of the model increases the data, and this increases the number of instantiated objects that are present in the object space of the image. As the size of the Smalltalk image increases, it makes more demands on system memory and may need to extend itself into virtual memory. As the memory usage becomes more complicated, performance degrades. Increasing the volume of program entities that are fully supported as objects also increases the message traffic to fetch and store objects in other objects and the additional storage required to carry the object description of each object.

Offloading certain functions to user primitives alleviates some of the pressures on object space by eliminating the proliferation of objects that are needed to carry out intermediate tasks in a larger functionality. For example, the user primitive that replaces the **transformASurface** method described above takes as its arguments a **FloatVector** object (an instance of class **FloatVector**, whose storage methods for arrays of floating point numbers are implemented as user primitives) representing the 16 values of the current transformation matrix, and a **FloatVector** containing the data itself as x, y, and z values in column order. The **FloatVector** object is a less expensive way of representing the data than our original approach (a **Matrix** object storing **Triplet** objects of **Float** objects). One user primitive performs the total graphic transformations required to produce display coordinates representing a three-dimensional wireframe figure on a two-dimensional surface in perspective space. This includes normalizing the data, clipping to viewport space, and transforming the resulting perspective space coordinates to window (Smalltalk **View**) space. The primitive code, written in C, performs all these functions, iteratively, on whatever volume of data is passed to it.

As indicated above, we have written user primitives to speed up graphic operations for two-dimensional (GKS equivalent) transformations, three-dimensional transformations, hidden line removal, contouring, and vector representation. The graphics performance of the tools can be enhanced by including graphics primitives that exploit the native graphics repertoires that may be available in workstations. However, while the linked-in user primitive strategy is adequate in situations where a procedure can operate on arguments passed into it *each time it is called*, this technique cannot be used to offload functionalities that require preservation of the "offloaded" context information from one call to another. User primitives, as they are currently available in Smalltalk, are not reentrant. Thus, they are not suitable for situations where we need to maintain large amounts of information in memory for access by objects in the Smalltalk image but where that access is intermittent. This requirement is basic to our abilities to interact with large three-dimensional data sets of complex computational objects. For such "reentrant" situations, we have devised the *remote primitive* or *distributed primitive* strategy.

The Distributed Paradigm: Remote Objects

A remote primitive is a program that operates as a process independent of the Smalltalk image and that communicates with the Smalltalk image through interprocess communication support provided by the system environment. We use the locution *primitive* to emphasize the similarity between the remote process and the locally linked primitive strategies. While they differ in implementation mechanisms, both kinds of primitives are invoked as methods of Smalltalk objects and, therefore, are extensions of front-end methods. Presently, as the majority of our Smalltalk workstations run a Berkeley compatible version of UNIX, the interprocess communication is implemented in sockets. Alternate development might make use of Linda®, a parallel processing system; development on the Macintosh will be able to make use of interapplication communications under System 7. Since the paradigm does not constrain *where* the remote primitive may be operating (it could be on the workstation itself, on one or more serial computers, or on one or more parallel systems) or how many remote primitives may be open concurrently, it is more informative to call them *distributed* primitives.

Central to this strategy is the belief that the *logic* of an object-oriented design transcends its implementation. Or put another way, the functionalities that make object-oriented systems so useful can be preserved and/or simulated in unorthodox environments (for example, a distributed system of workstations, single processor computers, and massively parallel computers) using conventional languages (such as C) in innovative ways. Basically, SCENE makes use of Smalltalk's total object-oriented capabilities *in Smalltalk*. During the prototyping phase, inheritance and dynamic binding play critical roles. The visualization classes that we have added were developed and continue to be enhanced using the full repertoire of services (such as the Browser and the Debugger). Because the behaviors of our classes are prototyped to the point where we wish to use them as production tools to explore scientific objects, we seek to convert their graphic representation and data management functions to primitives, a conversion that requires strict datatyping and loss of dynamic recompilation. Presently, the extended methods of user and distributed primitives are developed manually in C as needed. We are working toward automating that process so that, in a future version of SCENE, Smalltalk objects will be able to write their own primitives. Although that automatic capability is not fully in place, the distributed services environment is in use.

The distributed paradigm uses a *dual* representation of objects: Objects in SCENE may be implemented both as classes in Smalltalk and as *structs* in C. From the standpoint of the user, the behavior of a remote object is identical to its behavior in Smalltalk. What the user sees and deals with is the object in its Smalltalk persona. What the user does not see is the "back-end" computational behavior supplied by the distributed resources to support the appearance of the object in the visualization tool. To offload large amounts of numerical information so that it is managed in a remote primitive but remains accessible to the user interface tool, we have designed a dually implemented object called a *warehouse*. On the back-end facility, a warehouse is a C program whose data structures implement the computational behavior and storage of a specific kind of computational object whose visualization is controlled by a user interface tool running in Smalltalk. On the front end, a Warehouse class is subclassed off the graphics class whose visualization behaviors are most relevant to the specific computational object. Methods to support user queries are written side by side in C and in Smalltalk. A substantial library of C routines to support search and retrieval of two-, three-, and three-dimensional-in-time data sets of computational objects has been implemented and is now being generalized to be automatically configurable to newly defined computational objects.

Color Plate 6 shows a visualization tool opened on a warehouse of **VorticityVector** objects. The data, organized in a *remote process warehouse*, represents velocities and vorticities in a 32 by 32 by 32 computational model of vorticity tube behavior. The visualization tool, running on the front end, allows the user to select the axes orientation of the volume and to request a view of values on a selected plane. The warehouse computational objects are **VorticityVector**s. Each vector is individually inspectable. In this view, the user has requested that vorticity magnitudes for plane 17 be presented as a contour plot. XY plots have been generated in response to user queries about the vorticity magnitude at a given x (column shown in red) or y value (row marked by blue line) in that plane. The inspection box at the left shows the actual data values of the object (vector) closest to the user selected position (marked by the black dot at the center).

Distributed Graphics Objects

The visualization classes we have been describing constitute a group of *informational* rather than *representational objects*. It may appear surprising that we do not include geometric structures as objects. We have not fashioned classes of objects based on types of spatial behaviors (such as spheres, polygons, and surfaces). Rather, we treat spatial presentations (surfaces, planes, volumes, or contours) as *consequences* of querying and manipulating computational objects. The computational objects we define are based on the conceptual needs of the scientific model the user is investigating with SCENE. SCENE is, after all, an environment for numerical experimentation with simulated physical phenomena and its visualization needs are rooted in its computational structure. The typical computational structure of a scientific model involves a two- or three-dimensional mesh at one or more time steps. The computational objects to be visualized are the data values that have been computed at each node in the mesh. The information to be visualized is self-organizing; it is inherently spatial (and may be spatio-temporal). The mesh itself provides the structure for representing the values at its nodes as a surface, a contour on a plane, or a volume. Figure 8.5 illustrates this concept using a 5 by 4 by 3 mesh. Each 5 by 4 section represents a plane of objects. The three planes are stacked front to back. The object at each mode of the mesh is a **VorticityVector**.

The data management strategy we have developed for such computational models has been described in Walther [1991]. Briefly, the strategy

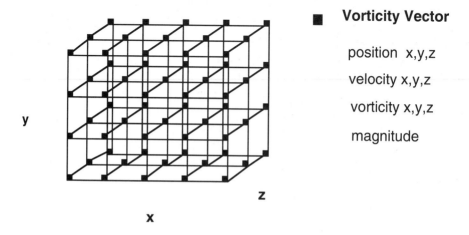

■ Vorticity Vector

position x,y,z

velocity x,y,z

vorticity x,y,z

magnitude

y

z

x

Figure 8.5: Diagram of a volume of objects

rests on constructing hashing maps to a data set of objects (the computed values at each mesh point). The maps are based on the unique spatio-temporal coordinates of each object. The information structures (and, therefore, the primary graphic structures) are planes, volumes, and time series. A plane is a two-dimensional array of objects; a volume is an array of planes; a time series is an array of volumes. The indices of the arrays are mapped to the mesh values of the computation along the relevant axis. *The computational model is, effectively, a numerical object-oriented database.* The computational mesh is the hashing key to the objects. All queries about the data are resolved into queries about the maps that represent the mesh. All visualizations are constructions of graphic displayable entities (such as polygons, triangles, and contours) from selected values of the computation objects in relationships defined by their mesh positions.

Some excerpts from the back-end code in C that supports a warehouse are useful to illustrate how this strategy is implemented. The basic components of every warehouse are:

1. The *key* comprising the spatio-temporal coordinate unique to each object. The key can be a two-dimensional, three-dimensional, or four-dimensional coordinate. The keys are datatyped as follows:

```
typedef struct {float x,y} 2dPoint;
typedef struct {float x,y,z} 3dPoint;
typedef struct {float x,y,z,t} 4dPoint;
```

2. The *maps* incorporating the mesh for two, three, and four dimensions. To manage a spatio-temporal data set, we need data structures for planes, volumes, and time series. These data structures can be dimensioned for the maximum expected size. We are using a mesh size of 100 by 100 by 100 by 100 as our current maximum.
A *plane map* is defined as

```
typedef struct {int plane[100][100];} XYmap;
```

A *volume map* is defined as

```
typedef struct {XYmap volume[100];} VolumeMap;
```

A *time series* is defined as

```
typedef struct {VolumeMap timeslices[100];}
    TimeSeries;
```

These data structures are the same for any type of computational object. The data structure for any specific computational object is defined by the user. The only requirement is that the definition include a field named *position* and that field be typed using one of the above defined keys. Otherwise, the object can have any number of fields of any type.

3.   User-defined *computation object.*

For this example, let us define an object as:

```
typedef struct {3dPoint position,velocity,vorticity;
                float magnitude;} VorticityVector;
```

Let us also declare a storage element for these objects, defined as

```
VorticityVector *dataVectors[1000000];
```

The data itself can be dynamically organized into the database format while it is computing, or it can be collected and organized from a file or files for postprocessing. As the raw data is accessed, each set of values for a mesh-point (in this case, a "record" is 10 floating point values in sequence of position, velocity, vorticity, and magnitude) is organized into a **VorticityVector** object and is placed in its storage array in the order in which it is encountered. This means that the data objects can occur in any order provided that the internal order of the elements of each object is preserved. Thus, data can be accepted from a randomly accessed set of inputs. Input can come from precomputed files, from distributed sensors, or from segments of models computing concurrently. If the mesh indices are given along with the actual data values for the spatial coordinates, the steps that identify the positional mesh are not needed. However, for nonCartesian coordinate systems, we require the indices to be given as well as the positions.

For Cartesian coordinate data, as the data is "typed" into objects, the positional mesh is identified by making collections of the coordinates for each dimension. In this example, since the position coordinate is a **3dPoint**, we would make an *x* collection, a *y* collection, and a *z* collection. The collecting routines are written to filter out duplicates so that by the time the datatyping has been completed, we have captured the unique values in each dimension. Sorting these sets of unique coordinates recaptures the gridding for each dimension of the computation. The maps are then constructed by inspecting each data object to identify for each position coordinate the *ordinal number of the value* in the grid for each dimension that matches the *value* of the position coordinate of each dimension. The code for setting up a **VolumeMap** follows.

```
organizeVolumeMap(n)
int n;                       /* total number of objects */
{ int i, xindex, yindex, zindex;
  VorticityVector *V;
  for(i = 0; i < n; i++) {
    V = dataVectors[i];
    xindex=findIndex(V->position.x,xgrid,xgridsize);
```

```
yindex=findIndex(V->position.y,ygrid,ygridsize);
zindex=findIndex(V->position.z,zgrid,zgridsize);
volume[zindex].plane[yindex][xindex] = i;  }
   return;  }
```

Note that the value i in the map is the *index* of the object in the object array. The maps reference objects by their storage locations so that the actual data objects can be physically located anywhere in a distributed system. (The maps are declared as "globals" and can be queried by any function). The **findIndex** function searches the grid (ordered set of grid values) supplied as an argument to find the value in that set that matches the position value given as an argument. It returns the index of the matched value. The matched indices are the position key of the object in the map. These searches can be done concurrently. In fact, the entire mapping process can be parallelized easily since the mapping of each object is "encapsulated" and does not depend on the mapping of any other object.

Figure 8.6 illustrates a simple hashing map. The table "OBJECTS IN ARRAY" represents an array of six data objects and shows the x and y coordinates of the objects at each index in the array. The 5 by 4 mesh at the left represents a map of a plane. The columns labeled "xorder" and "yorder" represent the ordered sets of values of the x and y grids. The plane map is set up by finding the ordinal of the coordinates of the data object in their respective grids and using those ordinal numbers as the row and column designation in the matrix. Thus, the data object at array[1], whose x coordinate (2.0) matches the fourth value in xorder (at x4) and whose y coordinate (1.2) matches the first value in yorder (y1), is mapped into the plane map at row 1 (y1) column 4 (x4).

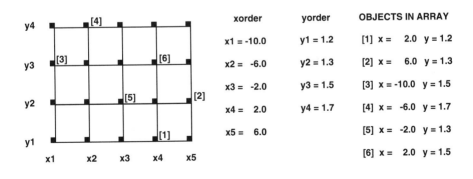

	xorder	yorder	OBJECTS IN ARRAY
	x1 = -10.0	y1 = 1.2	[1] x = 2.0 y = 1.2
	x2 = -6.0	y2 = 1.3	[2] x = 6.0 y = 1.3
	x3 = -2.0	y3 = 1.5	[3] x = -10.0 y = 1.5
	x4 = 2.0	y4 = 1.7	[4] x = -6.0 y = 1.7
	x5 = 6.0		[5] x = -2.0 y = 1.3
			[6] x = 2.0 y = 1.5

A matrix 4 rows by 5 columns

Figure 8.6: Hashing map of a plane of objects

As a hashing table, the maps resolve queries about a data object to one reference. In Color Plate 6, the user, wishing to inspect a computation object, has indicated a place on a contour plot. Clicking the mouse at that display location causes the visualization tool (running in Smalltalk) to decode the screen coordinates into data coordinates by procedures explained in the prior sections. The data coordinates are matched against the grid sets to determine the ordinal values (the Smalltalk tool maintains its own copies of the grids for local matching), and that information is passed to the back-end warehouse with a request that the complete information present in the data base for that coordinate equivalent be returned for displaying. Retrieving the object at that coordinate is accomplished by this type of code:

```
usertype *findObject(x,y,z)
int x,y,z;
{   index = volume[z].plane[y][x];
    object = dataVectors[index];
    return(object);} /* return pointer to object */
```

An important benefit of this strategy for graphic manipulations is that one search procedure services contour plots, surface plots, and two-dimensional vector plots of any selected plane for any selected parameter. Graphical objects, such as polygons, triangles, and meshlines (for wireframes), and simulated physical objects, such as pathlines, streamlines, and streaklines, can be constructed out of simple queries to the maps. For example, the following code segment accesses all objects on a plane p by rows:

```
for(r = 0; r < rowsize; r++) {
    for(c = 0; c < column; c++) {
        object = findObject(c,r,p)}};
```

Once a set of objects is retrieved, specialized routines operate on appropriate fields in the objects to produce the requested visual and informational effect. Color Plate 7 shows a sample of supported graphical queries on a warehouse storing a 32 by 32 by 32 volume of **VorticityVectors**. First, the user has selected the option to structure the volume so that the y-axis represents the depth dimension. At the top right, after restructuring the map, **vorticitytool** has produced a contour plot of the data on plane 15 according to the value of the vorticity magnitude of each vector in the plane. The contour option extracts the data for that representation and opens a **surface-tool** on that same data (upper left). The original **vorticitytool** (upper right) is then asked to spawn a vector view of plane 15 (although it could have been of any plane). Another **vorticitytool** opens on the warehouse and uses the vorticities of each object in the plane to represent vector arrows. Finally, the user selects a vector to inspect by clicking the mouse at a displayed arrow.

The warehouse responds by finding the requested object and sending it back to the tool where it is presented as a Smalltalk inspection view on an object.

A library of service routines has been developed to access the mesh, retrieve object values, and constitute *intermediate* computational or geometric objects. Polygons are established by accessing objects at adjacent mesh columns for every two rows. Triangles are established by bisecting polygons. The streamlines shown in Figure 8.3 require accessing values from objects at the four corners of a 2 by 2 mesh region (in a plane) that encloses an interpolated point. Interpolation of streamlines in a volume requires accessing values from objects that are at the eight corners of a cube defined by adjacent rows and columns at two adjacent planes.

Future Work

SCENE tends to add to its repertoire as users express needs. Therefore, the automatic generation of code to change and/or add remote objects, remote object fields, and remote object services is a high priority in our continuing work. Currently, we are implementing procedures whereby a scientific object defined in Smalltalk by the user (using the Smalltalk compiler) can write a C version of itself as a *struct* or can change a struct that has already been defined in back-end source code. The C equivalent object will update a "dictionary," which will be relinked to the back-end libraries of support services. Those libraries are being generalized to support indirect referencing of objects in data structures and in function calls. In this manner, newly defined objects will be able to tap the services of existing back-end utilities. Such a procedure is needed most typically when a user wishes to add a field to an existing object and have that field be selectable by a back-end graphics routine such as contour plotting.

The ability to add or change methods on the back end by defining them in Smalltalk is also under development and is already in place in one of SCENE's computational tools, a differential equation solver. Extensions to this capability will help fulfill the goal of *computational steering*, the ability of the user to alter the model (by altering its specification on the front end) and to have those changes automatically incorporated in "back-end" behavior and reflected in the visualization they return to the front end. As the repertoire of back-end services is implemented on a variety of parallel facilities, we expect to make the computational objects "intelligent" enough to request services from the type of remote system best suited to the operation requested.

Finally, many more graphics features will be added to SCENE. As we integrate faster graphic systems into front-end service, we intend to include user primitives to support z buffering, lighting, and shading of three-dimensional surfaces. We are experimenting with a Macintosh IIfx™ to which a Tektronix M88000-based graphics processing system has been added. Image processing and pattern recognition capabilities will also be included as we develop parallelized algorithms to support the compute-intensive aspects of those functions. In any case, we will continue to operate using the object-oriented paradigm.

References

Peskin, Richard L., Sandra S. Walther, and Andy Froncioni [1989]. "Smalltalk-The Next Generation Scientific Computing Interface?" *Mathematics and Computers in Simulation,* October, 1989.

Walther, Sandra S. [1987]. "Strategies for Interactive Graphing of Numeric Results," *Proceedings*, 1987 International Symposium on AI, Expert Systems, and Languages in Modelling and Simulation (IMACS), Barcelona, Spain, North-Holland.

Walther, Sandra S. and Richard L. Peskin [1989]. "Strategies for Scientific Prototyping in Smalltalk," *Proceedings,* Object-Oriented Programming: Systems, Languages, and Applications, New Orleans, ACM, 1989.

Walther, Sandra S. and Richard L. Peskin [1991]. "Object Oriented Visualization of Scientific Data, " *Journal of Visual Languages and Computing,* Vol. 2, 1991, pp. 43-56.

Chapter 9

Ida: An Interactive Data Display System

Robert L. Young

Ida (Young [1987], Smith [1987]) is a class library providing a substrate for building interactive, 2D-graphics, application interfaces. It supports the display and manipulation of numeric data (as opposed to geometric models). Figure 9.1 is a typical Ida display. An object-oriented architecture has proven especially useful for Ida. As Ida's architecture is described, four important contributions will become apparent.

First, object taxonomies very naturally meet the need to organize and describe the basic types of elements in the drawing model. These model classes explicitly declare their attributes and operations, and the intrinsic relationships between different elements of the drawing model exploit inheritance quite profitably.

The second contribution is support for performing graphics operations. In Ida's drawing model, operations are realized as methods defined in appropriate classes. These operations are defined through inheritance for all model classes. Performing an operation on a display element is done by sending a message to that element. No knowledge of the identity of the recipient is needed. This polymorphism inherent in object-oriented programming provides both clarity and flexibility; the message identifies the abstract operation, yet each graphic entity can interpret the operation appropriately.

The third contribution is the simplicity of extending operations on individual elements to operations on aggregates. A display instance has an *orthogonal* (to the taxonomic) organization describing its part-whole com-

Without the vision and indefatigable efforts of Eric Schoen and Reid Smith, neither HyperClass nor Ida would exist.

position. For example, the presentation in Figure 9.1 is divided into the
x-axis labels, the *y*-axis labels, the data plotting area, and a message area.
The data plotting area, in turn, utilizes other parts that can produce the data
curve from the sets of data points. In Ida's model, each of these components
is an instance of a particular class of the model. Since model operations are

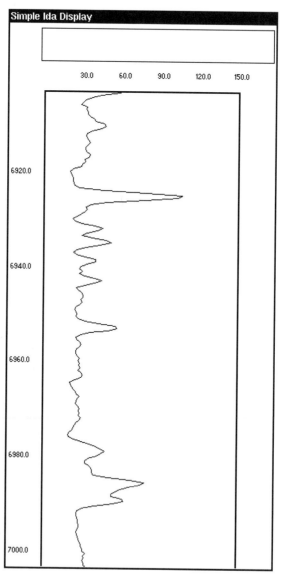

Figure 9.1: A simple Ida display

realized as messages, forwarding messages along the part-whole hierarchy effects execution of the operation for the entire complex. For example, drawing this presentation is done by the following event sequence: (1) The presentation instance is sent a **Draw** message; (2) it draws the presentation border and title, and then forwards the message to each of its sub-parts; (3) the axes labels and message area draw themselves directly, but the data plot requests its constituent elements to draw themselves. This sort of message passing among objects representing graphic components is a very straight-forward way to carry out graphic operations on complex entities.

The fourth contribution of an object-oriented graphics architecture is support for a highly declarative model supporting late binding of model object attributes. In Ida, the act of drawing a curve representing some data points will be controlled by that curve's current graphic attributes. Line width and pattern, point sampling interval, and the particular drawing operation are all curve attributes. When a curve object responds to a **Draw** message, it performs its drawing operation as specified by the current values of its attributes. Late binding of model attributes makes possible a wide spectrum of interactive alterations.

In addition to the modeling power of its object-oriented architecture, Ida illustrates how an object-oriented architecture can enhance reusability. Ida has been used to develop a wide diversity of interfaces. Although some of these applications were developed using only the basic model, many exten-sions to the model have been made by users other than the developer. The success and relative ease of making extensions attests to the enhanced reusability of a good object model.

Ida's development itself also illustrates reuse. Ida is implemented within HyperClass®, a LISP-based object-oriented framework composed of Class®, an object representation layer, and MetaClass®, a class library providing a user interface substrate described in Smith [1986, 1987].[1] Ida is a major extension to MetaClass. The ease with which relevant parts of MetaClass were reused further illustrates the potential longer-term payoff of well-designed object-oriented architectures.

In the next section, we discuss the data display problems that Ida addresses. Next, we introduce the LISP-based object-oriented environment in which Ida was constructed. The following two sections present Ida's drawing model: the static part of this model, including the important classes developed and their taxonomic organization, as well as the part-whole aggregation of instances underlying an actual display. Then we present the methods that Ida uses for performing the drawing model's graphic opera-tions, and describe the responses of different classes of objects to these basic messages. We also show how the part-whole structure provides the essential communication path for message passing. Next, we take a more careful look at the HyperClass environment and Ida's relationship to it. We discuss reuse of previously existing components, and how Ida's extensions fit into that existing architecture. We then survey Ida's development history and give some examples illustrating its diverse use. Finally, we return to the discussion of the impact of an object-oriented architecture on Ida.

The Data Display Problem

Ida was motivated by the need to display numeric data in easily customized formats, both for standalone examination and as part of the interfaces for interactive applications. Data sets that are a function of one variable are especially common in some of Schlumberger's Oilfield Services businesses, where Ida was developed. These data sets are well logs, which are collections of measurements made at depth or time intervals. Well logs are made and used in oil exploration and production. These data are measured by instruments called logging tools. Logs are made by lowering logging tools into a borehole and recording measurements made by the tools as they are raised to the surface. Logging tools measure a variety of petrophysical properties (for example, the resistivity of the rock surrounding the borehole). The resulting logs are sequences of values indexed by depth or time. Examination of original and computed logs help users infer geological properties of the formation in which the logs were made. Analysis of the data may involve viewing the data on different scales, correlating data from different logs (made by different instruments), and rapidly moving between different intervals of the data. Logs frequently contain tens of thousands of readings.

Figure 9.2 shows an example of an Ida display containing a small group of well logs. The presentation includes several plots based on the same two logs, both of which are functions of depth. One log, *GR*, measures naturally occurring gamma radiation. The other log, *RHOB*, measures bulk density. Both logs are plotted in summary form over the entire measured interval in plot area 10. (Referenced plot areas in the figure have identifying numbers circled in one of their right interior corners.) The logs span the interval 6254 through 7107 feet. *GR* is plotted as the lighter curve, and *RHOB* as the darker curve. The black rectangle in plot area 10 highlights a sub-interval of the logs (6900-7000 feet) plotted elsewhere in the presentation. Plot areas 6, 3, and 14 present different views of this sub-interval. Plot area 6 contains an

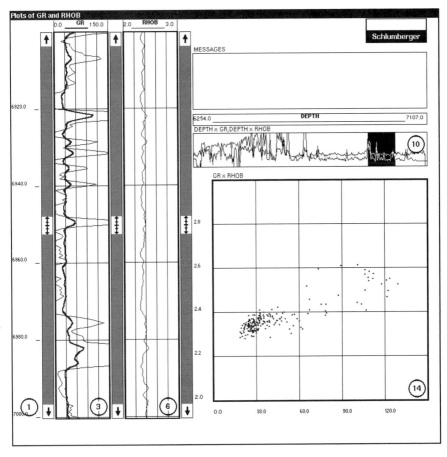

Figure 9.2: A typical well log display

expanded view of the *RHOB* log, with an *x* scale of two to three grams per cubic centimeter. Plot area 3 contains two differently scaled versions of the *GR* log over the same sub-interval. The darker curve is plotted with an *x* scale of 0 to 150 API, while the lighter one emphasizes curve character more by reducing the *x* scale to 25 to 50 API. Plot area 1 contains the *y*-axis depth values for both plot areas 3 and 6. The scatter plot in area 14 is a crossplot of the two logs over the sub-interval. Each plotted point corresponds to the values of the two logs at some common depth. These logs have been recorded at 0.5-foot intervals, so the 100-foot sub-interval yields 200 points to plot. The *GR* value is indicated by the *x* coordinate and the *RHOB* value by the *y* coordinate.

A standalone (not integrated into an application interface) Ida presentation provides a wide range of interaction functionality for the viewer. Where it makes sense, plot areas are active (pickable) and respond to mouse buttoning by presenting the user with a menu of possible actions. These actions include rescaling either axis of any contained plot, adding new plots, altering the visibility for the entire plot area (or for an individual plot drawn in that plot area), and soliciting a description of the identity and current state of everything in the plot area.

Scrolling is essential for interactively examining well logs. Logs have too much data to view meaningfully in their entirety, and there are no standard patterns of sub-interval viewing that would obviate the user's need to arbitrarily navigate through the data. Consequently, Ida supports a variety of scrolling capabilities. Figure 9.2 contains the two interaction display components by which a user can invoke a variety of scrolling actions. Ida's scrolling capabilities address two distinct needs. The first need is to quickly display "local data" (data adjacent to that already being viewed), and the second is to display any arbitrary portion of data. In both cases, the user is able to request these actions by interacting with the scrolling control mechanisms.

In Ida, scrolling to view local data is called immediate scrolling. Each of the dark vertical bars adjacent to plot areas 3 and 6 in the figure is an immediate scroll bar. If an immediate scroll bar is moused, the affected plot areas will begin scrolling immediately. The immediate scroll bar to the left of plot area 3 is declared to control plot areas 1 and 3. Several variants of immediate scrolling are provided. The portion of the immediate scroll bar moused determines which response the user gets. The available responses are: drag scrolling, where the data display scrolls continuously at the speed the cursor (mouse) is moving; variable speed scrolling, where the data display scrolls continuously at at a speed that varies with the location of the cursor; and jump scrolling, where the data display is instantly updated to show the immediately adjacent segment of data.

Elevator scrolling provides a mechanism to move to any arbitrary segment of the data. In the figure, elevator scrolling is available in plot area 10. The inverted area, as mentioned above, indicates the depth interval plotted in areas 1, 3, 6, and 14. Mousing area 10 allows the user to select a new sub-interval by moving the "elevator" in either direction. Summary logs are present in area 10 to make it easier to find the desired sub-interval of data. Once the new interval has been selected, the displays controlled by this scroll elevator are redrawn accordingly. Plot areas 1, 3, and 6 are updated to show the new sub-interval, and the crossplot in area 14 is redrawn based upon it.

In summary, Ida was developed to provide a tool for building data plots. Well logs, large sets of data that are recorded as a function of depth or time, are primary sources of the data that must be plotted. The data plots can stand alone, but can also be used as part of an interactive application's interface. The nature of well logs and their use mandated that easy ways to move around quickly in the data sets be developed. Ida's several scrolling schemes are a response to this need.

Ida's Implementation Environment

Ida was designed to run on conventional workstations without special graphics hardware. It was originally developed for black-and-white monitors, but support for color has been added. This class of machine was targeted because it was expected to be widely available among potential users. These workstations have enough CPU power and memory to support LISP; however, their graphics speed is not great enough that "brute force" techniques can be used while maintaining reasonable interactive performance.

Ida is written entirely in Common LISP (Steele [1990]) and was developed as an extension to HyperClass, a LISP-based, object-oriented framework. HyperClass includes three major software layers. At the lowest level is the Generic Window System (Schoen [1989]), a portable window interface for Common LISP programs. It provides windows, active regions within windows, text display, basic graphics, menus, and a graphics package. Ida's color version uses tools that extend Generic Windows to allow a color window to be treated as though it has a set of independent layers, each with its own color map (Schoen [1990]).

The second layer in HyperClass is Class, an object-representation system. Class provides a very flexible object model, taking advantage of LISP to provide late bindings for slot interpretation and inheritance. Class's multiple inheritance taxonomies can be changed dynamically. Class does not make sharp distinctions among the uses of an object's slots. Class and instance variables are not distinguished, and even determining if a slot is to be interpreted as a method is done dynamically. (A method is a slot with a LISP datatype and a value that is a LISP function.) There is also little distinction between classes and instances other than the restriction that instances may not be instantiated. One Class facility that is quite important in Ida is the existence of *Facets* as annotations on slots. They are much like property lists that can be attached to slots.

MetaClass is the third layer in HyperClass. It a class library providing a general and extensible substrate for interface design. It supports the construction of customized interfaces, which are specializations of its **Editor** class. MetaClass's notion of "editing" is quite broad, encompassing traditional text editing, browsing, program development, debugging, and end-user interaction. MetaClass's class for modeling workstation windows is **Editor Window**. We will discuss the MetaClass model (and how Ida made use of it) later in the chapter.

Static Drawing Model

In presenting Ida's drawing model, we will use standard graphics terminology, as used by Foley et al. [1990], where possible. In particular, a "real" picture exists in some arbitrary world coordinates. It is transformed into screen coordinates to be realized as pixels on a workstation screen. A clipping region in world coordinates delimits the portion of the picture to be drawn at any time. A region on the workstation screen that allows viewing a portion of the picture is a viewport. In graphics parlance, one meaning of a window is the portion of the picture in world coordinates that is projected into the viewport. However, we will not adopt the term window. Because "window" is also the term used for the entities created and managed by workstation window-management systems (such as NeWS, described in Sun [1987], or the X Window System, discussed by Scheifler [1988]), overloading the term would be confusing. Instead, we will use the term *viewed region* for the portion of the picture visible in the viewport and use window in the context of a window-management system.

We begin this section by introducing the entire drawing model vocabulary, since it is nearly impossible to discuss the model's elements in isolation. After this introduction, we describe the most important classes in detail.

Ida's drawing model is based on the following classes:

1. **Ida Window**—the class representing workstation windows for Ida displays.
2. **Data Display**—the basic display and interaction class, each instance of which possesses a viewport within the display window.
3. **Assembly**—a coordinated, arbitrarily large set of *Data Displays.*
4. **Presentation**—a set of independent *Assemblies* collected for dis-

play in a single window.

5. **Data Source**—the class from which all drawing objects are descended.

6. **Scale**—a class that represents a one-dimensional coordinate transformation used by data sources.

Assemblies provide the primary grouping mechanism for display elements. Each assembly defines a collection of elements for a display that is self-contained and independently usable. In a very simple case, an assembly might consist of nothing more than plot areas for data and axes. However, an assembly can become quite complex, involving numerous interrelated display elements. The examples in Figures 9.1 and 9.2 are each single assemblies. *Presentations* are collections of separately defined assemblies. Each presentation has a single window, and its component assemblies are all displayed together in that window. Each example in these figures is a single presentation, containing the single assembly mentioned above, and displayed in a single workstation window. **Presentation** and **Assembly** are each descendants of the MetaClass class **Editor**, and **Ida Window** is a descendant of the MetaClass class **Editor Window**. Further discussion of these relationships with the MetaClass model will be discussed later in the chapter.

The *data display* is the most complex entity in Ida's drawing model. A data display provides a viewport onto a stack of underlying pictures, drawn in screen coordinates on the data display's canvases. The pictures are translated and combined into a single image in the viewport. The intuitive image of a data display is a stack of transparencies viewed through a (possibly) smaller rectangular hole. The transparencies can be shifted or removed individually. An assembly is a spatially arranged collection of data display viewports. Figure 9.3 shows the collection of viewports for the assembly from Figure 9.2. Data displays are used for both dynamic display areas (such as plots and axis labels) and constant areas (such as titles), and their viewports may or may not be active regions. All permanent drawing is done onto data displays' canvases.

The descendants of the class **Data Source** are entities that draw or otherwise depict data (for example, printing text is also a way to depict data). Any number of data sources can be associated with each canvas of a data display's stack of canvases. These data sources always do their drawing onto their designated canvas. A typical Ida well log data display would have a stack of three canvases. One canvas is drawn onto by a data source that draws one data curve. The second canvas is like the first but is drawn onto by a distinct data source that produces a second curve. The third canvas has the grid, which is drawn by two data sources, one that draws vertical lines and

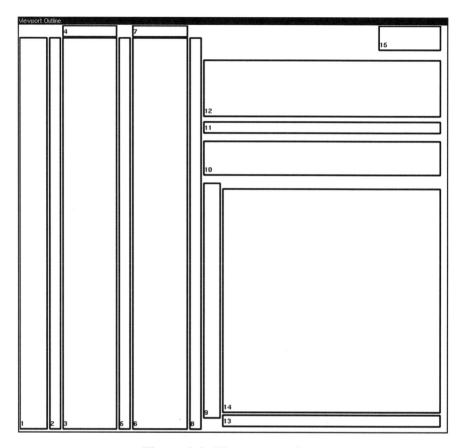

Figure 9.3: Viewport outlines

one that draws horizontal lines.

When transformations from world coordinates to screen coordinates are needed, a data source will have one or more scales associated with it. Each scale encodes the transformation from world to screen coordinates for a single dimension. (These transformations are restricted to scaling and translation.) A data source for a typical curve (such as the one drawing the curve in plot area 6 of Figure 9.2) has two world dimensions and uses two scales to represent its needed transformations to screen coordinates.

The principle reason for representing transformations with scale objects is to make the transformation easily referenceable. Ida displays frequently include multiple plots, drawn in different data displays but with a common world dimension such as depth. When transformation synchronization is required among these plots, it can be achieved by data sources using shared scales. Sharing the same scale instance means that it is impossible for the two to have different coordinate transformations.

Data Displays

Instances of the **Data Display** class underlie all display and interaction regions in an instance of an Ida **Assembly**. Some attributes are specified once for the data display and apply to its entire stack of canvases. These include:
1. A viewport within the assembly.
2. Buffer size factors (given as x and y values).
3. Border style.
4. Title and title location.

The viewport provides the viewing region for the data display, and no two data displays' viewports can overlap. (Overlapping viewports would require some kind of occlusion policy, which seems inappropriate for data plots.) The same viewport is used for the entire stack of canvases belonging to a single data display. Data display canvases have Pixmaps onto which drawing is done. Because the picture produced in the viewport is the result of combining the stack of canvases, the canvas Pixmaps are all the same size, and this size should be at least as big as their viewport. However, the size can be any real factor larger in either dimension. These are the x and y buffer size factors. For example, a factor of 3.0 for the y dimension creates a buffer three times higher than the viewport, thus providing enough already drawn (but not visible) display in screen coordinates to fill the viewport two additional times. This buffering provides support for immediate scrolling. The viewport can have a border and can have a title. Plot area 14 in Figure 9.2 has both a border and a title (*GRxRHOB* located at the top), while plot area 1 (with depth labels) has neither. The default title is a method that constructs the title from the data display's constituents.

Other data display attributes have independent values for every canvas of the data display. Some of these are:
1. A Pixmap stream for I/O.
2. A list of data sources using the canvas as a destination.
3. A viewing translation to map the viewed region to the viewport.
4. Current canvas visibility.
5. Current canvas scrollability.

Each canvas has its own Pixmap stream (as discussed above) that is completely distinct from all other canvases' streams. Each canvas explicitly identifies the data sources for which it is the destination. These data sources only draw onto that canvas. Any viewport-sized subregion of a canvas can become its viewed region. The viewed region typically changes as a consequence of scrolling. Hence, the appropriate viewing translation must be maintained for each individual canvas. (The question of how the viewed region changes, and how it can move "off" of a canvas is discussed later in the chapter.) Each canvas specifies its current visibility. When a data display's viewport image is composed, only canvases that are currently visible participate. (This image composition is also discussed later in the chapter.) Finally, each canvas has its own current scrollability. Immediate scrolling uniformly varies the viewing translations of all a data display's scrollable canvases while leaving those of its unscrollable canvases unchanged. In this way, one canvas's data sources can be "slid" over another's.

Each canvas of a data display is represented by a unique object instance. A data display always has one primary canvas, and that primary canvas is referenced directly by the assembly. All additional secondary canvases are referenced by the primary canvas rather than directly by the assembly, creating a part-whole structure as shown in Figure 9.4. The figure shows the part-whole structure of an assembly with two data displays; one displays a simple textual copyright notice, and the other has three layers for data plots. **CR-Log-Assembly-100** is an Assembly instance. Its two data displays are **DataDisplay-101** and **Text-DataDisplay-104**, each of which is a primary canvas. **DataDisplay-101** has two secondary canvases, **BackGround-Data-Display-102** and **Grid-DataDisplay-103**. The ordering of the two secondary canvases is significant.

We will continue, using the example in Figure 9.4, to illustrate important slots and values. Listing 9.1 shows the code of **CR-Log-Assembly-100** and its **DataDisplay-101** slot. The assembly has two slots, one for each of its data displays. The slots' values are the primary data display object instances.

DataDisplay-101 contains three groups of information, as shown in

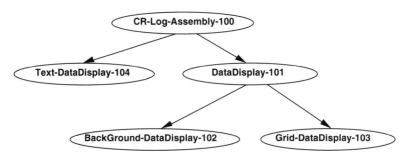

Figure 9.4: A part-whole hierarchy

```
CR-Log-Assembly-100
   Copyright-Display: Text-DataDisplay-104
   Plot-Display:  DataDisplay-101

DataDisplay-101
    ;; entire data display information
   viewport: window-region[origin: (50, 75);
            width: 100; height: 200]
   border: 2
   title-location: TOP
   title: default-method-to-compute-title-string
   x-buffer-factor: 1.0
   y-buffer-factor: 3.0

    ;; primary data display information
   background-plot:  BackGround-DataDisplay-102
   grid-plot:  Grid-DataDisplay-103

    ;; private data display information
   visible:  T
   scrollable:  T
   io-stream:  io-stream-for-DataDisplay-101
```

Listing 9.1

Listing 9.1. The first group of slots applies to the data display as a whole. This group includes the data display's viewport within the window, specification of a two-pixel border around this viewport, specification that there should be a title displayed at the top of the viewport region, and that the actual title string will be that computed by a default method. The canvases are all three times bigger in their y dimension than the viewport's height and equal in their x dimensions to its width. Since the viewport is 100 pixels wide by 200 pixels high (from the viewport window-region), the canvases will all be 100 pixels wide and 600 pixels high.

The second group of slots has information found only on a primary data display instance. It specifies the secondary canvasses. Here, **BackGround-DataDisplay-102** and **Grid-DataDisplay-103** are identified. The third group of slots is found on every data display. It includes the specifications that the canvas is both visible and scrollable. It also has a pointer to the actual Pixmap-stream used for drawing and displaying the canvas of **DataDisplay-101**.

As the above example illustrates, Ida represents a part-whole link with a slot in the whole, containing a pointer to the object instance, which is the part. Ida frequently supports arbitrary-sized part sets. Here, both the number of data displays an assembly may have and the number of canvases a data display may have are unlimited. Identification of the relevant slots and ordering information among them are both represented as slot annotations (as described earlier in the chapter). A particular facet—*Role*—is reserved to represent the kind of relationship a slot embodies. The slots of an object may be interpreted by using their Role facet, requiring no a priori knowledge of either the number of slots or their names. That is, there are methods that look at all of an object's slots and filter out all those that do not have a specific Role facet value. Another facet provides ordering information. This representational scheme is very flexible and is used many times in Ida, providing another form of late binding for model attributes.

In summary, Ida's model for data displays grew from the need to provide performant immediate scrolling, curve sliding, and visibility toggling, while keeping the model intuitive for users. Use of multiple canvases, each the destination for distinct plots and each of which can be shifted with respect to the others, addresses these requirements. Precedents for features of this model can be found in both hardware and software. Graphics hardware is commonly used to provide multiple canvases underlying a single viewport. Manipulation of video look-up tables for displays with multiple bits per pixel (Foley et al. [1990]) can provide image combination or rapid image exchange (double buffering). NeWS implements some similar constructs in software. Ida's drawing model incorporates these features in a uniform, object-oriented representation creating flexibility and richness that have proven extremely powerful.

Data Sources and Scales

A *data source* is a graphic object representing some "virtual plot" in its own world coordinates. Upon request, a data source will realize some portion of this virtual plot as an image on its destination data display canvas. The portion realized is determined by the data source's current world-clipping region. The image produced is determined by the current values of the data source's graphic attributes and by the current transformations from world to screen coordinates. The descendants of the class **Data Source** represent the known categories of "plots."

Data sources can vary widely in their attributes, so we will consider two specific data sources as illustrative: the **Simple Annotation** and the **Single**

Index Curve. They are quite different and suggest the range of possibilities that Ida's drawing model includes.

The **Simple Annotation** is a data source that only displays a single textual string. Its attributes include:

1. The text to display.
2. The font to use.
3. Current data source visibility.
4. Destination data display canvas.

The text will be displayed on the destination canvas using the specified font, whenever the data source is visible.

Single Index Curve is the specialization of a data source that displays data that is a function of one variable—the Index. The well log curves previously discussed are drawn by Single Index Curves. A Single Index Curve has the following attributes:

1. The data points (in world coordinates).
2. Data sampling interval.
3. Line width and pattern.
4. Drawing operation.
5. Data point marking symbol.
6. Data point coordinates to display.
7. Current data source visibility.
8. Destination data display canvas.

The data points are conceptually a table with one column of index values and one column of corresponding function values. For a well log where the index is depth, the log values at the those depths define the function. The data sampling interval specifies how frequently to sample the data for plotting. A value of one uses every point while a value of five uses every fifth point. The line description details the kind of curve, if any, to be drawn through the plotted points. If a line is being drawn through the points, it will have the thickness and pattern (for example, dashing) indicated. The drawing will be applied to its canvas using the indicated drawing operation (such as Paint or Invert). The plotted data points themselves can be marked with a point marking symbol. Valid alternative combinations include: a curve with its points marked with the marking symbol, a curve without marking symbols, and no curve with marking symbols (yielding a point plot). Each data point considered may be further annotated with some of its world coordinates. Thus, in situations where exact values are needed, the coordinates can become part of the basic plot. As with data displays, any data source may become invisible. When invisible, a data source is not asked to render itself. Finally, all data sources have a unique data display canvas onto which they draw their images. (That canvas could also be the destination for any number of other data sources.)

We will continue with the example in Figure 9.4, adding the data source information shown in Listing 9.2. Each of **Text-DataDisplay-104** and **DataDisplay-101** has a data source that draws onto its canvas. **Text-Data-Display-104** has an instance of **Simple Annotation** that displays a copyright notice. **Simple-Annotation-151** is currently displaying its textual copyright notice on the canvas of its destination data display.

DataDisplay-101 has an instance of **Single Index Curve** that plots a well log. **Single-Index-Curve-200** is currently visible and will render itself on its destination canvas. It does so using all the data points, painting a solid line two pixels wide between them. The data points are not marked, but they are annotated with their actual depth (y world coordinate) value.

In addition to graphic attributes, many data sources require transformations from world to screen coordinates. These transformations are represented by **Scale** instances attached to the data sources that use them. A Simple Annotation has no scales, because Ida's drawing model does not include scalable text. However, a Single Index Curve has two scales: an x and a y. **Single-Index-Curve-200** has references to two scale instances, **Y-Scale-202** and **X-Scale-201**. In addition to recording the current transforma-

```
Simple-Annotation-151
   text:  "Copyright Schlumberger, Ltd."
   font:  helvetica-bold-10
   visible:  T
   destination-canvas:  Text-DataDisplay-104

Single-Index-Curve-200
   y-data-array:  depth-values-array
   x-data-array:  log-values-array
   y-scale:  Y-Scale-202
   x-scale:  X-Scale-201
   data-sampling-interval:  1
   line-width:  2
   line-pattern:  solid
   drawing-operation:  paint
   data-point-marking-symbol:  NIL
   data-point-coordinates-to-display:  [Y]
   visible:  T
   destination-canvas:  DataDisplay-101
```

Listing 9.2

tion from world to screen coordinates for the relevant dimension, a scale also records the current world coordinate clipping interval for the same dimension. When an instance of Single Index Curve is asked to render its image (via a **Draw** message, discussed later in the chapter), it responds by producing the portion of that image on its current clipping region in its destination data display canvas, using the current values of its graphic attributes and according to the current coordinate transformations. Because **Single Index Curve** is a function of its index, it may use the current clipping region to draw only the interval of the virtual plot actually needed without any unnecessary work. For example, if the y dimension of a Single Index Curve is depth, and the data spans the interval 0 to 5000 feet, a current y clipping interval of 4000 to 4100 feet allows the Single Index Curve to draw only that 100-foot interval. Non-index dimensions, of course, have the usual difficulties utilizing a clipping region to reduce work.

Scrolling a display may require drawing different segments of its virtual plots onto that data display's canvases. This is accomplished by adjusting both the translation component of the coordinate transformation and the world coordinate clipping regions. These issues are discussed later in the chapter.

A sampling of other types of data sources Ida offers includes:

1. *Crossplot*—scatter plot correlating two well logs.
2. *Polyline*—multiple, connected 2D line segments.
3. *Grids*—rectangular grid lines.
4. *Axis labels*—the x and y labels.
5. *Area filling*—shading between curves.
6. *Elevator*—part of an elevator scroll control.

The variety of data sources shows that many kinds of data depiction fit into Ida's drawing model. Data sources can share scales with other data sources. The last four entries above all utilize scale sharing. Grids, axes labels, area filling, and scroll elevators all use shared scales because their transformations to screen coordinates are dependent on the transformation of some other data source used with them. For grids and axes labels, it should be especially clear that it is necessary for them to use the same transformation as the data source they are describing. Consider a Single Index Curve with its depth plotted in the y dimension. Its y-axis labels must be coordinated with it. A depth label of 4000 should print at exactly the same y position as a data point of the curve with a depth of 4000 feet. The same holds for a horizontal grid line that marks this depth. The three must remain synchronized through rescaling and scrolling and will always need to have identical transformations and world coordinate clipping regions. Rather than use some form of constraints to enforce this coordination, it has proven very effective to simply share scales. When a data source is instantiated, any scales that it will control (own) are instantiated with it. Then when a data source that shares scales needs one, it finds the scale and then declares itself a secondary user of that scale. These dependencies are recorded by the scale and used to notify dependents when a scale changes. Of course, the owner of a scale must already exist before any other data source can ask to share its scale.

In summary, data sources and scales provide Ida with the means to encapsulate important sets of graphic information. Data sources are virtual plots, while scales manage both coordinate transformations and world coordinate clipping regions. Scale sharing is a very useful facility that avoids the need for a more complex constraint system. Graphic attribute binding is always done at the time of drawing, allowing attribute alterations to appear immediately. The distinction between a data source and the image it draws is much like the one PostScript (Adobe [1985]) makes between a path and painting that path. However, PostScript paths are much more transient and are constructed by execution of a PostScript program, while Ida data sources are permanent representations.

Summary

Ida's drawing model reflects a tension between two separate goals. On the one hand, we have tried to "declare" as much of the drawing model in the object framework as possible, because we believe this produces a more flexible and understandable system architecture. On the other hand, there is almost always some performance cost associated with highly declarative architectures. We have addressed the performance issue with some very contained decisions. The data display model, in particular, relies on PixBlt capability to manipulate canvases. Additionally, excluding geometric models and image rendering obviates the need to perform general viewing transformations.

Presentations and assemblies provide flexible layout and display reuse capabilities. The multiple canvas buffering afforded by data displays enables performant implementation of operations like scrolling and visibility control. Data sources are self-contained repositories of drawing information. The sharp distinction between data sources and data displays provides flexibility; data displays are unconcerned with producing the images they contain, and data sources can draw themselves onto any data display canvas. Scales provide explicit representation of clipping regions and coordinate transformations and explicitly manage their shared use, thus providing a simple scheme for consistency maintenance.

Graphic Operations

We now define Ida's graphic operations, and see how they are realized using message passing among instances of the drawing model classes.

Ida has six basic graphic operations:

1. *Clear*—clear viewport.
2. *Erase*—erase data display canvas.
3. *Draw*—draw image onto canvas.
4. *Show*—compose drawn images from canvases and display in viewport.
5. *Range Reset*—change world coordinate clipping region.
6. *Update*—respond to scrolling.

Ida's operations are defined in two ways. They are operationally defined for some specific classes of Ida's drawing model, and they are transitively defined for other classes that may contain instances of the former group. For example, the **Clear** operation clears viewports, so only an entity that has a viewport can operationally define **Clear**. Only primary data displays have viewports. However, **Clear** is transitively defined by presentations and assemblies, because instances of both of these classes will contain primary data displays as parts. All graphic operations are carried out by message passing along the part-whole structure underlying an Ida display. This leads to blurring the distinction between an operator and the name of the method that performs that operation. A message can begin at any level for which it is defined, either transitively or operationally. The message is forwarded along the part-whole structure from its point of entry until it reaches the elements that actually execute the operation it is invoking. The level that operationally defines the message varies with the operation. The message forwarding is done in a broadcast mode; all appropriate parts will be sent the message. However, in addition to this standard forwarding protocol, there are options for all operations that allow a sender to inhibit normal message forwarding. These are useful in special cases where the sender knows from the context that forwarding the message is inappropriate or unnecessary.

Figure 9.5 expands the part-whole structure from Figure 9.4 with a presentation (**CR-Presentation-80**), two data sources (**Simple-Annotation-151** and **Single-Index-Curve-200**), and two scales (**X-Scale-201** and

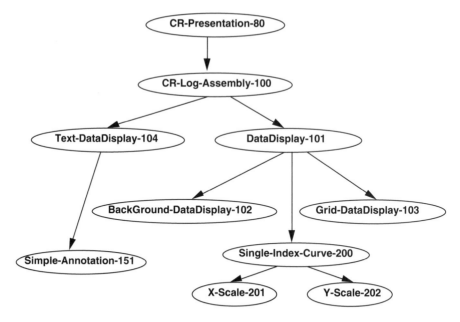

Figure 9.5: A complete part-whole hierarchy

Y-Scale-202). It illustrates all the part-whole relationships in Ida's model. The new relationships are: (1) an assembly is a part of its containing presentation, (2) a data source is a part of its destination data display, and (3) a scale is a part of the data source for which it provides a transformation. This figure will provide an example for our message-passing discussion.

Basic Operations

As mentioned above, the **Clear** operation clears data display viewports. It is operationally defined for entities that have viewports (primary data displays) and transitively defined for entities which contain primary data displays (presentations and assemblies). A **Clear** message sent to a presentation is forwarded to all component assemblies. Each assembly, in turn, forwards the **Clear** message to all its data displays. Each data display acts on the message by clearing its viewport on the screen, thus executing the operation. The message is not forwarded past the primary data displays because all the displays' secondary canvases share the same viewport. Similarly, the **Clear** operation is not defined for data sources or scales because they do not have viewports. A **Clear** message sent to an assembly clears only the viewports in that assembly, and a **Clear** message sent directly to a data display clears only that data display.

The **Erase** operation is defined to erase all the canvases belonging to a single data display. It is executed by both primary and secondary data displays and results in completely "blank" canvases. (Their Pixmap streams have been reset to the background color.) Like **Clear** messages, **Erase** messages are forwarded from presentations to their assemblies and from assemblies to their primary data displays. However, the **Erase** message is also forwarded from primary data displays to their secondary data displays. **Erase** is undefined for data sources and scales.

A **Draw** operation is a request to data sources to produce their images. A data source must produce the portion of its image within its current world coordinate clipping region as transformed onto its destination data display canvas. If a single canvas serves multiple data sources, the sources' images are produced in the same pixel buffer. This is typically done in an additive fashion (for example, OR-ing Bitmaps) for monochrome displays, but precedence of one pixel setting over another is more predictable for color displays. (Performing logical operations between pairs of arbitrary color codes will not typically produce a useful result.) **Draw** is transitively defined for presentations, assemblies, and both primary and secondary data displays; it is undefined for scales.

Invisible data display canvases are not forwarded **Draw** messages. Since the images that their data sources would produce are not visible, it is more efficient to bypass drawing them. When a canvas becomes visible, all its data sources that are not current will be asked immediately to draw themselves. Similarly, an invisible data source will not be forwarded **Draw** messages, even though it has a visible destination canvas. In this case, not only is it more performant to bypass the invisible data source, but it would be impossible to subtract only its contribution from the canvas.

The **Show** operation is defined for data displays. It composes and displays the existing images of all a data display's canvases into the viewport of the data display, along with the viewport's border and title. It is like **Erase** and operates on both primary and secondary data display canvases. Each currently visible canvas responds to a **Show** message by PixBlting its viewed region (as defined by its current viewing translation) into its viewport. The **Show** message is not forwarded to invisible canvases. The primary canvas is displayed first and is followed by all the visible secondary canvases in their defined order. The primary canvas displays the viewport's border and title, as well as its own canvas. For monochrome displays, the image from each canvas is typically combined additively by BitBlting with an OR combination of bits. However, other canvas combination operators are available. For example, Ida's elevator scroll bar utilizes this capability (see area 10 of Figure 9.2.) Its data display consists of two canvases. The primary canvas is used for drawing curves over which the scrollbar's slider passes. The background canvas contains the scaled, black rectangular slider image representing the currently visible interval. When the two canvases have been combined in their viewport, the background canvas uses an Invert combination operator to keep foreground curves visible where they pass through the slider. Color displays take advantage of the color window support to create window layers (with their own color maps) for each canvas. This allows each canvas's contribution to a screen pixel to be treated independently.

The **Range Reset** operation is defined to set world coordinate clipping regions. Scales are the actual repositories of world clipping regions, so it is at their level that **Range Reset** is operationally defined. As with the other operations, containing entities forward a **Range Reset** message to their appropriate parts. Clipping region adjustments can be either numerically or symbolically specified. Two useful symbolic intervals are "the world clipping region corresponding to the current viewed region" and "the world clipping region corresponding to the entire destination canvas."

Range Reset is the first operation defined for scales, so it is the first to be sensitive to the use of shared scales. When a data source is sharing a scale, it references that scale exactly like a scale it owns. When an action would change a scale, it is not applied to a shared scale. To honor this restriction, data sources only forward **Range Reset** messages to scales they own.

The **Update** operation requests a shift of the viewed region of a data display canvas in one or two dimensions. This operation supports scrolling, so the shift amounts are given in pixels. They are converted into world coordinates for affected data sources (those drawing into the scrolled data display canvases).

The initial sequence of operations for the example in Figure 9.5 will clarify the model. First, **CR-Presentation-80** is sent a **Clear** message to clear all its viewports. It is forwarded through **CR-Log-Assembly-100** to its primary data displays, **Data-Display-101** and **Text-DataDisplay-104**. These displays actually clear their screen viewports. An **Erase** message is then sent to the presentation. It is also forwarded to the primary data displays, but they, in turn, forward it to any secondary data displays. **Data-Display-101** has two secondary displays, so **BackGround-DataDisplay-102** and **Grid-DataDisplay-103** also receive **Erase** messages. All four data displays reset their canvases. The presentation is then sent a **Range Reset** message asking that the world clipping regions be set to correspond to their destination canvas sizes for all data sources' scales. It is executed by scales **X-Scale-201** and **Y-Scale-202**. (Because **Simple-Annotation-151** is an unscaled text display, its clipping region always includes the full text.) Next, a **Draw** message is sent to the presentation. It is forwarded to data sources **Simple-Annotation-151** and **Single-Index-Curve-200**. **Simple-Annotation-151** displays its text string in its destination canvas. **Single-Index-Curve-200** produces the interval of log needed to fill (in the *y* dimension) its destination canvas, **Data-Display-101**. In drawing this plot segment, it references its scales for the needed transformations. Finally, a **Show** message is sent to the presentation. It is forwarded to the primary data displays that draw viewport borders and titles as needed. The primary data displays also display their own current viewed regions before forwarding a **Show** message to their secondary canvases (which in this example have no images).

One variation in the operation sequence is used when the total plotting time will be noticeable to the user; it first produces the currently visible part of the display, and then iterates drawing portions not seen by the user. This is done by performing a **Range Reset** setting the clipping regions according to the sizes of the viewports—not the canvases. Hence, the **Draw** operation draws only the parts of the images lying in the viewed regions (where possible to do so). The **Show** operation then shows exactly these viewed regions. Then, the **Range Reset** and **Draw** operations are repeated as needed to complete the initially invisible portions of the canvases. This produces a presentation for the user as quickly as possible, then finishes drawing those portions of less immediate concern.

In summary, Ida's model produces a display by performing the sequence of operations: **Clear**, **Erase**, **Range Reset**, **Draw**, and **Show**. Obviously, many variations can be used. The specific existing state of the display, as well as the change to be made, determine the appropriate operation sequence. We consider some other common changes in the next section.

Plot Changes

Ida's model, as presented thus far, produces a fixed display. In this section, we briefly consider how changes to a display are accomplished. Changes we will discuss include rescaling data sources, adding and deleting data sources, and scrolling. Scrolling is invoked with scroll interaction elements as described in the explanation of Figure 9.2; all other changes are requested through pop-up menus supported by MetaClass.

Data source rescaling requires changing the transformations the data source is using, as recorded in its scales. Once the scales are altered, the data source must be redrawn. Furthermore, any other data sources sharing an altered scale must also be drawn. (The rescaling must be initiated from the data source that owns the scale. This seems more consistent with the notion of scale ownership, but would be easy to alter in Ida.) When a data source needs to be redrawn, its entire destination canvas needs to be redrawn, as well. So, for each data source using the altered scale, it and all of the data sources sharing the same destination canvas must be redrawn. No other canvases—even other canvases within the same data display as the canvases being redrawn—need redrawing. After the redrawing, a **Show** message to each affected data display produces its revised image.

Adding a new data source is very straightforward. It is added to the list of existing data sources sharing the same destination canvas it will use. Only the new data source needs to be drawn. Its interaction with the image already present on its destination canvas is the same as if it had been drawn along with the data sources that produced that image (as will be the case once it has been added). The entire data display of the affected canvas then receives a **Show** message. Making an invisible data source visible again is done in exactly the same way as adding a data source, except there is no need to add it to the list of data sources.

Deleting a data source requires removing it from the list of data sources, then redrawing all data sources that previously shared its destination canvas (like rescaling). A **Show** message is then sent to the data display to display the new image. Making a visible data source invisible is done in exactly the same way as deleting a data source, except there is no need to remove it from the list of data sources.

Scrolling is another way to change the state of an Ida display. Elevator scrolling is really just an easy way for a user to specify a new world clipping region. Once the new clipping region is selected and installed, redrawing is much like drawing. However, immediate scrolling requires some additional support. Ida's mechanisms for immediate scrolling assume that they will be used with the additional buffers afforded by canvases that are larger than their viewports. (The amount of buffering is completely under the presentation designer's control.) Once immediate scrolling begins, the image is scrolled by varying the viewing translations of the scrolling canvases. When scrolling stops, the new viewing translation will be offset by some number of pixels from the starting translation. This is the **Update** operation shift amount. All data sources that have been scrolled will have been changed by the same number of pixels. Interpreting the change in pixels requires asking the scales of the affected data sources to perform inverse transformations. This computation determines the scrolled amount in world units. One of

Ida's immediate scrolling strategies is to center the viewed regions of the canvases after scrolling. Having the scrolled amounts in both pixels and world units allows recentering to be done. The image in each scrolled canvas is shifted by the update amount in pixels, using PixBlt. This removes a certain amount of the old image at one end of the canvas and creates an equal amount of newly available erased canvas at the opposite end. The scroll amounts in world units are then used to establish the new world clipping regions for all sources that need to redraw onto these shifted canvases. The affected data sources are all redrawn. A **Show** operation is not actually needed because the scrolling itself has left all viewports looking exactly as they would after being updated and shown. There are many details of scrolling that we are ignoring, but this brief overview gives the flavor of how it fits into Ida's model.

Interactive Elements

We now briefly discuss Ida's approach to interactive display elements. Ida's environment provides support for defining rectangular active regions within windows, as well as recognizing mouse events in window backgrounds and titlebars. Ida's model uses the MetaClass mechanisms to provide general pop-up menus in response to appropriate buttoning in a window's titlebar or background, and defines activeregions for the viewports of data displays that are active. MetaClass sends a **Select** message to the data display owning an active viewport that has been buttoned. Standard data displays are active and respond to middle buttoning (and the consequent **Select** message) by presenting the user with a menu of possible actions such as rescaling a data source, changing the visibility of a data source or canvas, adding or deleting data sources, or generating a description of the current state of the data display and all of its data sources. Most of these choices have secondary menus and may solicit additional input from the user.

It is also important to be able to interact with the data sources that are drawing onto one of a data display's canvases. For example, if a user indicates a desire to rescale a data source, it should be easy to have the user then pick the desired data source with the mouse by buttoning some part of the visible plot. Of course, the data display may have multiple canvases, each with multiple data sources, visible in the same viewport. Ida provides this functionality by extending the MetaClass **Select** protocol with a "**Select?**" method for data sources. The data display **Select** method sends "**Select?**" to each of its visible data sources, providing the data sources with the coordinates of the picked position. Each data source responds by examining itself to see if the picked position is close enough to its image to qualify. If yes, the "**Select?**" method returns an affirmative answer. Each affirmative responder receives a **Select** message indicating that it has been picked. Separating the query from final picking makes it easy to disallow ambiguity. If a specific context allows only one selected data source, the user can be asked to disambiguate with a menu or told to retry the pick before any **Select** message is sent.

Reuse of Ida's Environment

As discussed earlier in the chapter, Ida is built on HyperClass. The Generic Window System and Class object-representation system were both implementation tools. They each provided needed functionality, and neither was changed to support Ida. On the other hand, MetaClass, the third part of HyperClass, provided a class library and interaction model within which Ida's model was developed. It is the relevant component to examine for reuse assessment.

As mentioned earlier, MetaClass' model of interaction is built around the metaphor of "editing," but encompasses traditional text editing, browsing, program development, debugging, and end-user interaction. MetaClass contains five classes as its basic building blocks. They are:

1. **Editor**—the central mediator of interactions between the user and the edited entity.
2. **Editor Window**—manages the screen context of a collection of editors.
3. **Property Display**—presents a view of (part of) an edited entity in a window.
4. **Menu**—messengers between the user and an editor.
5. **Operations**—objects which group methods that perform the commands defined for an editor.

MetaClass also provides a large number of specializations of these basic classes. Ida extends the MetaClass framework with the classes needed to implement its own drawing model. Quantitatively, Ida added more than 100 classes to a MetaClass library of more than 250 classes.

Ida Editor is a specialization of the **Editor** class, and **Presentation** and **Assembly** are further specializations of **Ida Editor**. **Ida Editor** only provides a convenient ancestor for Ida's specialized editors; it adds nothing conceptually to MetaClass's **Editor** class. An Ida display is always managed by an instance of a **Presentation**, and each associated **Assembly** is a sub-editor of this managing presentation. Similarly, **Ida Window** is a trivial specialization of the **Editor Window** class. The **Data Display** class is a specialization of the **Property Display** class. This is appropriate, because data displays extend the notion of viewing data, and both classes provide the managers of activeregions within windows.

Ida's drawing model makes a distinction that was not needed in the MetaClass model: the distinction between creating and displaying images. This separation of responsibility for creating images from responsibility for displaying them leads to the creation of a new portion of the taxonomy rooted in the **Data Source** class. These new kinds of entities are not closely related to previously existing classes in the MetaClass library.

Drawing Object is a mixin defining the methods for drawing operations (such as **Draw**, **Erase**, and **Show**). None of these operations exist in MetaClass, so **Scale**, **Data Source**, **Data Display**, **Ida Editor**, and **Ida Window** are all descendants of **Drawing Object** to inherit the drawing methods.

There were many advantages to building Ida as an extension to Meta-Class. The data display problem divided nicely into a part that could be done using the existing MetaClass functionality, and into another part that required totally new functionality. The first part includes all the mechanisms for editor creation and deletion, windows, menus, and operators, while the second part was the data graphics, *per se*. Fortunately, the new functionality could be effectively designed as either elaborations of existing MetaClass classes, or as completely new classes that blended well with the existing ones.

How Ida Has Been Used

Ida and HyperClass were developed in a research laboratory. Both of them were motivated by the belief that tools for building user interfaces quickly and easily were needed badly. HyperClass already existed when Ida was begun. Ida was developed to enlarge the set of interface types that could be built; specifically, its main target was interfaces involving the kinds of data displays needed for working with well logs. HyperClass and Ida were used in the laboratory to construct interfaces for many programs and experimental prototypes.

It is also interesting to see how Ida (with HyperClass) has been used away from "home" (both organizationally and geographically). Ida was used in one of the Schlumberger engineering centers to develop prototype interfaces for a new family of workstation-based products for processing and interpreting well logs. The project required a number of new display types, as well as building interfaces for interactive applications such as well log editing. In this instance, Ida's developer interacted closely with the engineering staff to help them get started. Once the staff understood the basic architecture, they did a great deal of unaided experimentation. This first commercial version of the system was then implemented using NeWS for the user interface.

Schlumberger's Sedco-Forex drilling business has used Ida in its MDS drilling management system. MDS is a new production system, used when drilling on offshore platforms. This project also involved making a significant number of extensions to Ida, but was done almost exclusively by the MDS™ developers, without assistance of Ida's developer.

The Ida version of the MDS interface will be used for the foreseeable future, but there are no new applications under development. This outcome is connected with the decision to abandon LISP-based systems.

Conclusions

An object-oriented architecture is very well-suited for Ida's data display problem. Let us review why this is true. A good solution requires developing the right drawing model. Object taxonomies very naturally meet the static modeling needs of the drawing model. Implementing the drawing model operations as methods of these objects has proven to be a very clear way to structure the system. The polymorphism offered by object-oriented models is especially valuable when there is a small set of basic operations that operate over a large set of entity types. Ida's model must also include arbitrarily large and deep part-whole aggregations. Organizing these aggregations with instances, and using message broadcasting along this hierarchy, provides a straightforward interpretation for aggregate operations. Late binding is a very useful characteristic for a display system like Ida and was made easier to implement by the LISP-based development environment.

Our experiences with Ida are very encouraging about the positive impact on reuse of a well designed object-oriented architecture. Ida is a reusable class library that a number of people in various settings have used extensively. Additionally, MetaClass is also a reusable class library that made the development of Ida a much smaller problem. It is important to point out that Ida's reuse of MetaClass was not done merely by having Ida "sit on top of MetaClass" but rather by Ida significantly extending MetaClass's model. Some of these extensions were in ways that were never anticipated by MetaClass's developers. They were developed through "growing the model" in a number of different places. A major extension such as Ida would have been much more difficult to design in a non–object-oriented environment.

Notes

1.   Class was previously called Strobe, and MetaClass was called Impulse.

References

Adobe Systems Incorporated [1985]. *PostScript Language Reference Manual*. Addison-Wesley, Reading, MA, 1985.

Foley, J.D., A. van Dam, S.K. Feiner, and J.F. Hughes [1990]. *Computer Graphics: Principles and Practice*, 2nd edition. Addison-Wesley, Reading, MA, 1990.

Scheifler, R.W., J. Gettys, and R. Newman [1988]. *The X Window System*. Digital Press, Maynard, MA, 1988.

Schoen, E. [1990]. *Color Layering Tools for Lucid Common LISP*. Technical documentation, Schlumberger Laboratory for Computer Science, Austin, TX, October 1990.

Schoen, E., R.G. Smith, and A. Atkinson [1989]. *The Generic Window System Reference Manual*. Technical Documentation TD-89-15, Schlumberger Laboratory for Computer Science, Austin, TX, November 1989.

Smith, R.G., P.S. Barth, and R.L. Young [1987]. "A Substrate for Object-Oriented Interface Design." In *Research Directions in Object-Oriented Programming*. M.I.T. Press, Cambridge, MA, 1987.

Smith, R.G., R. Dinitz, and P. Barth [1986]. "Impulse-86: A Substrate for Object-Oriented Interface Design." In *Proceedings* of the First ACM Conference on Object-Oriented Programming Systems, Languages, and Applications, pp. 167-176, Portland, OR, September 1986.

Steele, G.L., Jr. [1990]. *Common LISP: The Language*. Digital Press, Maynard, MA, 1990.

Sun Microsystems, Inc. [1987]. *NeWS Technical Overview*. Sun Microsystems, Mountain View, CA, 1987.

Young, R.L. [1987]. "An Object-Oriented Framework for Interactive Data Graphics." In *Proceedings* of the Second ACM Conference on Object-Oriented Programming Systems, Languages, and Applications, Orlando, FL, October 1987.

Chapter 10

Object-Oriented Ray Tracing: A Comparison of C++ Versus C Implementations

Karl D. Melcher
G. Scott Owen

Great claims have been made for the improved development productivity and greater ease of maintenance for software systems produced by object-oriented languages as compared to traditional languages. The purpose of this project was to test this claim in the development of a moderately complex computer graphics program. The test program generates graphical images by the technique of ray tracing. This program is a particularly good test case since a simple ray tracing program can be very small, but as new rendering features are added, it can become large and complex. It is also desirable to enhance the program by adding new types of geometric objects and by replacing older rendering algorithms with new ones. Thus, an ideal ray tracing program should be easy to modify and extend.

The first version of the program was written on am IBM PS/2™ in Turbo C® version 2.0, and then was rewritten in Turbo C++®. We compared the resulting C and C++ versions for ease of development and enhancement. In particular, we wanted to know if using objects with the properties of encapsulation, inheritance, and polymorphism would allow for easier maintenance of the system. We also tested the runtime efficiency of the two programs to determine if there was a performance penalty associated with using objects. This is especially important for a ray tracing program, since generating only a moderately complex image can require hours of CPU time.

Our results verified the claims for object-oriented languages. We found the C++ version much easier to develop and enhance. Although much of the improvement was due to the use of objects, some was due to non–object-oriented features of C++, such as operator overloading and inline function expansion. We also found no performance penalty with the C++ version. This paper provides a detailed comparison of the two implementations and the improvements due to the use of objects and their associated properties, such as inheritance and polymorphism. We also present images that have been generated by the programs.

A note on terminology is in order. C++ terminology will be used to describe object-oriented programming mechanisms. The *class* is a data structure that is composed of both data fields and member functions that manipulate the class, while an instantiation of a class is called an *object*. In our paper, a *geo_object* will be a visible geometric entity (geometric object) that will be rendered by the system

The ray tracer written in C is called RTC, and the C++ version is named RTCPP. In the following sections, we give a description of the design and capabilities of RTC and RTCPP. For input, both programs use a text file that contains a description of the image to be computed. Both programs then generate an output file that consists of three bytes of color information (red, green, and blue intensities) per pixel. With suitable post-processing, the output of both ray tracers could be displayed on any device of any resolution and up to eight bits per gun color intensity.

The Design of RTC

The design of both RTC and RTCPP is based upon Heckbert's article in [Glassner, 1989]. Thus, even RTC was designed in an object-oriented fashion. RTC is a conventional ray tracer based on the recursive method of ray tracing. The general algorithm is as follows: For every pixel on the screen, a ray is created that originates at the camera position (a primary ray) and projects through the pixel. The ray is tested for intersection with every geo_object in the scene. The nearest ray–geo_object intersection is considered the visible point for this pixel and is shaded. The shading for a pixel is determined by the color of the geo_object hit, the illumination of the geo_object by the light sources, and any reflected or transmitted light. The transmitted and reflected light contributions are calculated by casting new rays (secondary rays) in the directions of the reflected or transmitted angle. The colors are then combined and assigned to the pixel on the screen.

The time-consuming portion of this process is the ray–geo_object intersection computation, which can consume 75 to 95 percent of the total computations required [Whitted, 1980]. In RTC the objects in the scene are stored in a simple list. As each geo_object is considered for intersection, a switch statement is used to invoke the appropriate intersection function.

Input File for RTC

A simple Image Description Language (IDL) was developed for RTC and was extended for RTCPP. The input can be grouped into three categories: screen control, lighting control, and geo_object control. The screen control and lighting control sections are identical for RTC and RTCPP, but the geometrical section is quite different.

   Screen Control: In this section, the spatial resolution, spectral resolution (number of computed color bits per pixel), window size, camera position, and viewing direction are given. The number of levels of computed reflection is also an input parameter. There is also the option of supersampling (non-adaptive; four evenly spaced rays per pixel).

   Lighting Control: The ambient light level, background color, and light sources (position and color; up to 10 independent point light sources) are defined here.

   Geo_object Control: There are three types of input objects: spheres (unit sphere centered on the origin), boxes (unit cube centered on the origin), and squares (two-sided unit plane centered on the x-z plane). Each input geo_object can be translated, rotated, and scaled. An advantage of using these primitives is the simple ray–geo_object intersection tests, but this would be lost if the object were distorted (for example, if a sphere were extended along one axis by differential scaling). To maintain the simplicity of the ray–geo_object intersection tests, the rays were transformed into the coordinate system of the geo_object before the intersection test. This section of the input file was changed for RTCPP, as described later.

The Design of RTCPP

RTCPP was designed to use the object-oriented capabilities of C++, while retaining the fast execution speed available with C. The initial conversion from C to C++ was a natural evolution, because the existing code could be recompiled using C++ with changes to only two lines of code out of 2000.

However, we then made major changes to take advantage of the object-oriented capabilities of C++.

Geometrical Objects

The most fundamental change made was the development of a hierarchical geo_object database composed of primitive geo_objects and composite geo_objects. The database is implemented as a n-ary tree with all nodes derived from a base class **geo_object**.

Class geo_object

The base class **geo_object** (see Listing 10.1) defines the interface for all the functions necessary for derived geo_objects. Note that all functions are declared virtual to allow for late binding of the call to the correct derived class. Class **geo_object** is never to be instantiated itself. It is only used as an abstract base class in a hierarchy of derived geo_objects.

From **geo_object** are derived two classes, **prim** for primitive geo_objects and **comp** for composite geo_objects. From primitive geo_objects, we derive geo_object coordinate system primitives (**ocs_prim**), where the ray–geo_object intersection calculation is in the geo_objects' own coordinate system, and world coordinate system primitives (**wcs_prim**), where the ray–geo_object intersection calculation is in the world coordinate system. The ocs_prims currently include **Sphere**, **Cube**, **Square**, and **Cylinder**. An example wcs_prim would be **Polyhedron**. Once a composite geo_object has been defined it can be transformed by translation, rotation, and scaling, just as a primitive can. This allows new objects to be defined and then manipulated as easily as any primitive.

The new composite geo_objects are defined in the input file using the IDL. The IDL uses the keywords "define" and "end" to mark the beginning and end of a list of sub-objects that will make up a new composite. The sub-objects can themselves be composites or primitives. Each sub–geo_object can be transformed by using the scale, rotate, or translate operations. Each operation listed after a sub–geo_object is applied to the last sub–geo_object encountered. The surface of the sub–geo_object can also be specified or modified by using surface objects. An example IDL file, for the image JACKS (Color Plate 8), is given in Listing 10.2. In this example, a jack

```
//———————————————
//  Geo_object base class
//———————————————
class geo_object {
public:
    // Data Members
    char *name;
    struct lnode *link_ptr;
    surface *surf;
    bound_t bound;
    // Member functions
    virtual geo_object* copy();
    // find intersection
    virtual int  hit(Ray &r, Intersect &isect);
    // calc surface norm
    virtual void calc_norm(Intersect &isect);
    virtual void map(Intersect &isect, double &u,
        double &v);
    virtual void rotate(char axis, double angle);
    virtual void translate(double x, double y,
        double z);
    virtual void scale(double x, double y, double z);
    virtual void print(int level=0);
    virtual bound_t calc_bound();
    friend void define_geo_object(safeifstream& infile);
};
```

Listing 10.1: The definition of geo_object

consists of two crossing rod_and_spheres, each of which consists of a cylinder and two spheres. The total image consists of six of these jacks surrounding a ball on a checkered surface.

In RTC, each geo_object had an associated set of ambient and diffuse
red, green, and blue reflection coefficients, a similar set of specular reflection coefficients, and a Phong number (for Phong shading). In RTCPP, we
modified this and gave each geo_object the appearance of plastic, metal, or
an overlaid checkered pattern. Again, there is a set of diffuse and specular
reflection coefficients. For a plastic or checkered surface the specular reflection is the color of the light source, while for a metal surface it is the color of
the surface itself. Usually a metal surface has no diffuse reflection, but we
decided to include this for flexibility. The computation of shadows, using
shadow rays, was also added in RTCPP.

```
*_____
* Notes:   1. Lines starting with an asterisk are
*             comments.
*          2. Screen and lighting control removed for
*             clarity.
* This image will demonstrate the following primitives:
* square, sphere, cylinder. It produces an image of six
* jacks surrounding a  ball on a checkerboard square
*_____
define rod_and_spheres
  * A cross rod with a sphere on each end.
  sphere
     *           r    g    b    Kd   Ks   Kt    Ph
     plastic   0.8  0.8  0.8   0.3  0.7  0.0   60
     scale 0.3 0.3 0.3
     translate -0.5  0   0
  cylinder
     *           r    g    b    Kd   Ks   Kt    Ph
     plastic   0.8  0.8  0.8   0.3  0.7  0.0   60
     rotate z 90
     scale 1 0.15 0.15
  sphere
     *           r    g    b    Kd   Ks   Kt    Ph
     plastic   0.8  0.8  0.8   0.3  0.7  0.0   60
     scale 0.3 0.3 0.3
     translate  0.5  0   0
end
define jack
  rod_and_spheres
    rotate y -45
    rotate z 45
    translate 0 -0.1 0
  rod_and_spheres
    rotate y 45
    rotate z 45
    translate 0 -0.1 0
```

(continued)

Listing 10.2: IDL file for the image JACKS

```
  * The center rod with no ends
  cylinder
    *             r     g     b     Kd    Ks    Kt    Ph
    plastic    0.8   0.8   0.8    0.3   0.7   0.0    60
    scale 0.15 1 0.15
    rotate y -45
    rotate z 45
    translate 0 -0.1 0
end
define image
  jack
    translate 0 0 -1
  jack
    rotate y 33
    translate 1 0 1
  jack
    rotate y 180
    translate 0 0 1.5
  jack
    rotate y -20
    translate -1 0 1
  jack
    rotate y 120
    translate -1 0 -0.65
  jack
    rotate y -120
    translate  1 0 -0.65
  sphere
    *             r     g     b     Kd    Ks    Kt    Ph
    plastic    0.5   0.2   0.2    0.8   0.1   0.0    5
    scale 0.7 0.7 0.7
  square
*             Num       color0              color1
*                       r    g    b    r    g    b   Kr   Ks  Phong
Checkered_2d 15 0.4 0.9 0.5   0.4 0.5 0.9 0.7  0.0       50
  scale 10 1 10
  translate 0 -0.5 0
end
```

Listing 10.2 (*continued*)

N-ary geo_object Tree

As the objects in the scene are read in from the IDL file, they are stored in a n-ary tree structure, which is built into the geo_objects rather than being an object itself. Perhaps it should be an object, but this would take a significant revision (next time). The root of the tree is a composite geo_object called **IMAGE**, which must be defined in the input file. Each composite geo_object has a list of pointers to child objects. Child objects may be other composite objects or primitive objects. Since each geo_object is derived from the base class **geo_object** and defines the member functions required of a geo_object, traversal of the geo_object tree is easy. For each child geo_object, the member function **hit()** is called. Since **hit** is defined by each derived geo_object, the correct **hit()** function is called. This uses the polymorphism feature of C++ to bind the desired function call to the child pointer at runtime.

Before performing a ray–geo_object intersection with objects derived from **ocs_prim**, the ray must be transformed from the world coordinate system (WCS) to the object coordinate system (OCS). Each derived class of **ocs_prim** has its own WCS to OCS transformation matrix. The coordinate transformation involves a significant number of floating point multiplications, but it enhances the shading capabilities and allows simpler intersection calculations in the OCS. For intersections that must be shaded (such as the closest intersection), the surface normal must be computed in the OCS and transformed into the WCS.

Bounding Hierarchies

Bounding volumes, which were added in RTCPP, are used to accelerate the process of finding the closest geo_object intersected for a particular ray. We have defined a **bound** class (six-sided slabs [Kay, 1986] that tightly surround the geo_object), and each geo_object, both primitive and composite, has an instantiation of **bound**. These slabs are more costly to test than spheres, but they provide for a smaller volume and are easier to combine. The intersection test between a ray and the bounding volume is much faster than the test with the primitive objects, because the ray-bound intersection test is performed in the WCS and does not require that the ray be transformed to the OCS. A significant time savings is also realized by bounding each geo_object in the geo_object tree.

The bounding volumes are hierarchical and are tested at each branch in the hierarchy for composite objects. The bound for a particular geo_object is calculated so that it tightly encloses all child objects. Thus, if a ray-bound intersection test fails, all objects below the current geo_object in the tree need not be considered further. If this occurs high up in the geo_object tree, many objects can be removed from further consideration. Since **bound** is a class, a change in bounding volume type (for example, to spheres) involves only changing the member functions and definitions with no external code changes.

Math Classes

For RTCPP, we rewrote the mathematics package that implements all vector, matrix, and ray calculations. We created a **Vector** class, a **Matrix** class, and a **Ray** class. By making these into classes, we could reduce the complexity of the source code. We overloaded the standard operators (+, −, *) to perform the desired **Ray**, **Vector**, and **Matrix** operations. For example, subtracting vectors in RTC is done by the function call

```
vect_sub(new_vector, vector_a, vector_b)
```

In RTCPP, it can be done by the infix notation

```
new_vector = vector_a - vector_b
```

In addition, C++ allows for the overloaded operators to be expanded into inline code. This increases the runtime efficiency by not having the over-head associated with a function call. This is especially important on functions that implement very few lines of code, such as the vector operators.

Screen Class

The screen is also represented as a class. The **screen** class encapsulates all screen-oriented data, such as the spatial resolution, spectral resolution, image aspect ratio, window location and size, and camera location and orientation. It is responsible for generating the primary rays and performing optional supersampling. In addition, it creates the output file and outputs the final pixel information.

Surface Class

A class called **surface** is used to shade the surface that is intersected by the ray. **surface** is an abstract class that defines the interface for all surface shading classes. It has some private member functions that are used by all surface shaders. Currently, we have derived classes to shade plastic, metal, and a 2D checkered pattern. Each derived class defines the data members necessary to shade the surface. They also are responsible for reading all parameters from the input file when the particular surface class is encountered by the input file parsing routine.

Other Classes

There are a few other miscellaneous classes used in the program, such as a modification of the standard I/O class to improve input error detection. Also, there is a statistics class that accumulates runtime data on the image generation (including the number of rays, number of hits, and total runtime) and passes it to the output file.

Object-Oriented Description of the Ray Tracing Process

The process of ray tracing was reworked in RTCPP. It was no longer necessary to use switch statements to ensure the correct functions were being used. Late binding (polymorphism) ensured that the correct member functions were called based on the **geo_object** or **geo_object** pointer at hand.

The program is started by calling it with the name of the image description file on the command line. RTCPP initializes itself and then loads the data file. The data file contains parameters to specify the camera, screen, lighting, and commands to build the **geo_object** database in the n-ary tree.

The process of image generation starts with the main program sending the **RayTrace** message to the **Screen**. The **Screen** then creates a primary ray for each pixel that makes up the final image. The ray is passed as a parameter in a "**Hit?**" message sent to root of the n-ary tree of geo_objects. The "**Hit?**" message is then recursively sent to each sub–geo_object in the tree. Each geo_object contains an instantiation of the bound class. A "**Hit?**" message is sent to the bound object to see if further consideration is required.

Once the nearest ray–geo_object intersection is found, it must be shaded. Intersection information was accumulated by "**Hit?**" for the ray–geo_object intersection nearest the origin of the incoming ray. Since each geo_object contains a pointer to a surface object, that pointer is among the intersection information saved. The pointer to the surface of the nearest geo_object is used to invoke the appropriate surface class member function called **Shade**. The message **Shade** is sent to the surface object pointed to by the saved surface pointer. The surface object then determines the shading for the intersected point by considering the light sources and surface characteristics. For shiny or transparent surfaces, the reflected or transmitted color can be from other geo_objects in the scene. Secondary rays must be created and tested against the root of the n-ary geo_object tree. A limit is imposed on the number of levels of recursion allowed in determining the color of the screen pixel.

Advantages and Disadvantages of C++ and C

Advantages

C++ simplified the creation of the objects to be rendered by the system. By defining a base class **geo_object** and deriving all other objects from it, extension of the objects to new primitives was easy because of polymorphism. Traversal of the **geo_object** database did not have to be modified to deal with new primitives.

Inheritance was used for creation of new objects and surfaces. Objects can be linked into the program and are automatically available for use. The routines that interface with the objects did not need to be modified to allow for the new **geo_object** since the new **geo_object** is derived from a base **geo_object** that is already handled by the routines.

Automatic **geo_object** initialization was used to ensure that new primitives and surfaces were added to the list of available primitives and surfaces scanned by the input file parsing routines. It should be noted that the automatic initialization was added and later removed from the **vector** and **ray** classes. It was determined that whenever these classes were used, they were immediately assigned values. Because they are a fundamental part of the system and were being unnecessarily initialized, automatic initialization had a detrimental impact on runtime.

We did not notice a degradation of runtime performance for similar procedures in both languages, and in some cases for C++, runtime performance is better because of the inline expansion of functions. It is possible to expand function calls with macros in C, but overloading cannot be done with macros.

Overloading of operators for ray, vector, and matrix manipulation allowed cleaner implementation of many algorithms since high-level operators can be expressed more closely to the mathematical notations found in textbooks, as shown in the example for vector subtraction on page 273.

Disadvantages

The switch from C to C++ can be performed as an evolutionary process in an application. One problem initially encountered was the tendency to use the design method of functional decomposition rather than object decomposition. This was to be expected, since the object-oriented paradigm is new. As we gained experience, it became easier to think of the program as a set of interacting objects, not functions acting on data structures. C++ requires more effort to see what data and member functions are available in a derived class, because one must look at all classes in the particular derivation tree and the access modifiers at each level.

A minor inconvenience is the increased compilation time caused by more rigorous type checking and forced prototyping. This is necessary because the entire derivation tree for classes must be analyzed to compile each program module. Overall, the benefits gained from being able to derive new classes far outweighs the increased compilation time.

Conclusions and Future Work

We found the C++ version of the ray tracing program to be a much simpler program than the C version. Even though it incorporated more advanced techniques for image generation, it was simplified by using inheritance, polymorphism, and operator overloading. New primitives and surfaces can be added much more easily than with the C version.

One area where the program will be expanded is in the collection of the primitives available. We hope to add primitives for cones, tori, hyperboloids, polyhedrons, and surface patches. Each of these can be directly derived from the **ocs_prim** and **wcs_prim** classes.

Several new surfaces will be added, some of which are based on using pseudo-random noise functions [Perlin, 1985]. Noise can be used for wood, marble, granite, and other surfaces. We also would like to extend the IDL to allow creation of a shading method in which both the texture and surface normals can be controlled. This would allow bump mapping as well as texture mapping. We are currently adding specular transmission with refraction to the plastic surfaces. We also plan on moving RTCPP to other systems such as our Silicon Graphics 4D/380 and IBM RISC System/6000™.

References

Glassner, A. [1989]. *An Introduction to Ray Tracing.* Academic Press Inc., San Diego, CA, 1989.

Kay, T. and J. Kajiya [1986]. "Ray Tracing Complex Scenes." *Computer Graphics*, (20)4, 1986, pp. 269-278.

Perlin, K. [1985]. An Image Synthesizer. *Computer Graphics*, 19(3), 1985, pp. 287-296.

Whitted, T. [1980]. "An Improved Illumination Model for Shaded Display." *Communications of the ACM*, 23(6), 1980, pp. 343-349.

Chapter 11

Design of a Mathematicians' Drawing Program

Dennis Roseman

Drawings As Mathematical Symbols

Consider a knot. Figure 11.1a shows a knot that could be physically constructed from a circular rope. In Figure 11.1b we see the same knot represented more abstractly by a closed polygonal path. A drawing of a knot is, in fact, a symbol that represents it. Furthermore, there is a graphical "calculus" of allowable manipulations one can perform on such symbols. These ma-

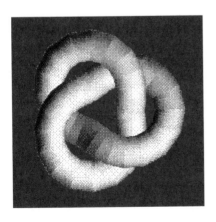

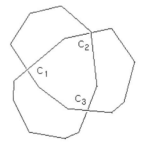

(a) a knotted circular piece of "rope"

(b) corresponding knotted polygonal curve. Crossing points labeled C_1, C_2, and C_3

Figure 11.1: A knotted circle

nipulations are frequently done in an interactive manner, and our project, TopDrawer, is a program for such graphical symbolic manipulation.

Our goals are to achieve a thorough and flexible analysis so that every graphics aspect implied by a diagram can be expressed using our hierarchy of classes. In a standard drawing program, the user enters graphical objects and then interacts with the program by manipulating these objects. Such a program is designed to display a certain graphical image. In our program, the user interacts mostly with graphical objects computationally derived from those that were entered. We want to enter these symbols, perform corresponding symbolic manipulations, and display the graphical image resulting from these calculations.

Our project is intended to develop computational tools, some of which are graphic, to aid in the mathematical investigation of certain aspects of four-dimensional space. Our focus is the topological investigation of surfaces and "motions" of such surfaces in four-dimensional space (see, for example, [Roseman 1989]).

As a first step, we reduce our four-dimensional problem to a three-dimensional problem. There are two standard methods to do this. The first, called *projection*, results in a self-intersecting surface in three-dimensional space. The second, called *slicing*, results in a sequence of knotted and linked circles in three-dimensional space. In either case, we will call such a depiction a diagram of the unknotted surface, and it consists of a labeled three-dimensional picture or a sequence of labeled three-dimensional pictures. The labelings are mathematically very important. What we discuss here is only a "slice" of our problem that we must then integrate into a much larger structure. This paper focuses on the development and implementation of the graphics portion of our project for such slices.

TopDrawer is written in Objective-C on a NeXT® computer. We designed it so that the programs developed would be of general use to mathematicians. For example, we would like to be able to handle many of the well-known pictures of knots and surfaces in [Francis 1987]. Object-oriented programming has been fundamental in our design, allowing us to achieve considerable flexibility and extensibility. In our work, we have developed two new groups of classes. The first is a foundational collection of classes that will handle the graphs and graph methods that are fundamental to the combinatorial approach, and the second is a collection of graphical entities which are derived from user-entered graphics. This chapter describes the part of our program that handles figures depicting one-dimensional polygonal objects in three-dimensional space, such as knots, links, and knotted graphs. Roughly, a knotted graph is a realization of a graph in space on which the graph edges can be represented by polygonal paths. Our object-oriented design makes extensions to more complex figures relatively easy.

New Types of Graphics Objects, or Finding Out More Than You Ever Thought You Wanted to Know About a Drawing

For better or for worse, mathematicians always seem to look at things differently. Complicated things are described in very simple ways, and simple things are explained in very complex ways. There are sound mathematical reasons to do this, and the result is a very different view of what classes and methods are considered to be basic. In our drawings, the points and edges entered by the user are familiar items in everyone's graphics vocabulary and program. However, the derived classes are not standard, although they do correspond to things we see when we look at the finished figure.

Consider Figure 11.2a. The drawing was made by clicking the mouse at the 19 points seen labeled in Figure 11.2b. Corresponding objects were created called *Dpoints* (drawn points), and these were labeled by the program in the order drawn. In the process, three crossing points were generated and labeled C_1, C_2 and C_3, as seen in Figure 11.2c. When we look at this drawing, we see two "pieces": a quadrilateral, labeled A, and B, formed by the remaining edges (see Figure 11.2d). We call these pieces *Webs*. We also organize the drawing into "paths" and say that the order of a Dpoint is the number of edges that meet that point. A *Path* is a connected collection of edges such that, except for a first and last point, all other Dpoints have order two. In this definition, we will ignore the crossing points, because they were not given as input. Thus a Path can "contain" crossing points.

Figure 11.2c shows the four paths P_1, ..., P_4 for our example. The path P_1 is the quadrilateral, and each of the other three paths has the points numbered 6 and 10 as endpoints. In our figure, we see regions enclosed by polygonal boundaries, and here we *do* wish to consider crossing points as corner points of these regions. For example, we have labeled "f" the region enclosed by the circuit that begins at C_1 then goes to these points, in order (counterclockwise): 4, 3, 2, 1, C_3, 10, 11, and then back to C_1, as shown in Figure 11.2b. We call such a region a *Shard*, referring to a broken piece of pottery. Although this boundary curve has many edges and vertices, the points C_1 and C_3 are clearly distinctive. We can describe the boundary of our shard more simply by saying that it is made up of two *oneCells*. These oneCells are arcs. The first goes from C_1 to C_3 and contains points 4, 3, 2, and 1; the other goes from C_3 to C_1 and contains points 10 and 11. In Figure 11.2b, we label the shards a, b, …, g, where g is "the outside shard." Shard b is more complicated since its boundary is the union of two disjoint circuits,

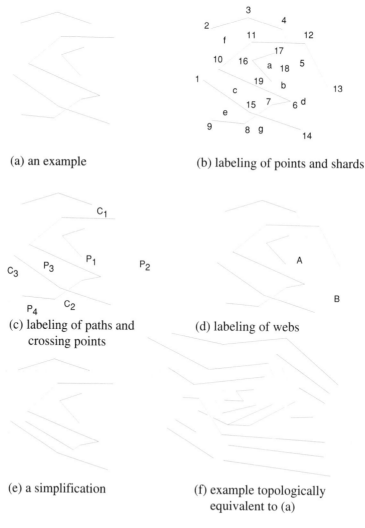

(a) an example   (b) labeling of points and shards

(c) labeling of paths and   (d) labeling of webs
crossing points

(e) a simplification   (f) example topologically
equivalent to (a)

Figure 11.2

one of which is a quadrilateral. The boundary consists of two circuits reflecting that this shard is, topologically, of a type known as a "disk with one hole," and thus quite distinct from shard f, which, topologically, is a "disk." Our program must do this analysis and update as much as possible while the drawing is entered by the user. There are other objects of a graphical nature that we use, but they are more important to the mathematical analysis than to the graphics display.

The point of all this analysis is to be able to answer questions such as whether the cursor position is presently in a shard that has exactly two oneCells for its boundary. For example, we might wish to make an allowable simplification of a diagram such as in Figure 11.2e. Such a search is a first step in finding a possible simplification. Or we might inquire of the program how many shards have boundaries made up of exactly three oneCells. (In Figure 11.2b, there is only one—the "outside" shard labeled g.) Furthermore, we might want the program to indicate these graphically on the screen.

We show a complicated figure in Figure 11.2f and ask whether this is equivalent to Figure 11.2a. In our case, "equivalent" has a topological meaning in terms of the way shards and oneCells are assembled. This equivalence allows the elements of the drawing to be movable and flexible, and the answer is yes.

By restricting ourselves to consideration of polygonal line drawings, our analysis can be done with reasonable programming and CPU time, and these piecewise-linear techniques extend readily to the higher dimensional case of self-intersecting polyhedral surfaces in space.Why do we need a computer to do this? Why not use pencil and paper and forget the machine? One reason is that we wish to use the program interactively and use the machine to help keep track of the results. Keeping track of the results for us means not only recording changes, but also being able to relate objects in an original diagram with corresponding ones in a new diagram. Some types of manipulations we will consider are illustrated in the diagrams of Kauffman [1983], [1989].

Design Problems

To implement these analyses with computer graphics, we needed a design that would satisfy the following three requirements:

1. *Objects*: we needed to represent mathematical objects and connect these to the corresponding graphical objects which are on the screen.

2. *Methods*: we needed methods that made two sorts of changes in our structure.
   a. One set of methods needed to be interactive. When the viewer makes changes on the screen image, our objects must record these changes and alter the underlying mathematical object accordingly.
   b. A second set of methods consists of computational algorithms applied to the mathematics objects, and these altered objects must be able to display themselves on the screen in a reasonable way.
3. *Error management*: we needed a "smart cursor." For the interactive methods mentioned above, there will be certain possible viewer inputs that are not mathematically allowable and must result in an error message. To have a reasonable user interface, these errors must be reported very quickly, thus requiring swift analysis of the cursor's position with respect to the underlying mathematical structure.

In addition, we have the following problems to confront:

4. *Drawing speed and ease*: sometimes we want to do a preliminary sketch of a diagram. To do this, we must be able to suspend the symbolic methods that update the diagram's representation.
5. *Human-computer interface*: we want to have certain minimal "ordinary" drawing tools available, and we need a flexible user-controlled capability to prepare diagrams for publication.
6. *Portability*: we wish to maximize portability, especially for all objects and methods that are not directly connected with display.

Design Solutions

The Overall Design of the Program

The program is designed in three layers:
   Level 1—The basic combinatorial level
   Level 2—A virtual interface
   Level 3—A graphical interface

In the first level, we find objects and methods to describe abstract graphs and collections of sub-graphs. In the second level, we find objects corresponding to points, edges, and regions. Typical methods are adding, deleting, or searching for points and edges, as well as defining regions. In Level 2, we provide support for the interactive methods. In the third level, we have the resident graphical interface of the machine. Here the methods deal with manipulating menus and windows, handling events, and displaying graphics on the screen. All significant calculation is done entirely within the first two levels, and these objects and methods are easily portable. Thus the portability problem is reduced to connecting a new version of Level 3 to Level 2.

In Figure 11.3 we show the total class hierarchy of our project, including NeXTstep® classes, classes of the NeXT application Draw, and our own classes.

Level 1

All of the mathematical problems that we consider can be abstractly described in terms of graphs, lists of sub-graphs, and manipulations of these graphs and lists of sub-graphs. These graphs are not just graphs composed of Dpoints and Edges as entered by the user, but also associated abstract graphs. For example, the set of Shards and oneCells give rise to a graph (the dual graph of the planar graph, which is the union of the oneCells). We combine these and many other related graphs into one very large object, which is also a graph.

Representing a graph by a data structure is a standard thing, and data structure texts discuss several such representations. However, none of these representations are powerful enough to handle the incorporation of lists of sub-graphs in a uniformly extensible way.

Most classes in Level 1 are subclasses of **Link**. **Link** generalizes the standard concept of a link in a doubly linked, circular list. A standard link includes the concepts of a next link and a previous link. In **Link** each object may have several different pairs of next links and previous links, and this set of possible directions is defined at runtime rather than compile time. In each such direction, **nextLink** and **previousLink** will be defined and will be instances of **Link**.

Some **Link** methods involve the concept of list headers. Traditionally, a linked list has been represented by two sorts of objects: a header (an object that represents the list) and links (which represent elements of that list). In our system, we make no such distinction; a header is also a subclass of **Link** and is represented as a distinguished link in a list, associated with a given direction. Thus, any link object can find what lists it is on by traversing links in a given direction from itself until it encounters the header. It is easy to have such a link function as a traditional header, and it is possible that a list have no header at all.

There are many other methods for the class **Link**. For example, a **Link** can find what directions are defined for it, search the list in such a direction, find the header (if any) in this direction, add a new direction, insert itself into a list in a variety of different ways, and remove itself from a list in a variety of ways. All link objects have a label (a user-defined integer) for identification, and an integer called "searchMark" used to indicate whether or not the link has been visited by various search methods.

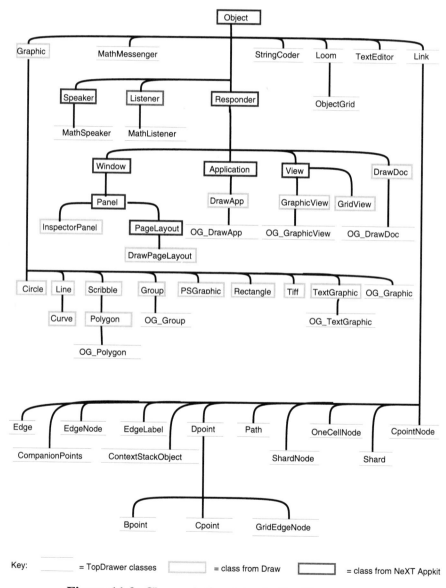

Figure 11.3: Class relationships in TopDrawer

The basic class that uses **Link** is called a **Loom**. Roughly, a **Loom** allows us to "weave together" different linked lists. It contains two objects of note: a root (a designated "first link" of the loom) and an instance of the **Navigator** class. Figure 11.4 shows the root and navigator of a loom; the object root is of type link. The basic function of a navigator is to facilitate complex searches in a loom. The navigator maintains a collection of objects that provide a partial log of calls made to the navigator. This is to allow backtracking along search paths. Each log is of class **Context**. Each context is a list of objects called *ContextStackObjects*; **ContextStackObject** is a subclass of **Link**.

Level 2

In the second level, our basic class is called **ObjectGrid**; this is a subclass of **Loom** and has the functionality of a virtual graphical interface. The links associated to an objectGrid all have some geometric meaning within a coordinate system, such as the objects corresponding to points, lines, and regions. All these links are interconnected via the **Loom** so, in principle, any link can locate any other link and send a message to it. Complex searches of this kind are facilitated by the navigator of the objectGrid. Thus, an edge can send a message to both its endpoints, a point can send a message to any edge on which it is an end point, and so on. Typical methods are adding points and edges to the grid and defining regions. We also have methods to search for certain kinds of objects within the grid, and we provide support for the interactive methods. Although we describe here an implementation of **ObjectGrid** that is basically in the realm of two-dimensional graphics (a fixed projection of a three-dimensional polygonal line drawing), the design is used for higher dimensional objects as well.

Two types of methods are needed in Level 2—local and global. Local

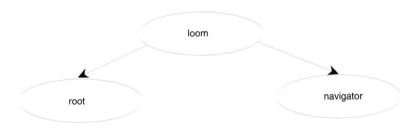

Figure 11.4

methods relate a given object to other objects near it in the coordinate system and geometrically related to it. Such methods are generally implemented as methods of that given object. Global methods relate the given object to the entire collection of objects associated to an objectGrid, and these methods are implemented as methods of **ObjectGrid**. (See example of message flow, discussed below.)

Level 3

In the third level we have the graphical interface, and the methods deal with manipulating menus and windows, handling events, and displaying graphics on the screen. At this level, we also handle runtime relations of TopDrawer with other programs. For example, we establish runtime interactions with Mathematica®, using the Speaker/Listener pair of objects supplied in the NeXTstep environment. In Figure 11.5 we show how the Level 3 objects are connected to the other two levels. **OG_GraphicView** is a Level 3 class that handles the mouse events and graphic displays. An instance of **OG_Graphic**, which contains an instance of **ObjectGrid**, is an object in the graphics list of the application. We will discuss little detail of this third level, because it is heavily dependent on the operating system and the available windowing system.

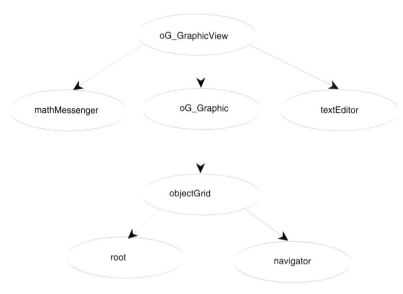

Figure 11.5

An Example of Message Flow

In following the message flow, we will focus on Level 2 objects and messages. To see how all this fits together at runtime, consider the following scenario. We are making a very simple drawing, which at the moment consists of two paths (**P** and **Q**) and a point **A** (Figure 11.6a). These paths have been oriented so that the first edges are at the left of the drawing. The most recent event has been the creation of the point **A**. For the next event, we will move the cursor to the point **B**, an interior point of path **P**, and add a new edge, **E**, to the drawing from **A** to **B**. The resulting drawing is shown in Figure11.6b. Now we have a new edge, and there are two other basic changes we will have to deal with. The first is that the point **A** is no longer an isolated point; the second is that the structure of our paths has been changed.

A Dpoint such as **A**, which is not a vertex of any edge, is an important special case both symbolically and in terms of screen display. An objectGrid maintains a list of such Dpoints by means of an ISOLATED_POINT_LIST. The method of objectGrid that adds edge **E** to point **A** sends the message to point **A** to remove itself from this list of isolated points.

Before the introduction of **E**, there were two paths; afterwards, there are four. One new path, **S**, consists only of the single edge **E**. The path **P** is now split at the point **B** into two sub-paths, one which is still denoted **P**, the other **R**. See Figure 11.6b. The objectGrid maintains a list of all paths.

The mouse click in the view sends a message to a corresponding instance of **oG_GraphicView** that causes several messages to be sent to the objectGrid associated with this view. First we do an error check by sending

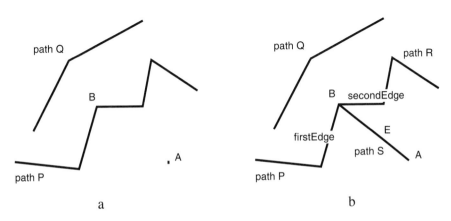

Figure 11.6

the message **-isGeneric**. If there is no error position, the next task is to locate the path **P**. Point **B** is a **Dpoint**, and every non-isolated Dpoint is on a list of edges on which it is an endpoint; this list corresponds to a direction called EDGE_LIST. Point **B** is a vertex of exactly two edges, which we next need to locate. By a series of messages, we have the navigator search this edge list and determine these two edges, which we call **firstEdge** and **secondEdge**. The order of these two edges is the same as the order in which these edges occur along the path **P**. To find the path **P**, the message **-toListHead** is sent to the navigator. In this method, the message **-nextLink:PATH_EDGES** is sent repeatedly by the navigator to itself until the current link is of class **Path**; this will be the path **P**.

To split the path **P**, the navigator sends itself **-splitListAfter:firstEdge**. This results in messages sent to the link's **firstEdge**, **secondEdge** and path **P** to do this splitting. Other messages are also sent to path **P** to tell it that the path has been shortened. Next a message **+newPath** is sent to **Path** to create and initialize the path **R**. Then path **R** is sent two messages:

```
-insertSelfBefore:secondEdge inDirection:PATH_EDGES
-insertSelfAfter:path_P inDirection PATH_LIST;
```

This integrates the path into the objectGrid. Finally, the message **+newPath:E** is sent to the class **Path** to create a path, **S**, with single edge, **E**. Then the message

```
-insertSelfAfter:path_R inDirection: PATH_LIST
```

finishes our modification of the paths.

The message flow diagram, Figure 11.7, shows some of the objects and messages flowing from the original message **-addEdgeToPaths:**.

Pens and Pencils: Two Drawing Modes

The method **-addEdgeToPaths:** outlined above is only one of several messages sent if we want to add an edge to an objectGrid. Clearly, it may not always be desirable to update the entire object grid for every mouse click, since this computational overhead can obstruct the flow of interaction. Also, in making a large drawing, it is most natural to draw small portions, readjust them, and assemble these parts into the final drawing. Our solution to this is to have two methods of drawing—a "pencil" mode and a "pen" mode. Having these modes also allows a drawing to be stored efficiently.

For simple drawings, one can simply enter points and edges directly onto the objectGrid. This is the "pen" method. In the pencil mode, the user

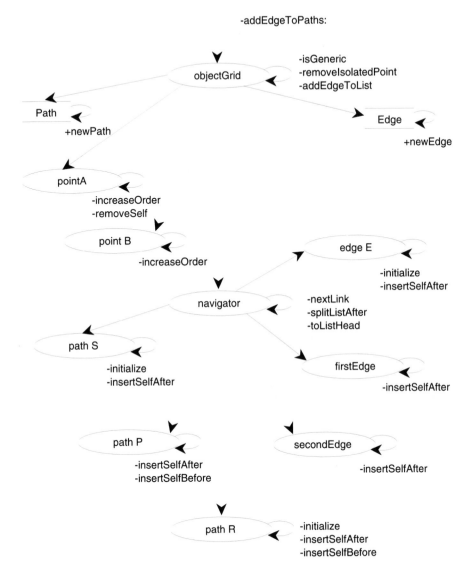

Figure 11.7: Portions of method flow of -addEdgeToPaths:

draws polygonal paths (instances of the class **Polygon**, a modification of this class from Draw). These paths appear on the screen in grey and are not entered into the objectGrid, so no calculation is required. Besides the usual resizing, repositioning, and grouping methods of the class **Graphic**, we have added the methods of geometric reflection. When a selected collection of polygons has been assembled, the message **-inkIn** is sent to **oG_GraphicView**. This enters these polygonal paths into the objectGrid.

What Are the Benefits of Object-Oriented Design in TopDrawer?

Object-oriented design provides the general organizational benefits such as data encapsulation and memory management. Because almost all of our classes are subclasses of **Link**, even such diverse objects as **Dpoint**, **Shard**, and **ContextStackObject** have common inherited methods to which they respond. This makes such polymorphic structures easy to construct and maintain and allows us to have uniform search procedures. Also because of this polymorphic structure, our code has a high degree of reusability. For example, it is very easy to extend the two-dimensional ObjectGrid to a three-dimensional one; one need only add a third coordinate and extend the methods to include messages involving this third coordinate. It is also easy to add a "solid" two-dimensional triangle to our considerations. We need only introduce a new object, **Triangle**, and add its three vertices (as **Dpoints**) and its three **Edges** to the ObjectGrid. These seven objects would then be connected to form a sub-graph of the ObjectGrid.

Another kind of extension is also important to us. We are not interested in just one drawing but a collection of interrelated drawings. Since each drawing is a graph object containing other objects, our class structure allows us to assemble these into one large graph and add edges to express important relationships between graphical objects in different drawings.

Each drawing is itself an object of class **OG_Graphic**. This has allowed us to insert it easily into an existing graphics program (Draw on the NeXT), thus inheriting all of Draw's window management. This includes event handling, as well as the use of more traditional graphics capabilities such as being able to add editable text to our screen.

Why Object-Oriented Design?

We are in an excellent position to evaluate the advantages of object-oriented design. During 1987 and 1988, we wrote a program in C that developed a graph-based data structure to describe a knotted sphere in four-dimensional space and do some of the mathematical manipulations we needed. We used traditional structs, pointers to structs, pointers to pointers to structs, and similar constructions for our data structures. Although the program worked, the code was inflexible and it was difficult to make improvements and extensions. We then began to rewrite this code in C++ during 1988–1989. Being able to easily code polymorphic linked lists was a great improvement, and as a mathematician, operator overloading seemed very natural and intuitive.

We had learned the basic methods of object-oriented design, and C++ was working out well. However, we abandoned this project after a few months because we obtained a NeXT computer as part of a National Science Foundation equipment grant in the spring of 1989. This machine and its software provided an excellent environment for program development and unique opportunities for development using computer graphics.

We decided that a fresh start was in order and turned our attention to the computer graphics aspect of this project. This was done in Objective-C, the native language of the NeXTstep environment of this computer. The advantages we saw were:

1. The NeXT interfaceBuilder™ that allows easy handling of graphics objects in building an application.

2. A reasonably good debugger (gdb) that could handle objects and methods.

3. A drawing application (with source code) that gave us objects we could reuse to construct our own drawing program.

The benefits also included relative freedom from having to worry about memory management and freedom from many (but not all) of the null-pointer coding errors that plagued us in the early stages of our development.

Object-Oriented Design Experience: The Good, the Bad, the Ugly

Our project is large, and we are trying to do many novel things. As a result, we encountered problems at several stages in our design development that necessitated major fundamental design changes. Several times we found that, because of the object-oriented design, very little recoding was needed. This was quite a pleasant surprise compared to our experience with our former "straight C" code.

When we began, our idea was to borrow code from the NeXT application, Draw, and customize it for our own use. But looking at the structure of Draw, we noted that, as with many object-oriented drawing programs (see for example, Stroustrup [1986]), it basically maintained a list of graphics objects. So "all" we had to do was to insert our own object into this list (our **OG_Graphic**), and we would have all these general objects and (most importantly) the general methods available to us.

However, it was not so easy. Although we could easily incorporate our object into the larger collection of objects, there was a problem with using the given methods. In a computer graphics image, what you see is not always what you have. In order to speed up the redrawing process, some graphics packages translate an image by translating the origin of its frame of reference. This indirect method has the advantage that coordinates of the given graphics object do not have to be recalculated and the result, as displayed, looks correct. This is, however, at odds with our needs to have the objects communicate their relations with one another. We need to recalculate coordinates. This illustrates one of the standard reusability problems for methods: An implementation that is faultless in one use may be inadequate in another. Our solution was to override these methods with our own, but it points out the importance of having source code available to pinpoint and correct these problems.

Overall, we have been pleased to date with our work with the NeXTstep and Objective-C on the NeXT and recommend it enthusiastically for development of programs such as ours. There have been three serious problems, though. The first is the general issue of source code availability, especially for the fundamental objects such as **Object**. The second is that NeXT has strayed from its initial intention of using an implementation of Objective-C compatible with the original Stepstone version. To avoid the portability problems this implies, we were forced to ignore many NeXT classes and methods and implement our own versions. Also, in each new release NeXT has changed the fundamental class **Object**. Each such change caused nontrivial, sometimes subtle, damage to our code.

One of the benefits we sought to achieve was flexibility of our basic design. We were pleased that this proved to be the case in at least one instance. Probably the most powerful program yet written to analyze knotted circles and links is *Snappea*, written by Jeff Weeks (for a review, see Adams [1990]). After we had written much of our code, we were asked if our program could produce the coding of diagrams used in that program. We have done this, and it was quite painless in spite of the fact that the diagram coding we use does quite a different analysis. Because all basic geometric concepts were represented as classes through the Loom structure, we were able to locate the objects and send the appropriate messages. This made it easy to write the code for the new problem.

Progress to Date (as of May 1, 1991)

This project is in progress as we write; a substantial portion has been written. It consists of about 21,000 lines of Objective-C code. About 13,000 lines are original code; the other 8,000 lines are borrowed from the NeXT application, Draw, and have been updated to run on version 2.0 of the operating system.

The basic portion for entering the drawing of an arbitrary graph and analyzing it are completed; we plan to add some additional editing methods. Improvement of the input system to accept a true third dimension is being implemented. Connections to Mathematica are in place and are being used to produce three-dimensional graphics derived from basically two-dimensional inputs. At present, we are working on writing methods for other mathematical calculations. Some of these involve Mathematica, while some are more topological in nature. For example, the methods involved with the discussions of Figures 11.2e and 11.2f are soon to be implemented.

References

Adams, Colin [1990]. "SNAPPEA, the Weeks Hyperbolic 3-Manifolds Program," *Notices of the American Mathematical Society*, **37**(3), 1990.

Francis, George K. [1987]. *A Topological Picturebook*, Springer-Verlag, New York, 1987.

Kauffman, Louis H. [1983]. "Formal Knot Theory," *Mathematical Notes* 30, Princeton University Press, Princeton, NJ, 1983.

Kauffman, Louis H. [1988]. "New invariants in the theory of knots," *Amer. Math. Monthly*, **95**, 1988, pp. 195-242.

Roseman, Dennis [1989]. "Spinning knots about submanifolds; spinning knots about projections of knots," *Topology and its Applications*, **31**, 1989, pp. 225-241.

Stroustrup, B. [1986]. *The C++ programming language*, Addison-Wesley, Reading, MA, 1986.

Index